THE PRIEST WHO PUT EUROPE BACK TOGETHER

THE PRIEST WHO

PUT EUROPE

BACK

TOGETHER

Sean Brennan

The Life of

FATHER FABIAN FLYNN, CP

The Catholic University of America Press

Washington, D.C.

The paper used in this publication meets the minimum
requirements of American National Standards for Information
Science—Permanence of Paper for Printed Library Materials,
ANSI Z39.48-1984.

∞

Library of Congress Cataloging-in-Publication Data

Names: Brennan, Sean (Sean Philip), 1979– author.

Title: The priest who put Europe back together : the life of Father
Fabian Flynn, CP / Sean Brennan.

Description: Washington, D.C. : The Catholic University of America
Press, [2018] | Includes bibliographical references and index.

Identifiers: LCCN 2018018727 | ISBN 9780813230177 (pbk. ; alk. paper)

Subjects: LCSH: Flynn, Fabian, 1905–1973. | Passionists—
United States—Biography. | United States. Army—Chaplains—
Biography. | Catholic Relief Services—Biography.

Classification: LCC BX4705.F61353 B74 2018 |
DDC 271/.6202 [B] —dc23

LC record available at https://lccn.loc.gov/2018018727

To Semion Lyandres and Bill Miscamble

A young historian could not have asked
for better mentors and advisers

CONTENTS

ILLUSTRATIONS

ACKNOWLEDGMENTS

It all began on March 13, 2010. I was attending the American Catholic Historical Association Spring Meeting at Princeton University, and a torrential downpour had spoiled my plans to explore the beautiful Ivy League campus. I passed the time reading through brochures on display about various Catholic historical archives and institutions. One that caught my eye was from the Passionist Historical Archive, then located in Union City, New Jersey. Since it was not too far from my home in Scranton, and on the advice of the director, Father Rob Carbonneau, I paid the archives a visit. Father Carbonneau informed me that numerous Passionists served as chaplains in the United States' Armed Forces during the Second World War. I had been hoping to write an article on such chaplains to be published in a historical journal.

Eventually I helped bring the Passionist archive to its current home, the Weinberg Library at the University of Scranton. Not long after the removal of the archives to Scranton, and in the course of examining the records of the Passionist military chaplains, I discovered the remarkable figure of Philip Fabian Flynn. Clearly, he would be the subject of my second book, my first biography.

Many different people and institutions made this biography possible. I first want to thank the Provost's Office of the University of Scranton and the American Catholic Historical Association, each of which provided financial support for my visits to various archives in the United States and Europe. I also want to express my gratitude to all the staffs at all the institutions I visited, especially the Archives of the University of Notre Dame, the Salzburg Archdiocese Archive, and the Archives of the United Nations High Commissioner for Refugees. I am grateful also to those who generously granted me permission to use photographs of Flynn in this book. I thank my academic colleagues at the rotating panels on religious history for the Association of Slavic, East European, and Eurasian Studies (ASEEES)—David Doellinger, James Felak, Robert Goeckel, and T. David Curp—who allowed me to present the early versions of chapters on Flynn's refugee work at various ASEEES conferences over the last decade. At my academic home, the University of Scranton, I am grateful to all my departmental colleagues—especially Bob Shaffern, Roy Domenico, and most of all Lawrence Kennedy—who provided invaluable advice on the history of early-twentieth-century Boston, especially its Catholic community. I thank also the special collections librarian, Michael Knies, who helped me bring the Passionist Archive to our university and assisted me every step of the way.

The Passionists were incredibly helpful, most of all Rob Carbonneau, CP, who was always available to answer my questions about the rules and teachings of his order. Flynn's family members gave my biography their blessing from the beginning and were always ready with a new story about him whenever I asked. I specifically want to express my deepest gratitude to Suzanne Birdsall and Patricia Chisholm. It is my sincere hope this biography does their beloved "Uncle Phil" justice.

The Catholic University of America Press demonstrated endless patience and encouragement during the process of turning my writings into a manuscript, especially the director, Trevor Lipscombe, and my editor, Susan Needham, without whose invaluable suggestions and assistance this book never would have been completed. The comments of the two anonymous reviewers also were extremely helpful.

Finally, I thank all my family members and friends who have cultivated my love of history over the years. Most of all, of course, is my dearest friend and most capable adviser, my wife, Lisa. Over the years, she has shown endless love and support as we invited Fabian Flynn into our lives and I spent many long weeks at distant archives on both sides of the Atlantic to tell his remarkable story. I could not have completed my second book without her.

ABBREVIATIONS

AES   Archiv der Erzdiözese Salzburg (Archive of the Salzburg Archdiocese)

AEF   Allied Expeditionary Force

ANY   Archdiocese of New York Archive, St. Joseph's Seminary, Dunwoodie, New York

AVH   Allam Vedelmi Hatosag (State Defense Authority-Hungarian Political Police)

BLS   Boston Latin School

BPL   Boston Public Library

CLA   Center for Legislative Archives, National Archives, Washington, D.C.

CMS   Center for Migration Studies, New York City

CRALOG Council of Relief Agencies Located in Occupied Germany

CRS   Catholic Relief Services (see WRS below)

CUA   The Catholic University of America Archives, Washington, D.C.

HUA   Harvard University Archives

IMT   International Military Tribunal at Nuremberg

IRO   International Refugee Organization

JDC   Jewish Defense Council

KPO   Kommunistische Partei Österreichs (Communist Party of Austria)

LWF   Lutheran World Federation

MDP   Magyar Dolgozok Partja (Hungarian Workers Party)

MRTC	Medical Replacement Training Center
NARA	National Archives at College Park, Maryland
NATO	North Atlantic Treaty Organization
NCWC	National Catholic Welfare Conference
NPRC	National Personnel Records Center, St. Louis, Missouri
OSA	Österreiches Staats Archiv (Austrian State Archive-Vienna)
OVP	Österreiches Volkspartei (Austrian People's Party)
PHA	Passionist Historical Archive, University of Scranton, Weinberg Library
SLA	Salzburg Landesarchiv (Salzburg Provincial Archive)
SPO	Sozialistische Partei Österreichs (Socialist Party of Austria)
UND	University of Notre Dame Archives
UNHCR	United Nations High Commissioner for Refugees
USAHEC	United States Army Heritage and Education Center, Carlisle Barracks, Pennsylvania
USEP	United States Escape Program
WRS	War Relief Services (renamed Catholic Relief Services in 1954)

INTRODUCTION

Rev. Fabian Flynn, CP, was unique. Who else could claim to have given last rites at Omaha Beach on D-Day; heard the confessions of Nazi war criminals at the Palace of Justice at Nuremberg; and smuggled supplies to Hungarian revolutionaries in communist-era Budapest? These events were among the most important events of twentieth-century European history, and Flynn played a vital part in all of them. Yet his participation in them constitutes only a small portion of his long and diverse career in the U.S. Army and with Catholic Relief Services. Flynn's role was not accidental. He chose it for himself, as a consequence of his deeply held belief that the Catholic Church must be active in the pivotal conflicts of good and evil in the world.

Flynn was indispensable. Not immediately on the moment he joined the U.S. Army in October 1942, but he gradually became so. During his service with the 26th Infantry Regiment, Flynn provided spiritual leadership to thousands of soldiers, Catholic and non-Catholic alike. And, like hundreds of other Catholic, Protestant, and Jewish clergy in the American military during the Second World War, Flynn's role as a military chaplain was multifaceted, as he shared the experiences of his men, including active combat.

Following the end of the war, Flynn's prominence steadily increased, especially after he was appointed to be the Catholic chaplain of the International Military Tribunal at Nuremberg in the fall of 1945. Even more importantly, though, Flynn administered the Witness House for the U.S. military authorities—the house that sheltered both the crucial witnesses for the Nuremberg prosecution and the family

members of many of the defendants. As he also became for many of
the inhabitants of the city, in his role as pastor of the Antonius Kirche,
Flynn was the symbol of the American military occupation.

From the time he joined the War Relief Services (WRS) of the National Catholic Welfare Conference (NCWC) in 1946 until his retirement in 1972, Flynn ranked among the key members of the organization, especially with respect to its European operations. His success
in the French zone of Germany led to his transfer to Hungary, at the
time one of the least stable countries in which the WRS operated. His
expulsion from Hungary in 1948—during the country's final stages of
transformation into a Stalinist-style dictatorship—led first to a brief
period in the American zone of Germany and then to his twelve years
in Austria. It was in Austria that Flynn directed aid to hundreds of
thousands of refugees, who arrived in Austria because of their inconvenient ethnicity in the new homogeneous states of Eastern Europe
or because of their political, social, and religious incompatibility with
communism. For the leaders of the WRS/CRS, Flynn was irreplaceable: less than a year after he returned to the United States to edit the
Passionist magazine *The Sign* in 1952, WRS leaders Edward Swanstrom
and James Norris basically demanded that the Passionists reassign
Flynn to Austria. Further evidence of his indispensability is indicated
by his having twice been awarded the Austrian government's Golden
Cross, in 1956 and in 1963; it is the highest honor Austria awards to any
non-Austrian. Flynn may not have put all of Europe back together—as
the *Catholic Herald* claimed in 1967—but a number of European countries, most importantly Austria, benefitted enormously through Flynn's
efforts during its two-decade-long refugee crisis.

This book seeks to place Flynn in the historical context of the military and diplomatic efforts of the United States government and the
charitable work of the Catholic Church, from the early 1940s to the early 1970s. More precisely, it discusses the life and career of Fabian Flynn
in five specific settings—that is to say, five historiographical periods
and their contexts. The first period of his adult life takes place in the
setting of the Passionists in the United States during the twentieth century. The second period unfolds within the broad context of military
chaplains who served in the U.S. Army in the European theater of the

Second World War. The First Infantry Division ("the Big Red One"), and particularly one of its three regiments, the 26th Infantry (which was at the front line of American combat against German and Italian forces for the entire duration of American involvement in the Second World War), provide the third context of Father Flynn's life.

The fourth context is the International Military Tribunal at Nuremberg, particularly as it affected the soldiers and officers of that same 26th Infantry Regiment (the "Blue Spaders"), who formed the American military presence at the IMT. Finally, the first two decades of the National Catholic Welfare Conference's Catholic Relief Services in Central Europe provide the fifth and last setting. The CRS crucially assisted in the reconstruction of Western Europe and provided aid for refugees from communist regimes and for ethnic Germans, who were expelled in accordance with the agreements made at Yalta and Potsdam in 1945.

No major *academic* study of the Passionists' activities in the United States has yet been undertaken, although there have been a number of works by their members, such as Cassius Yuhaus's *Compelled to Speak* and Roger Mercurio's *The Passionists*. Flynn is not mentioned in these works. His career at certain points exemplifies the direction the order took in the twentieth century (though sometimes Flynn was at odds with the order). During the Second World War, the Passionists were among the most active of American orders in providing chaplains for the U.S. Army, Navy, and Marines, and in this sense, Flynn's service with the Blue Spaders was unexceptional for a Passionist. Through the character of their founding, the Passionists were a not entirely monastic order, having established, since their arrival in the United States in the 1850s, Christian missions in Jamaica, Austria, Germany, and China (until their expulsion in 1950). However, unlike, for example, the Jesuits, Passionists were not permitted to conduct their spiritual work while living apart from the fellow members of their order, and in this regard Flynn's career working for CRS was highly unusual, as his superiors never let him forget.

Numerous books have been written on the role of Catholic chaplains in the American military. A sampling of them would include Harvey Cox's *American Chaplains: From a Religious Military to a Military*

Religion; S.K. Moore's *Military Chaplains as Agents of Peace*; Christopher Cross's *Soldiers of God: The True Story of American Military Chaplains during the Second World War;* Lyle Dorsett's *Serving God and Country: US Military Chaplains during World War II*; and Donald Crosby's *Battlefield Chaplains: Catholic Priests in World War II*, which briefly mentions Flynn's military service at Omaha Beach on D-Day. There have been many works about the Big Red One's role in World War II, and some, though not as many, about the Blue Spaders. Few works mention the role of the chaplains assigned to the division, despite the fact that they played a prominent role in the lives of most American soldiers.

Flynn's part in the Nuremberg trials has also been neglected. Tim Townsend's recent *A Mission to Nuremberg: An American Army Chaplain at the Trial of the Nazis*, about the Protestant chaplain at the trial, Captain Ralph Gerecke, omits any mention of Flynn.

Two books that depict personnel involved in the IMT do make some mention of Flynn: the first—Christopher Dodd's *Letters from Nuremberg: My Father's Narrative of a Quest for Justice*, concerning his father, Thomas Dodd, who was an assistant to the chief American prosecutor, Robert H. Jackson—mentions Flynn a few times, in the context of meetings between the elder Dodd and the American officers associated with the 26th Infantry Regiment.

The historical work that discusses Flynn to the greatest extent, though, is German journalist Christiane Kohl's *The Witness House: Nazis and Holocaust Survivors Sharing a Villa during the Nuremberg Trials*. This book details Flynn's actions that were pivotal in setting up a residence for witnesses for the prosecution as well as, counterintuitively, family members of several of the accused. It also discusses the friendship between Flynn and Ingeborg Kálnoky, the German-Hungarian noblewoman who governed the Witness House on behalf of the American authorities. Kohl's book was adapted in 2014 into a television film on the German channel ZDF, *Das Zeugenhaus* (The Witness House).

The lack of any major academic monograph on the history of Catholic Relief Services can reasonably be attributed to the inadequate condition of the organization's archival holdings. Although there are several books on the history of the American Catholic Church or on charitable relief during the Cold War that mention CRS peripherally, most of the histories of CRS were written by its own members. In most instances these books, rather than offering a history of the entire organization, have narrated the personal experiences of those members. One of few to have avoided this framework was Eileen Egan, herself a longstanding figure in CRS, in her book *Catholic Relief Services: The Beginning Years*. The book briefly discusses Flynn's service in the French zone of Germany, and his role in Hungary's 1956 revolution.

The sources for this present book come from every part of Flynn's life and career. For his youth, I examined the records of the Boston Latin School and his personnel files with the Passionist Historical Archive (PHA); I also conducted several interviews with his surviving relatives. His life as a member of the Congregation of the Passion is also covered extensively in the records of the PHA. For Flynn's military career, I fortunately had access to his files from the National Personnel Records Center in St. Louis. (His records were not among the many military records were destroyed in a fire at the facility in 1973.) I also examined the records of the 26th Infantry Regiment at the National Archives II in College Park, Maryland (NARA). Material from the NARA and the papers of Colonel Burton Andrus, the "Nuremberg jailer," held at the Center for Military History at the Carlisle Barracks in Pennsylvania, also proved useful in my research on Flynn's service for the IMT.

I was fortunate in finding an extraordinary variety of sources about CRS in archival collections throughout the country. These collections include the Center for Legislative Archives at the National Archives in Washington D.C.; the Catholic University of America Archives; the Archives of the Archdiocese of New York; and the Center for Migration Studies in New York. Also critical for my research were the Archives of the University of Notre Dame, which contains the correspondence of James Norris, Flynn's immediate superior in CRS. I was afforded the opportunity to explore Flynn's relations with religious and government officials in Austria through examination of the Austrian State Archive in Vienna, the Salzburg Archdiocese Archive, and the Salzburg Provincial Archive. Apart from the Catholic Church in Austria, no institution worked more extensively with CRS than the United Nations High Commissioner for Refugees (UNHCR), so I also examined their holdings at their headquarters in Geneva, Switzerland.

Flynn did not, as far as I could ascertain, keep a journal or a diary, but I have utilized his extensive correspondence with his family, his fellow Passionists, and his colleagues in the American military, co-workers in Catholic Relief Services, officials in the Austrian government, and clergy and laity from the Austrian Catholic Church. A selfless, brave, and generous man, but one of supreme ambition—and often angry impatience with those who failed to live up to his high standards—is easily perceived in his letters. His profound sense of personal destiny and his ideological commitment as a Catholic warrior against totalitarianism often annoyed those who worked with him. But these two personal characteristics undoubtedly enabled him to take part in extraordinary actions at some of the most important events in the history of the twentieth century. Flynn was one of the Americans who "put Europe back together." Leaders such as Roosevelt, Marshall, Truman, Acheson, Eisenhower, Dulles, Kennedy, and—in the CRS—Swanstrom and Norris, helped liberate Europe from fascism. Then, over the next two decades, they contained communism, which one day would collapse and give new birth to freedom in the eastern half of Europe. Yet these leaders would have achieved nothing without the actions, often against long and difficult odds, of men like Fabian Flynn. This is his story.

THE PRIEST WHO PUT EUROPE
BACK TOGETHER

∽ 1

YOUTH, 1905–1924

The World in 1905

Philip Flynn was born on June 21, 1905, in Boston, Massachusetts, to John Flynn and Julia (Ryan) Flynn, a middle-class Irish Catholic couple. He had been preceded by a sister, Elizabeth, who died aged one, two years before Philip's birth.[1]

The early twentieth century was a time of political, social, cultural, and religious transition. The United States and much of Europe were in the third decade of a "Golden Age," an era of seemingly endless economic growth and technological and industrial advancement. Dreams that this period of stability and prosperity could last forever, dreams shared on both sides of the Atlantic, were soon to be shattered.

The United States of America emerged on the world stage as a major imperial power following its 1898 victory over a fading empire, Spain. The Spanish-American War forced the Spanish out of two of their last colonies, Cuba and the Philippines. Although Cuba was grant-

---

1. He would take the name Fabian upon his entry into the Congregation of the Passion on February 8, 1931. For the sake of clarity, I will refer to him as Philip Flynn, his given name, until 1924, when, upon professing his vows to the Passionists, he took the name Fabian Flynn. Birth Certificate PHA—Passionist Historical Archive, University of Scranton, Weinberg Library, Record Group 379—Personnel Files, Box 29, File C—Fabian Flynn; hereafter, Record Group 379—29/C. Occasionally, when using a source collection I cite repeatedly, I will provide a full citation at its first use and will thereafter use an abbreviated form.

ed independence, which ostensibly had been the cause of the conflict between Washington and Madrid, American influence over the Caribbean grew stronger than ever. The Philippines passed from Spanish to American rule, although not until after the U.S. Army and Marines had put down a bloody two-year insurgency by Philippine rebels who were intent on securing their country's independence. The president who oversaw the American entry into the imperial club, William McKinley, in 1901 paid for it with his life, through an assassin's bullet fired by the anarchist Leon Czolgosz. McKinley's successor, Theodore Roosevelt, continued to exert a strong American presence on the world stage. In the summer of 1905—in Portsmouth, New Hampshire, not far from Flynn's native Boston—he helped mediate an end to the Russo-Japanese War. Re-elected the year before Flynn's birth, Roosevelt had a "speak softly, and carry a big stick" approach to world politics that was phenomenally popular with most Americans but disconcerted many of the European imperial powers, who were slightly uncomfortable with the vast potential of the emerging colossus across the Atlantic.

In Europe, the tumultuous twenty-three years between the revolutions of 1848 and the Franco-Prussian War in 1871 seemed a distant memory. The continent had never appeared wealthier or more powerful than it did in 1905. Most European states and all the great powers had taken some steps toward granting voting rights to non-property-holding males. There was a corresponding growth in political parties, as well as some progress toward the creation of a welfare state. Monarchs who exerted vast powers with relatively few checks remained in charge throughout most of Europe. In the Austro-Hungarian Empire, under the rule of the Habsburgs—one of Europe's oldest dynasties—Emperor Franz Joseph was in the fifty-seventh year of his reign. Since the death of Queen Victoria in 1901, no one better symbolized the permanence and stability of the European order than the man who was joint Austrian emperor and king of Hungary.[2]

2. The multiple tragedies of Franz Joseph's long life—his brother's execution by a Mexican firing squad in 1867; the 1889 suicide of his only son (with the son's mistress); the 1898 assassination of his wife by an Italian anarchist—hint at the underlying problems within the Habsburg domains, and perhaps, the later tragedies of Central Europe in the twentieth century.

Franz Joseph's unique position as a dual monarch derived from the *Ausgleich* of 1867, through which the Hungarians—the second largest ethnic group of the empire after the Austrians—became equal partners with the Austrians in the administration of an empire that stretched from central to southeastern Europe. Both countries were governed semi-constitutionally, although only Austria had universal male suffrage in 1905, something Hungarian authorities strongly resisted in their kingdom with regards toward their Romanian minorities. The various other nationalities of the empire—the Czechs, Slovaks, Slovenians, Croatians, Italians, Poles, Ukrainians, and especially the inhabitants of Bosnia-Herzegovina (not formally annexed until 1908 but effectively under Habsburg rule since 1878)—remained restless. Few believed this restlessness directly threatened the empire's existence, especially given the ambitious plans of Franz Ferdinand, the heir to both thrones, to reorganize the Habsburg domains as a "United States of Europe." In foreign affairs, Austria-Hungary's strongest rival was the Russian empire, and both desired to supplant the fading Ottoman empire as the new power in the Balkan peninsula.

Austria-Hungary's greatest ally—less generously, perhaps their sole ally—was the German empire, forged in "blood and iron" by the Prussian Chancellor Otto von Bismarck in 1871. By 1905, Germany had emerged as Europe's largest industrial economy, surpassing Britain. In the late nineteenth century, Germany belatedly entered races for territory in Africa and Asia, acquiring a handful of colonies in Africa and in the Pacific. The alliance between Berlin and Vienna was central to Bismarck's diplomacy; his diplomatic strategy was grounded in the *Realpolitik* that accepted Germany's destiny as a great European power, and it avoided policies that could drive any of the other great powers into alliance with France—Germany's permanent enemy since the German annexation of Alsace and Lorraine in 1871.

In 1890, the young and headstrong Wilhelm II removed Bismarck as chancellor. The Kaiser supported a foreign policy of *Weltpolitik*, designed to make Germany a great global power that ultimately would supplant Britain. This required a massive expansion of the German military, especially its naval forces, and attempts to expand aggressively on the imperial stage. Three months before Flynn's birth, Wilhelm II's clumsy attempt at "battleship diplomacy"—seizing control of the French colony of Morocco—led to a year-long diplomatic standoff, the Agadir Crisis, between Germany on one side and France and Britain on the other. The military and diplomatic ties between London and Paris were solidified through this crisis, and with those ties added to the alliance between Paris and St. Petersburg, Germany was hemmed in, to its west and its east, by potentially hostile powers.

Although they were certainly not fully constitutional monarchs, both Wilhelm II, a grandson of Britain's Queen Victoria, and Franz Joseph shared some power with the elected representatives of their subjects, especially in matters concerning the state budget and the passage of laws. The same could not be said of Tsar Nicholas II, the autocratic ruler of the vast Russian Empire. Nicholas and his predecessors—unlike the British, German, or Austrian monarchs—resisted entreaties to grant constitutions or create a parliamentary body (in the Russian case, a Duma). In January 1905, Nicholas's power was constrained by no constitution, nor did Russia have legal political parties. Revolutionary upheaval in 1905 shook the Tsarist empire to its foundations, as political chaos—following the country's humiliating defeat at the hands of Japan in the Pacific—culminated in Nicholas's decision, expressed in the October Manifesto, to grant certain freedoms to his subjects. With the Tsar's reluctant concessions, Russia had ceased to be an autocratic monarchy and had joined Germany and Austria-Hungary as a semi-constitutional state. Over the next few decades, all four of these countries—Russia, Germany, Hungary and Austria—would experience military defeat, revolutionary upheaval, and totalitarian dictatorships, in some cases in more than one form. All would exert an enormous influence on the life of this Boston infant in the years to come.

The second stage of the Industrial Revolution—of oil, steel, and electricity—was concluding in 1905. It had fundamentally transformed European social, cultural, political, and religious life. European societies, like the post–Civil War United States, became more urban; increasing numbers of people were engaged in industry rather than agriculture, although only in Britain, Belgium, and Germany were these the majority. The economic and political influence of the industrial bourgeoisie had grown significantly throughout the nineteenth century. Many European societies were more secular as well, with a corresponding growth in social democratic political movements determined to create a secular political and social order. The emergence of Christian mass political parties, especially in Roman Catholic regions of Europe—such as the Center party in Germany—were a response to this phenomenon.

The increasing secularism of urbanized Europe and the emergence of social democracy were of pressing concern to the Vatican and various leaders of the Catholic Church. The long-serving Leo XIII, whose papacy extended from 1878 to 1903, issued *Rerum Novarum*, one of the most important papal encyclicals in history; it was seen by many as the founding document of Christian democracy in Europe. In it, Leo XIII presented the Church's position regarding industrial capitalism, which was permitted and even encouraged if governments allowed for the creation of labor unions and worked with religious charities to provide aid for the poor. It also condemned socialism as an atheistic heresy that denied the inherent dignity of the individual and attempted to supplant God's role in the lives of men. Leo XIII's papacy was marked by constant reflections on how individual Catholics and the institutional Church should approach modern secular culture. The papacy of his more conservative successor, Pius X (1903 to 1914) was marked by a rejection of "modernism" in all its forms; close ties between the Vatican and the Catholic community throughout the world; and the uniform teaching of Catholic doctrine to every parish.

A conflict between traditional and modernist theology, as well as a struggle over the administrative role of the Vatican, played out in Flynn's native Boston during the years immediately before and after 1905. Toward the end of the forty-year (from 1866 to 1906) tenure of John Williams as the archbishop of Boston, the contentious issue of "Americanism" emerged, both in the archdiocese of Boston and throughout the country. Briefly, some clergy and laity (who acquired the name "Americanists") attempted to argue that the Church in America should go its own way administratively, independently of the Holy See, especially regarding the appointment of bishops.[3] Leo XIII condemned this idea;

3. Donna Murphy, *Boston Priests: A Study of Social and Intellectual Change* (Cambridge, Mass.: Harvard University Press, 1973), 171–73.

Williams and his successor, William Henry O'Connell, who would lead the archdiocese of Boston from 1906 to 1944, concurred with him on this matter. O'Connell stressed the Church's loyalty both to America and to the papacy and saw no contradiction between the two loyalties.[4] Americanism was a theme Flynn would deal with in his own writings.

The greater metropolitan area of Boston comprised more than 1,800,000 people. From the mid-nineteenth century to the early twentieth century, it was in a state of remarkable religious transformation. One of the oldest cities in America, Boston—and more broadly the colony of Massachusetts—had been established in the early seventeenth century by English Calvinists, better known as Puritans, the name derived from their desire to "purify" the Church of England's worship from all taint of "Romanism." They deeply influenced the colonial, revolutionary, and early Republican periods, and during these periods Boston was one of the most staunchly Protestant cities in America, if not the entire world. By the mid-nineteenth century, though, thousands of immigrants were coming to Boston each year to make new lives for themselves in America. Until the late nineteenth century, most of them were Roman Catholics from Ireland who were fleeing poverty and oppressive English rule in one of Western Europe's poorest countries. By the late 1800s, and early 1900s, other immigrant groups from largely Catholic regions of central, southern, and southeastern Europe gradually surpassed the Irish in numbers of arriving immigrants in Boston. In 1908 the archdiocese of Boston listed a census of slightly more than 850,000 Catholics.[5]

Through the massive waves of immigration, Catholics came to form the largest religious group in the commonwealth of Massachusetts and in the city of Boston. By the beginning of the twentieth century, 40 percent of the electorate of the city was, like the Flynn family, of Irish descent.[6] Other Catholic communities of immigrants from Italian,

4. Ibid, 193–95. O'Connell became a cardinal in 1907.

5. Thomas O'Connor, *Boston Catholics: A History of the Church and Its People* (Boston: Northeastern University Press, 1998), 201. The archdiocese was geographically larger than the Boston metro area.

6. Damien Murray, *Irish Nationalists in Boston: Catholicism and Conflict, 1900–1928* (Washington, D.C.: The Catholic University of America Press, 2018), 163.

Polish, German, and Croatian descent were also growing. During the ceremonies celebrating the hundred-year anniversary of the founding of the archdiocese of Boston on October 28, 1908, Cardinal O'Connell could confidentially assert, "The Puritan has passed, now the Catholic remains."[7]

This overstated the case. Boston's Protestant community had not disappeared, and the Boston "Brahmins" still exerted considerable economic and political influence, especially in the Republican Party, which dominated affairs in Massachusetts and much of New England. No family in Boston symbolized this more than the Lodges, including "Mr. Republican" in the United States Senate, Henry Cabot Lodge. There were also suspicions by the Protestant majority in the United States that American Catholics could never truly be loyal to the American government; their true political devotion had always been, and would continue to be, toward Rome, an attitude that persisted long into the twentieth century.

In the year of Flynn's birth, Irish Catholics could nevertheless legitimately claim they had reached the highest levels of political power in the commonwealth, exemplified by the swearing in of Daniel Whelton as the first Irish Catholic mayor of Boston on September 18, 1905. Whelton, like most Irish Catholics, belonged to the Democratic Party, which remained the party of a large majority of Irish Catholics throughout the twentieth century, culminating in the rise of Kennedys to political dominance first in Massachusetts and briefly in the United States during the early 1960s.[8] The archdiocese that Cardinal O'Connell now led was not a missionary outpost in a heavily Protestant city in a strongly Protestant country, but a respected and strong institution that represented a majority of Christians within the city. In his first decade as archbishop, O'Connell chaired meetings in Boston of numerous Catholic national organizations. Unlike his predecessor, Arch-

7. *The Boston Globe*, October 29, 1908, 1.

8. James O'Toole, "Prelates and Politicos: Catholics and Politics in Massachusetts 1900–1970," in *Catholic Boston: Studies in Religion and Community, 1870–1970*, ed. Robert Sullivan and James O'Toole (Boston: Archdiocese of Boston Press, 1985), 15–66, here 16–18. Flynn, an anomaly in most environments of which he was a part, would be a rare breed in Boston, an Irish Catholic Republican.

bishop Williams, O'Connell was a frequent guest at civic functions in the city, and met regularly with non-religious organizations. He was soon one of the most recognizable leaders in the city, for Catholics and non-Catholics alike.[9]

Under the auspices of Cardinal O'Connell, Catholic religious life in Boston emphasized regular attendance at Mass on Sundays and Holy Days, participation in various Catholic charitable and fraternal organizations, allegiance to the pope as the successor of Saint Peter, and veneration of the Virgin Mary. Mass on Sunday was the central event of religious life for most Catholic families in Boston, but the Church also played an enormous role in day-to-day life for most families. In the words of historian Thomas O'Connor:

> In every Catholic neighborhood (in Boston), the Church was an integral part of almost every aspect of family life. From the cradle to the grave. A large crucifix, along with pictures of the Sacred Heart of Jesus, the Blessed Mother and St. Joseph, was prominently displayed in almost every Catholic home, dramatizing the Holy Family as the universal model for all working-class (and middle-class) families. Religious pamphlets, inspirational literature, and copies of *The Pilot* were found in most houses, and entire families knelt together every night before going to bed to recite the decades of the rosary.[10]

Nor were Boston priests content to stay waiting in their churches for their parishioners to come to them. Parish theatrical, choral, and orchestral performances were common, and nearly every church had several sports organizations. The archdiocese operated an extensive network of charitable organizations, many tied to the National Catholic Welfare Conference following its founding in 1920. Priests and nuns were a frequent sight on the streets of Boston, as they guided the spiritual lives and moral attitudes of Catholic laity.[11]

---

9. James O'Toole, *Militant and Triumphant: William Henry O'Connell and the Catholic Church in Boston, 1859–1944* (Notre Dame, Ind.: University of Notre Dame Press, 1992), 81.

10. Thomas O'Connor, *Boston Catholics: A History of the Church and Its People*, 211. *The Pilot* was the official newspaper for the archdiocese of Boston.

11. Ibid, 213–15.

Philip Flynn's Youth, 1905–1924

It was in this milieu that Flynn spent most of the formative years of his life, not leaving the metro area of Boston for any great length of time until 1924. By all accounts, Flynn had a relatively normal childhood. Most Irish Catholic couples in Boston were famous for having multiple children, but Philip Flynn was essentially an only child, his older sister Elizabeth having passed away two years before his birth. Flynn had many cousins, all of whom also lived in Boston. His family was solidly middle class—his father John was a store manager in Faneuil Hall, then and now a historic shopping center in the heart of Boston. His mother Julia was a homemaker but occasionally provided maid services for other middle-class families. The Flynns lived for the entirety of Philip's youth at 485 Columbia Road in Dorchester, the largest of Boston's five neighborhoods.[12]

John Flynn was a typical store manager of the time, serious, industrious, thrifty, and level-headed. He lacked his son's driving ambition and global worldview. John rose from being a clerk to a store manager, staying at this position for most his adult life, never displaying a desire to expand his horizons far beyond Boston in general and Dorchester in particular. This is not to say father and son had nothing in common; Philip Flynn shared his father's sense of hard work and his practicality when it came to finances, as well as a lifetime love of the Boston Red Sox. His father rarely took time off from work except for illness, and there is no evidence that he ever had any difficulty in providing for his family. He acted as a firm father to his son but not a distant one.[13]

Julia (née Ryan) Flynn was the opposite of her husband in many ways. He was a practical man who maintained a detailed schedule for most of his days, whereas she was a free-spirited extrovert who loved spontaneity and the company of others, especially her extended family and friends. A lover of board and card games as well as practical jokes, Julia could frequently be found entertaining guests at her home or

12. Suzanne Birdsall, Interview with the author, February 12, 2015.
13. Patricia Chisholm, Interview with the author, June 8, 2015.

visiting them in turn. She was a woman of boundless energy and enthusiasm. She also possessed a sharp wit and a biting, although not cruel, sense of humor, traits inherited by her son. By all accounts, Julia Flynn doted on and was devoted to her only child, and Philip certainly never lacked maternal affection or guidance.[14]

Like most of their neighbors, the Flynns took their Catholic faith seriously, and that included the religious upbringing of their son. Philip Flynn was baptized a week after his birth on June 28, 1905, at the parish of Saint Margaret's in Dorchester, which would be the family parish for Flynn's childhood, until his teenage years, by which time the family had begun attending the larger Saint Peter's Church, where Flynn was confirmed at the age of thirteen on May 18, 1918.[15] The family attended Mass each Sunday as well as on holy days of obligation, and were active members of their parish, regularly participating in social activities. Flynn frequently took part in in parish sporting events, and, since he went to public schools, also attending Sunday school after Mass.[16]

While many Irish Catholic boys and girls in the Boston area studied at the various Catholic parochial schools, Flynn attended the Boston Mather School for his elementary education and then the Boston Latin School for secondary education. These were the oldest primary and secondary schools in the United States, founded in 1639 and 1635, respectively. In neither school in the early decades of the twentieth century did Catholic students form the majority. Both schools were famous for educating the sons of Boston's "Brahmin" elite, which were only slowly conceding political power in the commonwealth to the sons and grandsons of Catholic immigrants. The curriculum was based, like most public and private schools of the time, on a classical liberal arts model. Although these were public schools, religious instruction was an essential part of the curriculum, as it was in practically every school in the United States at the time. A middle-class Catholic in a school full of upper-class Protestants, Flynn made himself a visible presence at Boston Latin.[17]

14. Suzanne Birdsall, Interview with the author, February 12, 2015.

15. Flynn Family Baptismal and Confirmation Records. PHA Record Group 379—29/C. The reasons for the family's transfer to a different parish remain unclear.

16. Patricia Chisholm, Interview with the author, June 12, 2015.

17. See http://www.matherelementary.org/history.html, for a historical overview

Numbered among Boston Latin's famous alumni were Cotton Mather, John Hancock, Benjamin Franklin, Samuel Adams, Henry Knox, Ralph Waldo Emerson, George Santayana, and Joseph Kennedy. Later notable graduates were the composer Leonard Bernstein and the founder of the Air Force Academy, Brigadier General Robert McDermott. On September 4, 1918, Flynn was formally admitted to the school, where he was a student until May 24, 1923, when he left to enter the Passionists at Saint Mary's Monastery in Dunkirk, New York.[18]

Students at the BLS took either a four- or a six-year educational program, moving from Class VI, the equivalent of seventh grade in an American junior high school, in their first year, to Class I, the equivalent to senior year of high school. Some gifted students occasionally bypassed class levels and completed the six-year course of study in five years. Flynn was one of these exceptions, completing Classes VI, V, and IV in two years.[19] In transferring from the BLS to Saint Michael's Monastery, he simply moved from one educational institution to another to complete his intellectual training and satisfy his desire to join the Passionists.[20]

Academic and disciplinary records from the BLS reveal that Flynn was an above average student. He never received any of the prizes given by the school for outstanding academic work, but his parents were never notified of any poor academic performance on the part of their son on class assignments or, especially, exams. Nor did he appear to be a student with frequent discipline problems; indeed, the single instance of a behavioral citation for Philip Flynn, on March 25, 1920, notes that he "presented false notes to serve dismissal and forgery." Flynn's parents were called to the school and notified of their son's attempt at an early exit from the school day.[21] The course of study at the BLS, even

---

of the Boston Mather School, and http://bls.org/apps/pages/index.jsp?uREC_ID=206116&type=d, for a historical overview of the Boston Latin School.

18. Boston Public Library (BPL) MS 617—Attendance and Discipline Records for the Boston Latin School.

19. Boston Latin School Archives (BLS), Catalogue of the Public Latin School in Boston, October 1918.

20. BLS Catalogue of the Public Latin School in Boston, October 1922.

21. BPL, MS 617—Attendance and Discipline Records for the Boston Latin School. While John Flynn did not have the reputation of a strict disciplinarian, he did expect

by the standards of the day, was demanding and rigorous, and it certainly provided Philip Flynn with the intellectual foundations for his seminary work at Saint Mary's and beyond.[22]

Flynn excelled at foreign languages, history, and English. Fortuitously for his later career, Flynn opted for German language instruction at the BLS rather than Greek. His facility in French and German stayed with him throughout his life and supported his various missions; during the late 1940s, when the need arose he even developed some limited proficiency in Hungarian.[23]

Short for his age and slight of build, Flynn nevertheless made some time for athletics, serving on the BLS track team during his fourth year in 1921–22 and placing second in the fifty-yard dash. There were no indications yet of the physical problems that would plague Flynn for much of his adult life.[24]

---

his son to follow a code of responsible and honest behavior. Whatever punishment Philip received from his parents for this forging of a sick note certainly prevented his doing it again.

22. Pauline Holmes, *A Tercentenary History of the Boston Public Latin School 1635–1935.* (Westport, Conn.: Greenwood Press Publishers, 1970), 206–9. In their first year (as part of Class VI), students studied English, Latin, History, Mathematics, Geography and Science (Physiology and Hygiene). In year two, the curriculum included English, Latin, French, History, Mathematics, Geography, Science, and Physical Training. The third-year curriculum contained classes in English, Latin, French, History, Mathematics, Science, and Physical Training. The fourth year was English, Latin, French, Greek or German, Mathematics, and Physical Training. During the fifth year, Flynn's last at the school, students took courses in English, Latin, French, Greek or German, History, Mathematics, and Physical Training. The sixth year was slightly less demanding, with students taking courses in English, Latin, Mathematics, Physics, and a choice among German, French, Greek, or advanced Mathematics.

23. Flynn's School Records, BPL, MS 617—Attendance and Discipline Records for the Boston Latin School. The study of History at the BLS involved largely an examination of American and then British and to a lesser extent continental European History in the first three years. This was followed by a detailed set of courses on Classical Antiquity, with a roughly equal amount of time paid to ancient Greece and Rome. English classes involved everything from reading prose and poetry, to memorizing certain pieces and reciting them to the rest of the class, to composing original works of poetry and short stories, to exercises in Penmanship, spelling, and grammar

24. *The Boston Latin School Register,* March 1922, 30. Flynn's ultimate height would be 5'10" and his weight would be 155 pounds, according to his U.S. Army records during the Second World War. He had left his teenage shortness behind but would always be physically slight.

It was on the staff of the Boston Latin School's newspaper, *The Register*, where Flynn made a mark during his time at the school. Published once a month, *The Register* was a combination of the school's newspaper and a literary magazine.[25] His writings for that paper provide us an early view of his intellectual creativity, his strong work ethic, and his moral rectitude.

Flynn officially joined *The Register* during the beginning of his third year. The October 1920 issue is the first to list him as a member of the staff. This was the earliest he could have joined, as membership on the staff was not open to students from Classes VI through IV. Flynn reached Class III by this third year, and was on the lower totem of the newspaper staff as one of two "Class III" editors. He would remain on the editorial staff for the rest of his time at the Boston Latin School.

Flynn's first published article, "Concerning *The Register* and Subscriptions," appeared in the January 1921 issue. Thus began one of the main occupations of his life, as both a news editor and also as an editorialist.[26] Flynn returned to this career in the mid-to-late 1930s, and again briefly in the early 1950s. Even as a World War II army chaplain and then as director of Catholic Relief Services in Europe, Flynn always had time to write articles and editorials for various publications. It was an early and most dearly held passion.

His debut article was brief, but foreshadowed both the emotional investment Flynn brought to his writing and his occasional harsh tone. Flynn informs the readers that the staff of *The Register* made every effort to provide an outstanding issue each month. Yet compared to other school newspapers in Boston, *The Register* was not nearly as financially successful. Reminding his audience that the Boston Latin School's newspaper was the oldest in the United States, the students had a duty to make sure "this tradition does not fail." He concluded by urging the students "not to be a piker" and borrow another student's newspaper, but to "be independent and buy one on your own." The newspapers would serve as a reminder, throughout the rest of their

25. *The Boston Latin School Register,* October 1920, 2. Students could buy single copies for 10 cents, or apply for a year's subscription at either 75 cents to have it delivered to them at the school, or 85 cents to be delivered at home.

26. *The Boston Latin School Register,* January 1921, 12.

lives, of their happy experiences at the BLS. Almost issuing a command, Flynn ended: "Therefore in the New Year's let us see a large increase in subscriptions."[27]

Flynn's next piece, "That Runt," appeared in the November 1921 issue. A fictional sports story with an inspirational message, the main character was a diminutive teenager, Jack Nelson, who desired to play quarterback for his school, Fairfax Academy. His slight stature and lack of physical strength led many of his teammates to refer to him as a "runt" who played a "sissy game." Jack possessed a great deal of heart and some athletic ability, but seemed destined to spend his entire high school career on the bench. As if by a miracle, when Dick Shuyler, the star quarterback for Fairfax, goes down injured during a game against their rival Hillsdale Academy, Jack steps in and leads the team to victory. Alas, Jack has an undiagnosed heart condition, which causes him to collapse on the field at the game's end. His playing days over, Jack lies in a hospital bed next to Dick and is visited by classmates who congratulate him for his role in the team's victory, ironically the same ones who referred to him earlier as "that Runt." Jack magnanimously accepts their thanks, but reminds them of a quote from the English poet Martin Tupper: "A wise man scorneth nothing, be it ever so small or homely."[28]

It is fair to say the short, slight Philip Flynn, an Irish Catholic outsider at the Boston Latin School, saw himself in Jack Nelson, a tiny nobody who, when called upon by a twist of fate, rose to the occasion to be the man of the hour. Throughout his life, Flynn doubted neither his own potential nor that of the people with whom he worked to accomplish great things against long odds. We also see Flynn's trademark realism: because of his heart condition, Jack's role in the victory will not be repeated. This combination of idealism and realism is reflected in Flynn's later writings, and in his careers with the Passionists, the U.S. Army, and Catholic Relief Services.

Flynn's next work was "Such is Life in a Large City", which appeared in the June 1922 issue. The three-page short story was a combi-

27. *The Boston Latin School Register,* January 1921, 12.
28. *The Boston Latin School Register,* November 1921, 3–5.

nation of mystery and a crime procedural, set in the fictional large city of "Gninisso." The name of the city is a play on words, Ossining spelled backwards, the location of Sing-Sing prison. The story discussed themes of mistaken identity and the difficulty that former criminals encounter when trying to re-enter society. It lacks the Aesopian themes of "That Runt," but the story is a clever whodunit that also addresses themes of criminal justice in an urban environment, as well as the parallel societies developed by those who live outside the law. Both stories, interestingly, avoid any explicit statement of Christian themes. Unfortunately, these two short stories are all that remains of Flynn's efforts at fiction writing. Although his published output would be prolific, it would be entirely nonfictional analysis of national and international politics, military life, economics, and the role of the Catholic Church in the modern world.[29]

By his last year at the BLS, Flynn had been promoted to the position of Class II editor of *The Register*. In addition to the consequent editorial duties this position imposed, Flynn continued to contribute his own pieces. The character of those contributions, though, shifted from fictional to historical writing. In October 1922, Flynn published a short history of *The Register* in a piece entitled "Latin School Journalism." It discussed the publication of the school newspaper since its first edition in 1881. Flynn admitted that, in its early versions, *The Register* had been a simple chronicle of events on campus, but it had evolved into a combination of a detailed newspaper and a journal in which students could demonstrate and improve their literary abilities. As he had done in his first piece for the newspaper, Flynn concluded by calling on the students to subscribe to *The Register* and to give the staff the financial support they needed: "The editors of this year's *Register* hope to be able to present students a worthy, interesting, and readable paper. To do this, however, we call upon every pupil in the school to consider *The Register* his paper, and that it is his duty to help to make it a publication worthy of the children in common of one of the oldest, grandest, and most renowned schools in the world."[30]

29. *The Boston Latin School Register,* June 1922, 22–24.
30. *The Boston Latin School Register,* October 1922, 3–4. Flynn may have entered the school as an outsider from the social and economic environment of many of his fellow

During the summer of 1922, the Boston Latin School moved to its current address at 78 Louis Pasteur Avenue, right next to Harvard Medical School.[31] In commemoration of this event, in the December 1922 issue Flynn began work on a monthly history of the BLS, from its founding in 1635 up to the year 1923, with the idea that each issue of *The Register* until the end of the academic year would contain an article by Flynn discussing another era in the history of the school. In the initial article, Flynn wrote that his sources would be previous issues of *The Register,* issues of the Harvard University's *Register,* an earlier historical sketch of the school written by a former student named Henry Fitch Jenks, and numerous school records at the school's library. The initiator of this project was almost certainly Flynn himself, and throughout the rest of his fifth year, he published one story each month chronicling the history of the school.[32]

Many BLS students went on to attend America's oldest university, Harvard.[33] Others attended other schools in the Ivy League, such as Yale, Princeton, and Columbia, on their way to careers in law, business, medicine, journalism, or other fields. Perhaps Flynn would have followed this trajectory, as his experience at *The Register* had already given him a foundation in newspaper editing. By the summer of 1922, however, between his fourth and fifth years, Flynn was already nearing a decision about his future that did not involve study at any university at all. He was going to enter the Congregation of Saint Paul of the Cross, also known as the Passionists.

Paolo Francesco Danei, a Christian mystic from Piedmont in the Duchy of Savoy, who was beatified in 1853 as Saint Paul of the Cross, in 1720 wrote the rules for what would become the Passionist Order. In addition to the three usual vows of poverty, chastity, and obedience, Passionists would take a fourth vow, to promote a devotion to the Passion of the Divine Savior. In 1725, Pope Benedict XIII gave permission for Paolo and his brother Giovanni officially to found a congregation

---

students, but by his fifth year he clearly identified with the Boston Latin School and took a great deal of pride in his educational background.

31. Pauline Holmes, *A Tercentenary History,* 305.

32. *The Boston Latin School Register,* December 1922, 3–4.

33. BPL, MS 617—Attendance and Discipline Records for the Boston Latin School.

based on these spiritual rules. Both men were ordained as priests in 1727. The official name of the order is "The Congregation of the Passion of Our Lord Jesus Christ," but its members were often referred to simply as the Passionists; following the beatification of Paolo Danei it was sometimes known as the "Order of Saint Paul of the Cross." The more informal name, the Passionists, remains in broad use up to the present day.[34]

With the motto "May the Passion of Jesus Christ Be Forever in Your Hearts," the Passionists are a "mixed" congregation, a hybrid between a contemplative order, such as the Trappists, and a dynamic order, such as the Jesuits or Augustinians. The Passionists were officially recognized by the Holy See as a *congregation* in 1769. They maintain this designation to the present day. However, since their own members often refer to themselves as part of an order, I will use this designation as well.[35]

Passionists engaged in a strict life that combined missionary work and contemplation; their missionary work centered on giving spiritual retreats that focused on the Passion of Jesus Christ. The lives of Passionist priests—unlike the lives of priests of some Catholic religious orders and the lives of many parish priests, who usually had some leeway in determining how their days were scheduled and who often had a measure of financial independence—were strictly regulated by their provincial superiors; even small financial decisions had to be given the order's approval. Nor were Passionists expected to live or conduct spiritual work separate from the other members of their order; when this was permitted, it was for only a limited amount of time.[36]

Passionist communal life revolved around many traditional monastic practices, such as abstinence from meat, observing the Lenten Fast, walking barefoot, chanting the Divine Liturgy, and hours of silent contemplation and prayer, both alone and with other members. This did not mean the members of the order spent the entire day shut off from the rest of the community. They engaged in daily works of charity among the population, and were expected to lead the laity in prayerful

34. Roger Mercurio, *The Passionists* (Collegeville, Minn.: The Liturgical Press, 1992), 15–20.
35. Cassian Yuhaus, *Compelled to Speak* (New York: Newman Press, 1967), XIX–XXI.
36. Ibid.

reflection on the sacrifice of Jesus Christ. In the words of Paolo Danei, in the first rule he wrote for the order, the Passionists should "not only devote ourselves to prayer that we may be united with God in charity, but also lead others to do the same."[37]

Upon his death in 1775, the Passionists numbered about 180 members, nearly all of whom lived in twelve different retreats, most either in Genoa or in the Papal States. The congregation remained largely confined to Italian-speaking Europe for the next seventy-five years. It survived fifteen years of Napoleonic rule, during which time the Passionists, like nearly all other religious orders in Italy, were suppressed under the orders of the Corsican-born French emperor. After the final defeat of Napoleon in 1815, the congregation returned from exile and began growing substantially; by 1852 it numbered more than two thousand.[38] This was a significant year for the order, not only because Pope Pius IX began the beatification process for Paolo Danei, but also because Bishop Michael O'Connor of Pittsburgh, Pennsylvania, formally requested that Fr. Anthony Testa, the Passionist general in the Papal States, establish a Passionist community in his diocese.[39]

Long before their coming to the United States, the Passionists had been taking their mission work beyond the original European borders of the congregation. From the mid-1790s onward, the Passionists sent a few members of the order to Turkish-ruled Bulgaria, where they met with a small measure of success. In the 1840s they sponsored an ultimately failed attempt to conduct missionary work in an Aboriginal region in Australia. There was also a small Passionist presence in Britain—it was the Passionist Blessed Dominic Barberi who welcomed the legendary English convert Cardinal John Henry Newman into the Church in 1845. Later, in the late nineteenth and early twentieth centuries, the Passionists founded missions in countries as diverse as Jamaica, Germany, Austria, and most famously, China. (From 1921 until their expulsion by Mao Zedong's Communist regime in 1950, dozens

37. Mercurio, *The Passionists*, 23.

38. Ibid., 35–40. Like the Jesuits, the Passionists were originally organized along quasi-military lines, with a Passionist superior general as the order's leader, who answered directly to the pope.

39. Ibid., 75.

of Passionists from both Europe and North America established and maintained numerous missions in China's Hunan Province.) The creation of the Passionist monastery in Pittsburgh in 1853, named after Saint Paul of the Cross, was followed by more expansions: to Dunkirk, New York, with the founding of Saint Mary's Monastery in 1862; Saint Michael's Monastery in Union City, New Jersey, in 1864; Saint Joseph's Monastery in Baltimore, Maryland, in 1868; and Saint Ann's in Scranton, Pennsylvania in 1905. These foundations formed part of the Passionists' eastern province in the United States, also referred to as the Province of Saint Paul of the Cross.[40]

Despite the area's large Catholic population, the Passionists did not arrive in Boston until more than fifty years after their initial settlement in Pittsburgh. In 1908, the Passionist monastery of Saint Gabriel's opened in the Boston neighborhood of Brighton. It served not just as a monastery but also as a retreat center for both clergy and laity.

The first recorded contact between Flynn and the Passionist order was on July 8, 1922.[41] To Reverend John Carey, who had been instrumental in the founding of Saint Gabriel's and who was serving his second term as its Provincial, Flynn wrote: "I am very desirous of entering the Passionist Order this fall, if possible. I have read all the available literature on the Passionists and their rules of life, and I have thought everything over. Hoping that it is not too late to make an application."[42]

Flynn, as it turned out, was too late in his attempt to join the Passionist order for the following year, the deadline for entrance into the Passionist Preparatory Academy at Saint Mary's Monastery in Dunkirk having already passed. Flynn, though, did not easily give up his aspiration. Frequently throughout his life, this same determination emerged, for he rarely took no for an answer or gave up on any project in which he was engaged. On March 11, 1923, nine months after his first letter

40. Yuhaus, *Compelled to Speak,* 104–17. There was also a western province, known as the Holy Cross Province, which encompassed all of the United States west of the Ohio River; it contained Passionist churches in Cincinnati, Louisville, Chicago, Saint Louis, and Saint Paul.

41. Ibid, 134.

42. Letter from Flynn to Carey, July 8 1922. PHA Record Group 379—29/C. Unfortunately, the records contain only Flynn's writings to Carey; we do not have a record of Carey's responses.

to Carey, Flynn wrote that, as a result of a meeting the previous June between himself, Carey, and the parish priest at Saint Peter's Church, Father Gabriel Clement, he was convinced he should join the Passionists. Flynn added that his five years at the Boston Latin School provided enough time in academic preparation to enter the Passionist Preparatory Academy.[43]

A week later, having received encouragement from Carey, Flynn submitted a formal application to enter the seminary. Flynn noted his extensive studies in mathematics, history, Latin, English, French, and German. His Latin preparation was extensive: five years of courses (it was optional in his last year) and translations from Latin into English of the works of Julius Caesar, Cicero, Virgil, and Ovid. Flynn also mentioned he had never had any major health problems that would keep him from serving the order.[44] Having received a positive reception from the Passionists a week after sending in his application, Flynn wrote to Carey again, noting that he had completed the required medical examinations and was looking forward to entering the novitiate. Eager to begin, Flynn asked Carey to inform him of the date on which he should arrive at Saint Mary's, and "the sooner the better."[45]

One of his aunts on his mother's side, Margaret Ryan, wrote a formal letter of recommendation for her nephew Philip on April 12. Flynn, she wrote, came from "a good religious family, and he has always been a model of piety in his life and of industry and success in his studies."[46] On June 12, Flynn heard from Carey that he had been accepted into the Passionist novitiate and was expected to arrive in Dunkirk on August 17. His experience in the Passionists, which would lead him to tremendous accomplishments but also brought about severe financial humiliation, administrative mistreatment, and emotional pain, was about to begin.[47]

---

43. Letter from Flynn to Carey, March 11, 1923, PHA, Record Group 379—29/C. Passionists in Boston and elsewhere commonly visited local parishes to speak on the work of the order and invite young men to join the order.

44. Passionist Application Form, March 18, 1923. PHA Record Group 379—29/C.

45. Letter from Flynn to Carey, March 26, 1923. PHA Record Group 379—29/C. This would not be the last time Flynn would challenge his superiors.

46. Letter from Ryan to Carey, April 12, 1923. PHA Record Group 379—29/C.

47. Letter from Flynn to Carey, June 10, 1923. PHA Record Group 379—29/C. Also,

The World in 1924

As Flynn prepared to enter the Passionist novitiate, the "Golden Era" of the late nineteenth and early twentieth centuries had been swept away by the cataclysm of the First World War. The centuries-old rule of the Ottoman Turks, the German Hohenzollerns, the Russian Romanovs, and even the oldest dynasty of them all, the Austrian Habsburgs, had come to an end in the wake of military defeats and political revolutions. The first to collapse, the Russian Empire, was swallowed up in revolution and civil war from 1917 to 1921. Following a brief period of rule for eight months in 1917 by the democratic Provisional Government, Russia was transformed into a communist dictatorship by the Bolsheviks following their seizure of power in Petrograd in October 1917.

Led by Vladimir Lenin, the Bolsheviks were a tiny political group in 1914 who used the chaos during the collapse of Tsarist rule—and a series of mistakes made by the leaders of the Provisional Government and later the White Movement—to seize and hold onto power against seemingly unsurmountable odds. In the process of the Russian Civil War from 1918 to 1921, a humiliating peace treaty with the Central Powers was signed, Tsar Nicholas II and his family were executed, and the industrial and agricultural sectors of the Russian economy were nationalized. An attempt to export communism throughout Europe following the Red victory in the civil war was stopped in August 1920 at the gates of Warsaw by the armies of the reemerged Polish state, but the Bolshevik regime in Moscow never relinquished the goal of creating global communism through its umbrella network of communist parties, the Communist International, also known as the Comintern. In 1921 after the Civil War had concluded, Lenin was forced to make certain limited concessions to capitalism in his economic policy known as the New Economic Policy (NEP). Shortly afterward, Lenin's health seriously de-

---

Flynn was concerned to find out whether he had been admitted to Saint Michael's, so that his family would not have to pay the fees for the advancement exams and college entrance exams that were mandatory for every Boston Latin School student before they entered their sixth and final year. His family's solidly middle-class economic status is evident here, although there is no evidence he joined the novitiate because of financial considerations.

clined, and he died in January 1924. This set off a five-year succession struggle in the Soviet Union, from which the Georgian General Secretary of the Communist Party, Josef Stalin, emerged victorious.

Although Germany and its allies—Austria-Hungary, the Ottoman Empire, and Bulgaria—emerged victorious on the eastern front, setbacks in the Middle East, the Alps, and most significantly the western front at the hands of the French, British, and Americans, led to defeat in the fall of 1918. Wilhelm II avoided the dark fate of his Russian cousin, Nicholas II, by fleeing into exile in Holland, but Hohenzollern rule, and consequently the German Empire, came to an end in November 1918, and the declaration of the Weimar Republic followed. Initially under the leadership of the Social Democratic Party, the Weimar Republic in Germany brutally crushed attempts by the German Communist Party to seize power, by organizing soldiers returning from the war into paramilitary Freikorps to fight the communists.

The victorious allies of the United States, Britain, France, and Italy forced the Weimar government to sign a tough peace in the spring of 1919, the Treaty of Versailles. Under its terms, Germany gave up its colonies; ceded significant amounts of territory to France and Poland; reduced its armed forces significantly in size; and paid reparations to Britain, France, and Belgium—both for the costs of the war and the German occupation of the latter two countries. These actions were justified through the "war-guilt" clause in which Germany, along with its allies, admitted sole culpability for starting the conflict in 1914.[48] In the subsequent years six years, the Weimar Republic fought several brief border wars with Poland and lurched between various economic and political crises, including attempts by the military, as well as right and left-wing extremists, to overthrow the government.

The greatest crisis was the two-year French and Belgian military occupation of the Ruhr Valley, western Germany's industrial heartland, from 1922 to 1924, following Germany's failure to meet the scheduled reparations payments to Brussels and Paris. This exacerbated the infla-

48. As harsh as the Treaty of Versailles was, it was not nearly as harsh as the Treaty of Brest-Litovsk, which Germany had forced on Russia the year before. Nor was it even the toughest treaty forced on the defeated Central Powers—that was the Treaty of Trianon, which the Hungarians were forced to sign.

tionary crisis in Germany, reducing the Reichsmark to virtual worthlessness. It was, however, the only time the fractious elements of German political life were united during the history of the Weimar Republic. The new chancellor, Gustav Stresemann, helped negotiate the Dawes Pact in April 1924, in which—with the hope of paving the way for a return to economic and political stability—German reparations payment resumed and French and Belgian soldiers withdrew from the Ruhr.

A week before Germany's Wilhelm II abdicated, the last Habsburg emperor, Karl I, released his Austrian subjects from any allegiance to himself and left Vienna. Shortly thereafter, the Austrian First Republic was declared. Karl hoped to maintain his position as king of Hungary, but pressure from the Allied governments forced him to abdicate his Hungarian title and leave Budapest. He would die in exile in Italy a few years later. The new Austrian government initially avoided the violent political conflicts that plagued Russia, Germany, and Hungary following the military defeats, but it, too, had to sign a hard peace. The treaty of Saint Germain led to dissolution of all Habsburg domains except for those populated by its German speakers, and even there Austria lost the Tyrol to Italy and the Sudetenland to Czechoslovakia. A rump state remained, one without a clear national or political identity. For many Austrians, shorn of their ancient empire, the idea of unification with Germany was an appealing one, but both treaties signed by Berlin and Vienna with the victorious Allies explicitly forbade this.

Following Karl's withdrawal from Hungary, the country plunged into political chaos, as Hungarian Communists seized power and declared a Soviet regime in early 1919. Under the leadership of Béla Kun, the Hungarian Soviet Republic lasted only nine months, but during this time it attempted to nationalize the Hungarian economy fully, eliminate the Catholic and Calvinist churches, and conducted a Red Terror directed against political enemies. Kun's disastrous attempt to extend the Communist revolution by invading Romania led to the fall of his government, as the Romanian army halted the Hungarian advance, invaded the country, and occupied Budapest. Kun fled into exile in Moscow, and Miklós Horthy, the former Grand Admiral of the Austro-Hungarian Empire, led the reformed Kingdom of Hungary. Technically, Horthy served as regent for the absent king, since the Allies refused to allow Karl I to return and the Hungarian government never agreed to offer the crown to anyone else. Horthy's first task was signing the Treaty of Trianon in June 1920, which stripped Hungary of more than 70 percent of its pre-1914 territory and placed more than 30 percent of its pre-war Hungarian population in other countries, principally in Romanian Transylvania.

Hungary's bitter experience from 1918 to 1920—the fall of the old semi-constitutional order; a brief experience with democracy that was followed by a totalitarian and then an authoritarian government—mirrored much of Europe during the period between the two world wars. The various peace treaties at the end of the First World War left a legacy of embittered populations, intense infighting in domestic politics, and also territorial and ethnic conflicts between different countries.

The United States' entry into the First World War in the spring of 1917 turned the tide against Germany on the western front. President Woodrow Wilson arrived in France to cheering crowds two years later, seemingly indicating a significant American presence in European affairs. Yet Wilson, in his last two years in office, failed to accomplish his intended foreign policy, a "peace without victors"—this in the face of British, French, and Italian resistance—and he did not secure America's entry in the League of Nations, because of the intense opposition in the U.S. Senate that was led by Massachusetts Senator Henry Cabot Lodge Sr.

Just as Massachusetts had the most powerful senator in the country, it also had, after 1923, the presidency itself, as former governor Calvin Coolidge became president following the death of Warren Harding. Having made a name for himself in national Republican politics through his handling of the Boston Police Strike of 1919, Coolidge, perhaps the last (if not only) semi-libertarian American president, oversaw a period of substantial economic growth, as well the rapid social transformations of the "Roaring 20s." In Boston the institution of Prohibition was broadly unpopular (and led to frequent drinking trips to Montreal and other Canadian cities), but the city continued on its path of population growth and modernization, as the city airport opened in 1920, and the National Hockey League founded its first American team, the Boston Bruins, in 1924. The city's mayor, Democrat John

Curley, was in his second of ultimately four terms, once again demonstrating the strength of Irish Catholics in the city as many of the Protestant "Yankees" moved to the suburbs. The spectacular corruption of the "Curley machine" in the city's Democratic politics ensured none of these terms as mayor were consecutive.[49]

In the archdiocese of Boston, Cardinal William Henry O'Connell dominated as ever; he influenced every aspect of life in the Catholic Church, which continued to expand in terms of laity, clergy, new parishes, and new religious institutions. Yet his national and international reputation suffered grievous damage, through the scandal of the early 1920s involving his nephew Joseph O'Connell, who was also a priest and was the chancellor of the archdiocese. The younger O'Connell not only embezzled church funds, he also led a double life as a married man under a different name in New York City. What the cardinal knew about his nephew's activities and when he knew about them was sharply debated when the scandal broke (as it still is). Although his position as the leader of Boston's Catholics was unshakable, his aspirations to become the most prominent Catholic cleric in the United States were dealt a blow from which they never recovered.[50]

The city of Boston continued to have a strong influence on Flynn's life, but his entry into the seminary marked the end of his regular presence there. His journey as a priest in the Passionists, and later as an Army chaplain and a key member of Catholic Relief Services, would take him through America, Europe, South America, and even into North Africa. Through it all, his character as a tough-spirited, quick-of-mind and—when the situation called for it—sharp-tongued Irish Catholic from Boston was clear, and was a tremendous asset in the incredible adventure that was the rest of his life.

49. James O'Toole, *Militant and Triumphant*, 132.
50. Ibid., 197–201.

2

EARLY SERVICE WITH THE PASSIONISTS, 1924–1941

The Seminarian, 1924–1931

Philip Flynn spent the years from 1924 to 1931 in the Passionist seminary preparing to be ordained a priest. Unfortunately, the archival records for this period of his life are scarce, although a small number of records do reveal his activities. On January 21, 1924, following his first few months at the Passionist Preparatory Academy at Saint Mary's, Flynn received formal permission from Cardinal O'Connell to join the Passionist order. Seven months later, on September 14, 1924, Flynn professed his temporary vows as a Passionist at Saint Paul of the Cross Monastery in Pittsburgh, taking the name Fabian of Our Lady of Sorrows. His religious name had two parts. The first, Fabian, was an early Christian martyr who served as the Bishop of Rome from 236 to 250 AD; he was executed under the orders of the Roman emperor Decius. The second part, Our Lady of Sorrows, stems from the well-known Catholic devotion to the Seven Sorrows of Mary, which focuses on pivotal events in Mary's life. Although he would remain "Uncle Phil" to his numerous relatives and Philip to some of his Passionist friends, his name was now Fabian Flynn.[1]

1. Second Document Signed at Religious Profession, September 14, 1924. PHA Record Group 379—29/C. This is the name I will use for him for the remainder of this work.

Fabian Flynn would spend much of the next seven years at various Passionist monasteries and missions, but the bulk of the time was spent at the Passionist Preparatory Academy in Dunkirk; Saint Paul of the Cross in Pittsburgh; Immaculate Conception Monastery in Jamaica, New York; Saint Gabriel's in Boston; and Saint Ann's Basilica in Scranton. It was at this last post on September 14, 1927 (the Feast of the Exaltation of the Holy Cross), three years after professing his vows as a novice, that Flynn renounced usufruct—in other words, renounced wealth and all material possessions to the Passionist order. This meant Flynn was forced to beg his provincial superior every day for something as small as a dime to ride the subway. He also took the oath of perseverance, promising to follow the rules of the Passionists, and to maintain obedience to his provincial superiors. Finally, Flynn declared a perpetual profession of the vows as a Passionist, that he took his vows by his own free will, and that he would stay loyal to them throughout the course of his life. His career, especially after 1942, often took him far away from the company of his fellow Passionists, and, more importantly, away from the supervision of his superiors. Nor would it be suited for the strict vow of poverty. These vows would, decades later, cause a great amount of distress for Flynn, and at times, a virtual estrangement from his order.[2]

The Passionist Preparatory Academy in Dunkirk was in a rural area, at the western end of the State of New York, situated about forty-five miles southwest of Buffalo on the shores of Lake Erie. The city of Dunkirk had about 20,000 people in the 1920s, and was known mainly as a railroad and shipping hub. Seminary training in the Passionist order was characterized by a strong regimentation of life, divided between academic work, spiritual training, and service to the community. Every Passionist monastery had a parish church attached to it, and seminarians were expected to interact regularly with the lay population through service activities, amateur religious theatricals, instrumental and choral concerts, and sporting events. Each seminarian usually had a duty to perform around the monastery as well, from cooking to clean-

2. Third, Fourth, and Fifth Documents Signed at Religious Profession, September 14, 1927. PHA Record Group 379—29/C.

ing to gardening. Unsurprisingly, given his later duties, Flynn helped administer the retreat center attached to the school. For most students, the day began with a 6 a.m. Mass; it continued with meals, classes, spiritual exercises, religious services, and brief periods of recreation until lights out at 9 p.m. Classes were from Monday to Saturday, although Wednesday afternoons were free. Sundays were reserved for religious services and catechism lessons. Seminarians who were beginning their training were not allowed to visit home, but their families could visit them. Each year they were given two weeks of vacation, but they were expected to spend much of it at the seminary.[3]

In essence, the Passionist Preparatory Academy was a Catholic liberal arts college in all but name, and it was eventually credited as a two-year school, which benefited some students who began but, for a variety of reasons, did not finish seminary training. Each year, students had to complete a series of exams in June, at the end of the academic year, on everything they had studied. Failure to pass them could lead to being required to retake the entire course of study from the previous year.[4] In one of his military records, Flynn listed his primary area of study at the Passionist Preparatory Academy as theology. He also mentioned that, as he had approached the end of his own seminary training at the Academy, he had directed a few amateur theatrical productions and had taught English to first-year students.[5]

During this time of classwork instruction, students were gradually integrated into the semi-monastic life of the Passionists. This did not happen until a student demonstrated his spiritual and emotional maturity. Seminarians would often meet with Passionist leaders from around the United States, and in exceptional circumstances, from Europe, who would inform them of the various global activities of the order.[6] Flynn's grades, much like his grades at the BLS, were well above average, al-

3. Robert Carbonneau, "Life, Death, and Memory: Three Passionist Missions in Hunan China, and the Shaping of an American Mission Perspective in the 1920s" (Ph.D. diss., Georgetown University, 1992), 25–27.
    4. Ibid., 41–47.
    5. Ibid.
    6. Ibid., 83–86. Flynn opted to study both German and French, although he took far more German language courses.

though not at the very highest levels of his class. He was always able to pass his exams, and his contributions to the retreat center were noted as highly impressive, especially his organization of spiritual discussions and prayer sessions.[7]

It was toward the end of his time of seminary training that Flynn first began to experience severe kidney pains. These pains, which even resulted in a brief hospitalization, required him to curtail his activities as a retreat organizer.[8]

On February 8, 1931, Flynn's time in the seminary came to an end and he was ordained as a Passionist priest at the Immaculate Conception Monastery in Jamaica, New York. Although he was a full-fledged member of the order, he was not traveling to a new parish. Instead, he was officially assigned to serve as one of the retreat leaders at the Bishop Malloy House, which was located next to the Immaculate Conception Monastery. No matter their location, the Passionists were famous for conducting retreats for Catholic laity and clergy at their monasteries, and Immaculate Conception was no exception. It was the first of the many career-paths Flynn would follow as a Passionist.[9] One of the most remarkable vocations in the Congregation of Saint Paul of the Cross was about to begin.

The World in 1931

During his time at the Boston Latin School and at the Passionist Preparatory Academy, in the 1920s, democratic governments in Europe collapsed like dominoes and were replaced by totalitarian, authoritarian, or semi-authoritarian orders. Russia, Finland, Hungary, Italy, Poland, and Portugal all shared this fate, and more were to follow in the next decade. As Flynn began his career with the Passionist order, the entire capitalist and democratic world was reeling from the effects of the Great Depression, now in its second year.

7. Comments on Flynn's Seminary Activity. PHA Record Group 379—29/C.
8. Letter from Carey to Flynn, November 5, 1948. PHA Record Group 379—29/C. Carey refers to Flynn's kidney problems spiking up again in 1948, reminding him of Flynn's experience at the Preparatory Academy in Dunkirk.
9. Ordination Document, February 8, 1931. PHA Record Group 379—29/C.

What began as an American recession following the stock market crash of August 1929 became a global economic depression by 1930. Few countries were more deeply affected by these economic developments than Germany, whose economy was intimately tied to the Depression through American loans to assist the Weimar Republic in making its reparations payments.[10] The end of American financial assistance led to Germany's economic collapse under the burden of those payments. Economic weakness led to a corresponding political instability in Germany, as previously marginal parties of the left and the right, the Communists and the National Socialists, became the third and second largest parties, respectively, in the Reichstag after the disastrous parliamentary elections in July 1930. This effectively paralyzed the government in Berlin, as its president, former military hero Paul von Hindenburg, was unable to a form a majority government and essentially ruled by decree. Germany moved from parliamentary government to rule by presidential decree, a politically precarious situation that would last until the creation of a National Socialist government in January 1933.

In neighboring Austria, although the political crisis created by the Great Depression was not as large as what existed in Germany, Chancellor Karl Buresch governed through an unstable coalition of German nationalists (those who wished for the unification of Austria with Germany) and Christian Socials, a conservative party that rejected the idea of Catholic Austria joining largely Protestant Germany. A significant number of Christian Socials, led by Engelbert Dollfuss, were proponents of Austrofascism, which was modeled on Benito Mussolini's rule in Italy and also explicitly rejected the idea of unification with Germany.

On the political fringes in Austria were the communists and the Austrian Nazi Party; much like the Weimar Republic, the Austrian First Republic was a republic with few republicans. Street fighting between the right-wing paramilitaries the Heimwehr (the Home Army) and the left-wing Republikaner Schutzbund (the Defense Federation of the Republic) were common sights in Vienna as well as in Innsbruck, Graz, and Salzburg. There was a real possibility that a civil war could erupt between the different political extremes in Austria.

10. Amity Shlaes, *The Forgotten Man: A New History of the Great Depression* (New York: Harper Collins Publishers, 2007), 95–99.

There was little doubt about the nature of the Soviet regime in Moscow. In 1931, the USSR was in its third year of the "Revolution from Above," dictated by its leader Josef Stalin, who had emerged victorious in the half-decade power struggle to succeed Lenin. Stalin's Five-Year plan was to construct the largest industrial economy in the world and to do it in less than five years; "Complete the Five-Year Plan in Four!" was the Soviet slogan. Vast industrial sectors would be added to every Soviet city. Furthermore, model industrial cities would be built from the ground up. The most famous example would be the city of Magnitogorsk, in the southern part of the Ural Mountains. At the same time, the agricultural economy of the Soviet Union, which had been free from most state controls during the New Economic Policy of the 1920s, would be "collectivized"; that is, it would be placed under the strict monitoring of the Soviet government through state-administered collective farms—in other words, the Russian and Ukrainian peasantry would become serfs once more. The strong resistance of the peasants to these policies in 1930 led to a brief retreat in their implementation by the government in Moscow, but that reversal would prove no more than a temporary pause.

Isolated from the effects of the Great Depression, the two Soviet plans worked off each other: the collectivization of agriculture would allow Stalin to bring the peasants under the complete domination of the party-state, and their crops would be sold abroad, with the funds used to purchase advanced industrial equipment the Soviets needed. The limited toleration of "bourgeois specialists" in the Soviet economy during the New Economic Policy of the 1920s ended, as the secret police, the GPU (*Glavnoe Politicheskoe Upravlenniie*—Main Political Directorate) would massively expand their hunt for "wreckers, saboteurs, and counter revolutionaries" as described by the notorious Article 58 of the Soviet Penal Code.[11] Finally, the early 1930s in the Soviet Union were marked by the full-scale assault by all the organs of the party-state

11. As Aleksandr Solzhenitsyn and many subsequent historians have pointed out, Article 58 was used extensively by the Stalinist regime to justify massive violent repressions against "wrecking" and "sabotage"—everything from showing up late for work to criticizing the Communist Party to making a joke about the local collective farm chairman could qualify as a counter-revolutionary crime under the article.

in criminalizing and ultimately eradicating religious belief, as thousands of churches, synagogues, and mosques were razed to the ground, and thousands of clergy were arrested and sent to labor camps.

At the cost of enormous social, economic, and cultural, and personal suffering and destruction, Stalin's regime forged the Soviet model. Its main elements included a centrally planned economy, grounded in heavy industry and massive collective farms; a brutal hostility to religion, or indeed, any method of thinking or institution beyond the party-state's control; an omnipresent secret police force; and, increasingly, a massive cult of personality centered around Stalin. It was this system that the Soviets would impose on the countries "liberated" from Nazi rule by the Red Army after 1945.

The United States was under considerable strain from the Great Depression in 1931, as the unemployment rate was higher than 16 percent and more than 15,000 homeless men wandered the streets of New York City, with equivalent numbers in Boston, Philadelphia, Pittsburgh, Chicago, and Los Angeles. Nothing President Herbert Hoover did seemed to have any effect on improving either the health of the stock market or the GDP.[12] Liberal capitalism appeared to be in free fall all over the world, and this provided a unique challenge to the Catholic Church. As articulated by Leo XIII in *Rerum Novarum* and by thousands of clerical and lay Catholic leaders afterward, the Church had strongly rejected the solutions to the problems of capitalism offered by Marxists. Yet the effects of the Great Depression forced the members of the Catholic Church, including Fabian Flynn, to address more forthrightly than ever before the effects of the modern industrial economy on those who lived under it.

The Retreat Leader and Magazine Editor, 1931–1941

Flynn's first official position with the Passionists following his ordination was as one of the retreat directors at the newly established Bishop Molloy Retreat House, which was attached to the Immaculate Conception Monastery in Jamaica, New York. Located in the Borough

12. Shlaes, *The Forgotten Man,* 112.

of Queens in New York City, the neighborhood of Jamaica numbered about 45,000 in 1931 and was largely populated by Irish Catholics. In the Church of the 1930s, more and more orders and congregations were leading spiritual retreats for laymen; the Passionists were among the most active in this field.[13]

In the words of Cardinal O'Connell of Boston, addressing the Fourth National Catholic Retreat Conference in Latrobe, Pennsylvania, on December 29, 1930: "One of the greatest dangers in the materialistic world of today is the inadequate appreciation of the spiritual values of life, in fact, the failure of modern civilization to think of spiritual things at all. By providing havens of physical rest and spiritual refreshment in which Catholic men of the world can more readily obey God's injunction." The next speaker, the Right Reverend Alfred Koch, a Benedictine monk and the director of nearby Saint Vincent's College and Ecclesiastical Seminary, also noted: "Give us laymen, who see and understand with the mind of Christ, who love with the heart of Christ, men who earnestly strive to further God's plans for the extension and preservation of his Kingdom here upon earth."[14] Both quotes encapsulate the attitude Catholic clergy had toward the lay retreats, especially regarding what they were intended to accomplish in American society.

Weekend spiritual retreats, often for men of similar professions, were a common event throughout the 1930s at the Bishop Molloy House. From all over the tri-state area of New York, New Jersey, and Connecticut, doctors, policemen, sailors, firemen, lawyers, school teachers, businessmen, and various other professionals, as well as deacons, the Knights of Columbus, and even married couples would arrive at the retreat house and engage in prayer, spiritual exercises, self-reflection, and conversation with Passionist clergy and with the seminarians.[15] Flynn soon distinguished himself as one of the most

13. Carbonneau, *Life, Death, and Memory*, 41. The Passionist Retreat House was named after Bishop Thomas Edmund Molloy, the bishop of the Diocese of Brooklyn, in which the retreat house was located. Not a Passionist himself, Molloy was among the most influential Catholic clerics in the northeastern United States during his tenure as bishop, which lasted from 1921 to 1956.

14. Chronicle of events for Saint Paul of the Cross Monastery, Pittsburgh. PHA Record Group—Pitt 2002, Box 31, Folder 4, 98–100 (hereafter, 31/4).

15. Carbonneau, *Life, Death, and Memory*, 42. http://bishopmolloy.org/passionist

capable retreat leaders; his abilities as a spiritual counselor were especially notable.

Just as Flynn's work on the Boston Latin School's *Register* served as the foundation for his later work as a writer and magazine editor, his work as a spiritual counselor for a diverse group of individuals would be repeated on a larger scale during the 1940s, when Flynn would minister to many soldiers from all walks of life, many of whom were not even Catholics or Americans. As was the case for much of Flynn's career, each new path prepared him for challenges that would arise later in his life.

The provincial of the eastern province, Father Justin Carey, soon engaged Flynn's abilities as a writer, directing him to compose a retreat guidebook to be used for spiritual retreats all over the country.[16] The result of Flynn's efforts, published in 1932, was a pocket-sized book entitled *My Retreat*. It was a collection of prayers and spiritual readings, with short reflections on their importance. The book was meant to be given to each participant in the retreats offered at the Bishop Molloy House, or any other Catholic retreat, and then it could be taken with them at the conclusion. Reactions to Flynn's collection were positive, the Reverend Stephen Meaney, as the business manager of the Jesuit magazine *America*, wrote: "This Guide Book is a worthy contribution to the Lay Retreat Movement. Retreatants will find it a useful companion throughout various spiritual exercises of the weekend, and throughout the rest of the year."[17]

By the summer of 1932, Flynn's writing and editorial abilities had caught the eyes of the Passionists Harold Purcell and Theophane Maguire, the founder and second editor of *The Sign*, a monthly Catholic newsmagazine published out of the Saint Michael's Monastery in Union City, New Jersey. Harold Purcell founded *The Sign* in July 1921. It ran until 1982, and during its heyday of the 1930s to the 1960s it was one of the most popular center-right Catholic news magazines in the United States. Each issue of *The Sign* contained, in addition to articles

-history/ The Bishop Molloy House was located in a large and aesthetically striking facility in the heart of New York.

16. Fabian Flynn, *My Retreat*. PHA Record Group 379—29/C.

17. Advertisement for *My Retreat*. PHA Record Group 379—29/C.

and editorials on current events, stories on Catholic life in America and around the world, historical and theological essays, even prose and poetry. Its editor until 1934 was Harold Purcell. His life and career had many interesting parallels to Flynn. Born in 1881, he too had attended the Passionist Preparatory School in Dunkirk and had professed his initial vows at Saint Paul of the Cross, in Pittsburgh, in 1898. He was ordained a priest in 1904, and spent the next seventeen years as a retreat leader in the American South and West, working mainly with non-Catholics.[18]

Theophane Maguire also attended seminary training in Dunkirk; he had professed his vows in Pittsburgh in 1917, and he was ordained a Passionist priest in 1923. He spent the next six years at the newly founded Passionist mission in Hunan, China. Upon returning to the United States in 1929, he was first sent to the Saint Paul of the Cross Monastery in Pittsburgh, but he was then transferred to Union City to serve as an associate editor for *The Sign*.[19] Both Purcell and Maguire were impressed with Flynn's work on *My Retreat*. Flynn's provincial, Joseph Carey, approved his transfer to Saint Michael's Monastery in Union City at the request of Purcell and Maguire, and thus began Flynn's association with *The Sign*, which would last for more than two decades.[20]

Flynn worked from 1932 to 1934 as a personal assistant to Purcell. He assisted him in research for the editorial pages, selected artwork for the covers, and reviewed all submissions. He also served on the editorial board of the news magazine. During this time, in addition to articles from various Passionists, *The Sign* contained work from noted Catholic writers such as Hilaire Belloc, G. K. Chesterton, Enid Dennis, and Fulton Sheen. During this time, Flynn did not write any articles himself, although he did contribute to the editorial pages.[21] Another activity worthy of note was Flynn's decision to join a group in the New York metropolitan area known as the Celtic Circle. Little itself is known about this group, but it sent a letter on May 30, 1933, to the German ambassador to the United States, the German consul general,

18. Biography of Harold Purcell at the provincial website.
19. Biography of Theopane Maguire at the provinicial website.
20. Fabian Flynn's Personnel Records. PHA Record Group 379—29/C.
21. Fabian Flynn's Personnel Records. PHA Record Group 379—29/C.

President Franklin Roosevelt, and Secretary of State Cordell Hull, decrying attacks on German Jews by the Nazi regime, which had recently come to power in Germany: "no such campaign of bigotry as has been pictured as having occurred in Germany can be condoned."[22] While Flynn's anti-communism was more routinely expressed than his anti-fascism, this too was a part of his ideological makeup.

In the summer of 1934, the editorial board of *The Sign* went through a major overall. Purcell, its founder and editor, decided not only to step down from his position in the news magazine, but also to leave the Passionists. On July 28, 1934, Purcell officially left the Passionist congregation to found a Catholic community called the City of St. Jude, in Montgomery, Alabama, that was dedicated to the "religious, charitable, educational, and industrial advancement of the Negro People." Purcell worked at the community until his death in 1952.[23]

With Purcell's departure, Theophane Maguire became head editor, and Flynn took over Maguire's old position, which he occupied until health concerns forced him to withdraw in February 1935. Flynn was one of two associate editors, the other being his fellow Passionist Adrian Lynch. He continued most of the same duties that had occupied him over the past two years, but he now wrote regular sections of the editorial pages, most of which concerned foreign affairs and/or the threat of communism. In the September 1934 issue, Flynn's first as an associate editor, he wrote a brief column concerning the Austrian chancellor Engelbert Dollfuss, who had been assassinated two months before by Austrian Nazis in an attempted coup. Flynn praised Dollfuss as a "man of peace" and a devout Roman Catholic who strove throughout his life to create peaceful and stable order in Austria and Europe. Especially galling for Flynn was the fact Dollfuss, who took over two hours to die from the assassin's bullets, was denied last rites from a priest by the "Nazi Criminals."[24]

22. "Two Groups Add Protests," *New York Times*, March 30, 1933, 13.

23. Biography of Harold Purcell. Flynn would later write that his apprenticeship under Purcell had proved invaluable for his later career with *The Sign* and as a columnist for other newspapers.

24. "The Tragic Death of Dollfuss," *The Sign*, September 1934, 67. The fact that Dollfuss was an authoritarian leader who had done more than anyone else in Austria

Flynn wrote two significant editorials in the November 1934 and February 1935 issues. The November 1934 issue contained an editorial entitled "Communist Activities among American Youth." Flynn wrote that the Soviet government had been using every opportunity to recruit American youths into the communist movement since the Roosevelt administration had extended diplomatic recognition to the Soviet regime the year before. Flynn specifically referenced a pamphlet published through *The Young Worker*, the newspaper of the CPUSA's Youth League, that urged students to leave the United States and enter service in the armed forces of the Soviet Union. He wrote at the end of his editorial: "Any paper publishing such seditious rot should be suppressed. Yet *The Young Worker* circulates unhampered."[25]

"The Saarlanders Choose the Reich" appeared in the February 1935 issue, wherein Flynn expressed his concern that the largely Roman Catholic population of the Saarland had overwhelmingly approved unification with Germany in a recent plebiscite. This meant unification with Hitler; in spite of his "attacks on Christian Churches in general and the Catholic Church in particular, the ties of race and blood triumphed over every other consideration." Flynn hoped that those who had voted against the plebiscite would not be treated by the Nazi regime as traitors, and that the Nazis would learn to moderate their foreign policy, but perceptively he doubted this would happen.[26]

The February 1935 issue of *The Sign* would prove to be the last for Flynn as associate editor until another stint in this position in the early 1950s. As was the case through much of his life, health concerns forced Flynn to withdraw from his official positon. Not only had Flynn's kidney problems emerged again, but he was also experiencing serious pains in his stomach, occasionally coughing up blood. Flynn was trans-

---

to dissolve the democratic First Republic and replace it with the domination of the Christian Social party did not figure in Flynn's analysis. Dollfuss was better than Hitler, and that was what mattered.

25. "Communist Activities Among American Youth," *The Sign*, November 1934, 195. Flynn's point here is highly controversial, but it does fit with his tough views regarding communism and the threat it posed.

26. "The Saarlanders Choose the Reich," *The Sign*, February 1935, 387. Flynn would get a chance to work in the Saarland eleven years later, as the director of War Relief Services in the French occupation zone of Germany.

ferred to Saint Ann's Basilica in Scranton on February 14, 1935, to work as an administrative assistant at the Passionist monastery, where he would remain for the next three years.[27]

It was during this time that Flynn composed two lengthy pamphlets that were distributed all over the United States. The first, which appeared in 1936, was entitled *A Catechism of Communism for Catholic High School Students*; the second, written for an audience of Catholic lay adults in 1937, was named *Catholicism, Americanism, and Communism*. These two pamphlets provide some of the best insights into Flynn's own complex political philosophy. They are also his longest published writings, numbering twenty-three and thirty-eight pages, respectively. Flynn wrote these pamphlets at the request of Theophane Maguire and they were published by the Paulist Press. This Catholic publishing house, founded in 1866 by the Paulist Fathers, was and remains one of the largest distributors of Catholic literature in North America.[28]

Fabian Flynn was undoubtedly a conservative in his religious, social, political, and economic views. Throughout his life, he remained devoutly attached to Catholic doctrine as the best, if not sole, path to moral improvement in this world and to eternal life with God. Flynn saw the Church and the Passionists as a force for good in the world, and had little time or patience for those in or out of government who criticized or impeded them. He could also speak harshly of societies and countries that were not sufficiently devoted in spiritual matters.

Flynn's beliefs were also tempered by a realism that viewed the world as it was, not as he would have liked it to be. Certain political, social, and economic problems could not be permanently "solved," but their harsh effects could and should be ameliorated by those holding political and religious authority. At the same time, he exhibited at many times during his life a an strong inclination toward independence from his superiors; if he felt they were deficient in performing their duties, he would publicly call them out. As someone who had served on the front lines in Europe during the Second World War and the Cold War, Flynn felt those at the top issuing orders were often so

27. Chronicle of events for Saint Paul of the Cross Monastery, Pittsburgh. PHA Record Group—Pitt 2002—31/4, 153.

28. http://www.paulistpress.com/Pages/Centerright/150th_Anniversary.aspx.

immersed in the "big picture" that they neglected to examine how their directives affected those at the ground level, whether they were American soldiers in Sicily or ethnic German refugees in Austria.

Ultimately, he was no reactionary. He never wavered in his belief that fascism and communism, as two sides of the same totalitarian coin, were evil, but that it was not enough for the Catholic Church to declare them evil and thereby settle the matter. Instead, words had to be matched with action; the Catholic Church and its allies—including the American government—needed to demonstrate they could meet the great crisis of capitalism in the 1930s, or the great humanitarian crisis after 1945, and could do a better and more humane job in meeting these challenges than whatever might be offered by communists. Flynn followed these convictions throughout his career.

In the initial sections of *A Catechism of Communism*, Flynn justified liberal capitalism through political and theological arguments. He wrote that the Declaration of Independence offers a right to private property and that this idea was rooted in a belief in the Almighty. All people had a right to life, to a good name and reputation, and the right to hold property, as Jefferson argued. To violate any of these rights was a violation of the law and a "sin against justice." Flynn stated the right to property comes from God himself, the highest authority possible: "The first and fundamental source of all property rights is none other than God. The supreme dominion of proprietorship over the entire universe is his. Hence, He alone can give any part of the world to whom He Pleases. He may give much to one and little to another, for He is the Lord, the Creator and Ruler of all. Yet we will all share in the world's property."[29]

Each person is given a unique set of gifts, and by cultivating them and sharing them with others everyone can attain a share in the world's goods. Flynn pointed to the painter, the farmer, the landlord, and the businessman as examples of this. The plan of the communists to abolish private property was not only illegal, as it deprived Americans of due process regarding their right to property, it was also contrary to

29. Fabian Flynn, *A Catechism of Communism for Catholic High School Students* (New York: Paulist Press, 1936), 6–7.

"the mind of God and the teachings of the Catholic Church."[30] Flynn did not claim capitalism is divinely ordained, but in and of itself, it is not morally wrong, unlike communism, which is always morally wrong, a "cure worse than the disease."[31]

He conceded that capitalism could lend itself to abuses, such as the economic domination of the many by the few. Capital had a right to profit from labor, but only provided "it gives Labor a decent wage, good working conditions, and a reward for faithful service in some form of old age pension." The Church would always condemn the abuses of capitalism, and would work to harmonize the relations between capital and labor. The influence of Leo XIII and *Rerum Novarum* is especially prevalent here, and Flynn quotes the encyclical directly at the end of the pamphlet. Only after making this case does Flynn move on to the militantly atheistic nature of communism and how no Catholic could subscribe to Marxist-Leninist beliefs.[32]

Flynn suggested certain methods one might use to fight communism that might appear controversial today, such as immediately destroying any copy of *The Young Worker* that fell into one's hands. Yet he devoted considerably more time to emphasizing the positive things Catholic students could do to fight communism, noting that one productive act was to strive for racial equality in American society, since "the Communists are making special efforts today to win over the American Negro, whom we all know to be the victim of injustice and prejudice."[33] Catholic boys and girls should do what the Catholic Church had always done, work for the betterment of their fellow human beings, working in charitable activities and helping to create a humane and social economic system characterized by harmony between

---

30. Flynn, *A Catechism of Communism*, 9. He also provided a decent summary of the origins of twentieth-century communism as a philosophy, discussing the philosophies of Marx and Lenin's additions to them, although there are some mistakes—Vladimir Lenin is identified as "Nikolai Lenin" at one point.

31. Ibid., 10.

32. Ibid., 11.

33. Ibid., 16. Flynn did not often write or comment on racial issues in American society, but on the rare occasions when he did, he continually supported the idea of racial equality before the law, justified in the idea of the brotherhood of all races under God.

capital and labor. This should be matched by acting as a loyal son or daughter of the Church: "You must answer Communism by deeds. You must live as convinced Catholics. Keep the Commandments of God and the Church Faithfully. Only then can the menace of Communism, which disturbs the entire world, be defeated."[34]

Flynn's superiors in the Passionist order, especially the current head of the Saint Paul of the Cross Province, Colman Byrne, received with approval *A Catechism of Communism*. Since Flynn's health troubles continued to keep him from engaging in anything but minor administrative work at Saint Ann's in Scranton, he agreed to the request by Byrne, Cardinal Patrick Hayes, the Archbishop of New York, and the Paulist Press to write a longer pamphlet directed at Catholic adults in America, especially the elusive "man on the street." The result, published in March 1937, was *Catholicism, Americanism, and Communism*.[35]

Catholicism, Americanism, and Communism followed the same basic organizational format as his pamphlet for high school students, although his arguments were a bit more sophisticated, given his audience. At the beginning of the pamphlet, Flynn laid out the stakes facing not just Americans but everyone in the non-communist world: "Communism threatens to overturn the very foundations upon which our American democratic principles of government are founded, and to cover the entire world in their ideology."[36] Flynn urged readers to recognize communism already present in the midst of American society, and to avoid being "lulled into an unpatriotic slumber" by those who would dismiss the threat of communism, as a "Red Scare" or a "Red Herring." This conduct was the "basest form of political treachery." Returning to a common theme, Flynn wrote it was not enough merely to denounce communism; American Catholics had to "prove in everyday language and in an easily comprehendible way just why Communism is such an evil and why it must be opposed."[37]

After describing the actions and personalities of Karl Marx, Vlad-

34. Ibid., 22–23.

35. Fabian Flynn, *Catholicism, Americanism, and Communism* (New York: Paulist Press, 1937), 2–3.

36. Ibid., 3.

37. Ibid., 5

imir Lenin, Josef Stalin, and Earl Browder, the head of the CPUSA, Flynn returned to the words of Leo XIII and *Rerum Novarum*, arguing that capitalism was not immoral or unethical. It had "let itself be swayed by injustice and has more than once fallen into grave abuses." The solution was to create a social safety net for those who needed it. The Great Depression did not prove that capitalism had failed. Rather, it had "gone astray, led by a group of unprincipled and greedy men." The capitalist system needed a house-cleaning, not to be dynamited, as the communists were calling for. The forces of capital, according to Flynn, had a right to their profits as long as they, to quote Pope Pius XI, "provided a just share to their workers of the fruits of production." Flynn went on to say that capital owed the worker a living wage, decent working conditions, and old-age pensions. He pointedly noted the Soviet state had failed to provide these things in the "Workers' State"; neither had it abolished economic classes, for the Communist Party had become the new ruling class.[38]

He also pointed to the National Catholic Welfare Conference as one of the main organizations in the United States fighting to alleviate poverty and to assist those suffering from the effects of the Great Depression. He listed its various branches and the programs they offered, from immigration to health education. Its program of "Catholic Action," according to Flynn, promoted "Liberty, the arts, morality, social security, and the emancipation of women, the sanctity of the home, the right to a living wage, economic harmony, international peace and many other desirable social reforms." He urged his readers to remember that the Catholic Church, both in America and internationally, had fought to provide for impoverished industrial laborers long before "the Communists raised their hue and cry about the rights of the working man."[39]

Only then did Flynn move to discuss the explicit threat communism posed to religious faith and religious institutions. He warned American Catholics to reject arguments made by some members of the CPUSA that Catholicism and communism were compatible, or that

38. Ibid., 15–18.
39. Ibid., 25. War Relief Services was not yet part of the NCWC, for the WRS did not come into being until 1943.

communism was not actually militantly atheistic. Providing vivid and apocalyptic imagery, Flynn asked his readers to consider the effect of a communist revolution in the United States:

> Are you a good Catholic? Does your religion help you? Do you want to continue the practice of your religion unmolested? Do you want to see churches destroyed, convents sacked, schools burned? Do you want to see priests shot down in the streets? Do you want to see defenseless nuns whose entire lives and energies are spent in doing good for the sick, the poor, and the unfortunate, do you want to see these holy women insulted, raped, and murdered? Of course not! Then fight and expose this deadly Communist insincerity and deceit. Don't listen to their honeyed protestations of religious freedom. Think of Mexico! Think of Spain! Think of Russia![40]

After summarizing the essence of communism as violent, cruel, atheistic, and intent upon overthrowing the American government by force, Flynn outlined the best ways in which to fight it.[41] The best way, was to live a "good Catholic life," following the Church's teachings; to be knowledgeable of their faith and supportive of Catholic institutions like the NCWC and local Catholic schools, and to work to assist their fellow man through charitable endeavors. Prove communists wrong in their charges that the Church cared nothing for the world. The worst thing for a Catholic to be was apathetic: "Half of the recent trouble in Spain and Mexico, two so-called Catholic countries, can be laid directly at the door of ill-informed, indifferent, and unorganized laity. That an apathetic clergy was also partly responsible, it is idle to point out now. The damage has been done."[42]

Like its predecessor, *Catholicism, Americanism, and Communism* was distributed throughout the entire country and was favorably received by Flynn's Passionist superiors. By this point, his deteriorating health,

40. Ibid., 30. The reference to Spain refers to atrocities committed against the Catholic Church by forces of the Spanish Republic during the Civil War. Flynn, like nearly every conservative American Catholic, was a supporter of Franco and the Nationalist forces.

41. Ibid., 35. Unlike some other anticommunist American priests, such as Charles Coughlin, Flynn explicitly refused to link communism with Judaism.

42. Ibid., 36–37.

with its worsening pain in his stomach and kidneys, prevented him from writing any further educational pamphlets, or engaging in any active ministry at all. In late 1938, diagnosed with stomach cancer, Flynn needed emergency surgery to remove half of his stomach at St. Elizabeth's Hospital in Boston in January 1939. Because his doctors gave him at best five years to live, his superiors transferred him from Saint Ann's in Scranton to convalesce at Saint Gabriel's Monastery in Brighton, Massachusetts. His family and members of his order expected him to spend the rest of his presumably short life in Brighton.[43] At Saint Gabriel's from 1939 to 1941 he spent his time tottering on the verge of a coma, and was in nearly constant pain. Ironically, his lifelong habit of smoking a pack of cigarettes a day was one of his few ways of finding some relief.[44] By all accounts, it appeared Flynn would soon end his life with a tremendous amount of promise unfulfilled. Events at the other end of the world, as well as his sheer force of will to overcome his ailments and join the fight against totalitarianism, would ultimately send that life on a different trajectory.

The World in 1941

As Flynn was recovering from stomach cancer, the United States was drawing closer to involvement in the Second World War. Isolationist sentiment remained high throughout the country, for a variety of reasons, but most American diplomatic and military leaders, as well as the Roosevelt administration itself, realized that America's façade of "neutrality" in the face of Axis aggression could not be maintained for much longer, as the United States was already sending considerable military aid to Britain, the Soviet Union, and China.

In the decade between Flynn's ordination to the priesthood in 1931 and America's entry into the war in 1941, democracy collapsed in both

43. Register of Events, Saint Gabriel's Monastery, Brighton, Massachusetts, PHA, Box 204–7, Folder 5—Arrivals and Departures, 1929–1940. The archival records list only a few activities in which Flynn took part during this time period, such as attending an occasional spiritual retreat, as his poor health prevented him from engaging in anything else.

44. Patricia Chisholm, Interview with author, June 12, 2015.

Germany and Austria. In Germany, the decision by President Paul von Hindenburg to appoint Nazi party leader Adolf Hitler as chancellor of Germany in 1933 had, by the time of President Hindenburg's death nineteen months later in August 1934, led to the creation of a dictatorship under the National Socialist Party. Hitler's refusal to allow elections to go forward for a new German president, and his appointment of himself as *Fuehrer* (leader) of the German people, simply became the final steps in this process. Having purged the Nazi Party of its left-wing faction in the Night of the Long Knives the month before and thereby gained the acquiescence of the German military to the Nazi regime, Hitler began gradually but inexorably to implement the Nazi revolution in Germany, chauvinist, racist, and murderously anti-Semitic in tone, and he determined to reassert Germany's dominant position in Europe that he claimed had been lost through the Treaty of Versailles.

In neighboring Austria, from 1932 to 1934 the Christian Social Party under Engelbert Dollfuss—using a combination of legislative chicanery and the street muscle of their paramilitary faction, the *Heimwehr* (Home Army), and helped by sympathizers in the Austrian police and military—dissolved the democratic structures of the First Republic. Emerging victorious over the Social Democratic and Communist paramilitaries in Austria's brief civil war in February 1934, the Christian Social Party forced all political movements that were not banned to unify with them in the "Fatherland Front." This marked the beginning of Austrofascism.

Dollfuss had little opportunity to enjoy his position as Austria's leader, for six months later he was assassinated in the July Putsch by Austrian Nazis in their (ultimately unsuccessful) attempt to seize power in Vienna and then unify with Nazi Germany. The coup attempt was quickly crushed, partially due to the swift actions of Dollfuss's successor, Education Minister Kurt von Schuschnigg, but more directly because of Benito Mussolini's strong resistance to any German advancement into Austria, which Mussolini considered an Italian satellite; moreover, he was personal friends with Dollfuss. For one of the last times in his career, Hitler, who had been chancellor for only sixteen months and was still consolidating power in Germany, backed down. Four years later Italy's increasingly isolated position following their

1936 invasion of Ethiopia led Mussolini to a closer embrace of Hitler, and, by the beginning of 1938, the government in Rome had sent signals to Berlin that another German move on Austria would not face Italian opposition.

Having received the green light from Italy, Hitler moved swiftly in February 1938 to occupy Austria and incorporate it into the German Reich before Schuschnigg could hold an emergency plebiscite in support of Austrian independence, which the latter believed would strengthen his case in an appeal to the League of Nations. Despite the fact that the political unification of Germany and Austria was explicitly forbidden both by the Treaty of Versailles and by the Treaty of Saint Germain, Britain and France did not object to Hitler's actions, nor did most of the Austrians. Schuschnigg and his ministers were arrested and interned at the Dachau concentration camp, and the *Anschluss* between Berlin and Vienna was complete.

The next two years of Hitler's bid for European dominance are well known. Seven months after the *Anschluss*, the German government demanded that Czechoslovakia cede its western regions, the Sudetenland, to Hitler's regime in the name of reuniting all ethnic Germans (who made up the majority of its population) with their Teutonic Fatherland. This was a bigger gamble than the *Anschluss,* as Prague had security treaties with both France and the Soviet Union. Unfortunately, the idea of "collective security"—the idea that the non-Fascist powers should bury their differences in the name of containing Hitler and his allies— failed. Collective security could not work militarily without the active participation of the USSR, but it could not work politically with them, given the deep distrust of Moscow held by the British and French, as well as the refusal of the Polish and Romanian governments to allow the Red Army to pass through their territory to defend Czechoslovakia from a German attack.

Another factor was the refusal of Czechoslovakia's neighbors, namely Hungary and Poland, to come to its aid, as they decided instead to seize territory alongside the Germans. Desperate to avoid a repetition of July 1914, the British and French governments in November 1938 agreed to Hitler's demands for the transfer of the Sudetenland from Czechoslovakia to Germany, if Hitler promised no further territorial aggrandizement. The Czech government had no choice but to agree to this humiliating agreement.[45]

In March 1939, five months after making his promises at the four-power conference in Munich, Hitler seized the rest of the Czech lands, after having, as a pretext for this action, encouraged Slovakia to secede. Any further attempts at appeasement of the Nazi regime by British Prime Minister Neville Chamberlain and French President Edouard Daladier were thus effectively rendered impossible, as Hitler began to turn his attention to the "Polish Corridor." This was a strip of territory that, through the 1919 Treaty of Versailles, had been awarded to the re-emerged state of Poland. The strip divided the German provinces of West Prussia and Mecklenburg from East Prussia. It had a mixed German and Polish population and was therefore a logical next target for Hitler's ambitions. The Polish government, having witnessed the fate of Czechoslovakia, was determined to resist any and all of Hitler's demands. Equally wary of an alliance with Poland's other ancient enemy, the Russians, the Polish government received promises from both the British and the French that they would protect the country's territorial integrity.

The wild card in the summer of 1939 was the Soviet Union. By this time Stalin had overseen, from 1936 to 1938, a massive purge of the Soviet state, the Communist Party, the military's officer corps, and even the secret police. This was the end product of one of the essential aspects of Stalinism: the party-state itself must periodically be purged in blood in order to maintain its ideological fervor and ruthlessness. More than one million Soviet citizens were executed during this period; three times that number were sent to labor camps or exile colonies. The Great Terror had grievously, if temporarily, weakened the USSR as tensions were increasing all over the world, especially with the Soviet Union's neighbors and rivals Japan, Poland, and especially Germany. Desiring to avoid a conflict with his fellow totalitarian dictator Adolf Hitler, at least for the next few years, Stalin was uninterested in an al-

45. This decision would have a considerable effect on Flynn's career as director of Catholic Relief Services in Austria: the Czechoslovak government, upon regaining the Sudetenland in May 1945, began systematically to expel its ethnic German population, some of whom ended up in Austrian refugee camps.

liance with the Western democracies, correctly believing they wanted to divert Hitler's attention eastward. An alliance with the Germans, in comparison, despite the supposed ideological hatred between national socialism and communism, could effectively divide Central and Eastern Europe into mutually beneficial spheres of influence.

The result was the Nazi-Soviet pact in August 1939. Hitler's own deeply held desire to avoid a two-front war, which would involve Soviet Russia as well as Poland, France, and Britain, led to this non-aggression pact, which in reality was a tacit alliance between Berlin and Moscow. During the period from August 1939 to June 1941, Poland was overrun and crushed by Germany and the Soviet Union and was divided into western and eastern halves. The USSR also invaded the three Baltic republics—Estonia, Latvia, and Lithuania—and forcibly incorporated them, while also waging, from November 1939 to March 1940, an unsuccessful war to conquer Finland; this latter effort ended with the Finnish government ceding some territory to the Soviets while maintaining their independence. Eastern Poland as well as the Baltic states were brutally subjected to the Soviet political, social, and economic order; farms and industries were nationalized, churches closed, and hundreds of thousands of "counter-revolutionaries" shipped off to labor camps in Siberia or Kazakhstan or executed by special secret police (People's Commissariat for Internal Affairs, or NKVD) death squads, of which the massacre of Polish army officers at Katyn in April 1940 is only the most notorious example.

Germany barely engaged militarily with its western enemies during the next seven months, as the "Phony War" gave Germany time to consolidate its gains in Poland and prepare to defeat the western democracies with one swift stroke in the spring of 1940. In the space of six weeks, from April to May 1940, Germany—joined eventually by Italy—conquered Denmark, Norway, Luxembourg, Belgium, the Netherlands, and ultimately France. The remnant of the British Expeditionary Force was barely evacuated from Dunkirk in time to avoid total annihilation. Hitler's hope to crush the British through a massive aerial bombing campaign, followed by an amphibious invasion, in the Battle of Britain in the summer and fall of 1940, ultimately failed, thanks to the efforts of the Royal Air Force and Prime Minister Winston Churchill's stalwart leadership. Nevertheless, much of the continent was now under either Hitler's or Stalin's rule.

Horthy's Hungary was one of the handful of nominally independent countries after the events of 1940, and although the regime was certainly not democratic, it also was not totalitarian. Like its neighbors Bulgaria and Romania, Hungary found itself drawn into Germany's orbit in 1940 and early 1941, as Hitler's embrace was still, in their opinion, preferable to Stalin's; and of course in the example of Poland they saw what could be expected should they resist Nazi ambitions. As the Nazi-Soviet alliance began to sour following unsuccessful discussions between Hitler and Stalin's foreign minister Vyacheslav Molotov in November 1940, Germany's *Fuehrer* began drawing up plans for Operation Barbarossa, the invasion and conquest of the European part of the Soviet Union, to commence in the late spring 1941. Hungary was one of many countries that would provide soldiers to join the Germans in the invasion of Soviet Russia, which commenced on June 22, 1941.

With the Axis forces pouring over the Soviet border in June, Stalin ceased to be Hitler's ally and became allies with Churchill—and, tacitly, the American President Franklin Roosevelt, who had been sending Lend-Lease aid to Britain since 1940 and would soon provide economic support for the Soviets. Roosevelt, whose New Deal during the 1930s had not ended the Great Depression but had softened its worst effects, had wanted to bring the United States into the war in Europe since 1939, but he had faced continual isolationist opposition at home from many Republicans and some Democrats. On the other side of the world, the United States also inched closer to confrontation with the Empire of Japan in the Pacific, as the American government continued attempting to force Japan to end their war with Nationalist China, which had raged on since 1937. The joint American, British, and Dutch oil embargo on Japan in August 1941, the brainchild of Undersecretary of State Dean Acheson, was seen in Tokyo has an act of economic war, and Japan's military leaders decided to launch a massive attack simultaneously against all their rivals in the Pacific by the end of 1941.

The stage was then set for one of the most important fortnights of the twentieth century, at the beginning of December 1941. Although the German army and its allies had advanced rapidly into Soviet territory over the previous six months, the Axis advance finally ground to a halt at the gates of Moscow, and a counteroffensive of the Red Army under Marshal Georgi Zhukov saved the Soviet capital and drove the Germans back. This meant Hitler's gamble that the Soviets could be defeated in one six-month campaign in 1941, on which he had bet everything, had failed. The German government compounded its error by declaring war on the United States two days after the Japanese attack on the U.S. Pacific fleet at Pearl Harbor on December 7 without first receiving promises Tokyo would reciprocate with a declaration of war on Moscow. Germany now found itself fighting the British Empire, the Soviet Union, and the United States.

Japan's similar gamble also failed, as the surprise attack damaged but failed to cripple American naval power in the Pacific. Indeed, Japan's attack and Germany's and Italy's declarations of war served to unite most of American society behind Roosevelt in bringing the United States and its considerable resources into the war against the Axis powers. These world-shattering events in December 1941 would alter millions of lives, including that of Fabian Flynn, whose monastic life at Saint Gabriel's in Brighton was ended by his determination to join the U.S. Armed Forces as a chaplain. Within sixteen months of Pearl Harbor, Fr. Flynn would find himself in battle against the totalitarian evils of fascism, and then, over the next three decades, against communism.

∽3

MILITARY CAREER, 1941–1946

Father Monahan, when you received me recently into your office, you remarked that you would be on the lookout for my application when it came through. I do hope you recall me. I sure am anxious. They have me down for limited service; couldn't argue out of it. I trust that you won't brand me stupid or bold or seeking a favor before I am even accepted, but please take pity on this poor Passionist missionary. Don't relegate me to some post where I'll get no action or foreign service. After twelve years of giving missions, I'm ready for anything.[1]

As this letter of October 17, 1942, from Flynn to Father John Monahan—one of the administrators of the War Department's Office of the Chief of Chaplains—indicates, Flynn was desperate to serve abroad with American soldiers in combat. Although health issues required him to serve stateside during the first six months of his career in the U.S. Army, Flynn would get his wish in the summer of 1943, when he was transferred to the 26th Infantry Regiment, part of the First Infantry Division. The "Fighting First" would be at the center of combat in the western front of the Second World War in Europe. Although his health issues, compounded by the ill-effects that arose following the injury he had sustained during the Sicilian campaign, led to a six-month transfer away from the 26th Infantry Regiment from December 1944 to

1. Letter from Flynn to Monahan, October 17, 1942; NPRC Flynn Personnel File 0–501–418 (hereafter NPRC Flynn File).

June 1945, Flynn always considered the "Blue Spaders," as the 26th Infantry was known, to be his unit. He returned to them for the first year of the American occupation of Germany, and, as fortune would have it, he became the first of two Catholic chaplains of the International Military Tribunal at Nuremberg. Flynn would get his wish not only to pray for victory of the forces of Christian freedom against "pagan tyranny" but to participate in the fight itself, as a spiritual counselor to American soldiers in the greatest war in human history.

Entry and Training in the U.S. Army Chaplain Corps,
December 1941 to December 1942

American involvement in the Second World War changed forever the trajectory of Flynn's life and career. Clergymen had accompanied American soldiers into battle as early as the Revolutionary War, but the U.S. Armed Forces did not establish official standards and training for Army chaplains until the First World War. Even then, this happened only through the lobbying of numerous Catholic, Protestant, and Jewish organizations to make the Chaplain Corps a permanent part of the military.[2] Before the Japanese attack on the U.S. Pacific Fleet at Pearl Harbor, Hawaii, on December 7, 1941, the U.S. Army Chaplain Corps was, much like the rest of the armed forces, severely limited in number, having fewer than 150 chaplains on active duty and fewer than 700 in reserve as late as the fall of 1941.[3]

On May 25, 1918, Congress had authorized that every 1,200 soldiers be ministered to by at least one chaplain, and this rule remained in place throughout American involvement in the Second World War.[4] As the U.S. Army and Navy scrambled to build up their conventional armed forces following U.S. entry into war with Fascist powers in Europe and Japan in the Pacific, they had to do the same with mili-

2. Earl Stover, *Up from Handymen: The United States Army Chaplaincy, 1865–1920* (Washington, D.C.: Office of the Chief of Chaplains, Department of the Army, 1977), 222–25.

3. David Crosby, *Battlefield Chaplains: Catholic Priests in World War II* (Lawrence: The University Press of Kansas, 1994), xx.

4. Stover, *Up from Handymen*, 188.

tary chaplains to minister to Catholic, Protestant, and Jewish soldiers. Between 1942 and 1945, the U.S. Army commissioned more than 9,000 chaplains, about 35 percent of whom were Catholic priests. Despite this, the Catholic Church was never able to match the quotas requested of it by the Army and Navy.[5] Consequently, Catholic chaplains like Fabian Flynn would often minister to non-Catholics; this was a standard practice throughout the Armed Forces during the Second World War.[6]

Shortly after the United States entered the Second World War, Flynn asked his Passionist superiors if he might leave Saint Gabriel's Monastery and enlist as a military chaplain. The provincial, Edmund Walsh, had concerns that Flynn's health would prevent him from serving effectively in combat, but Walsh did eventually approve the request on October 2, 1942, the Catholic feast day in honor of the Guardian Angels. Flynn's health had slightly improved in 1941, as he was well enough to visit Passionist missions in both Canada and Mexico. He had a full physical examination under the supervision of the U.S. Army on October 9, 1942.[7] Like all other Catholic priests, Flynn then needed to appeal to the U.S. Catholic Church's Military Ordinariate, headed by the powerful archbishop of New York, Archbishop Francis Spellman.[8]

The Military Ordinariate gave its approval on October 10, and Flynn applied for his commission as an Army chaplain. Terrified that his health problems—which included not just his stomach and kidneys, but also, as his Army medical examiners discovered, a corneal scar in his right eye—might keep him stateside for the entire war, Flynn asked the Chaplain's Office to waive any recommendations for limited service.

5. Lyle Dorsett, *Serving God and Country: U.S. Military Chaplains in World War II* (New York: Berkley Books, 2012), 31.

6. Crosby, *Battlefield Chaplains*, xix. Among Catholic religious communities, the Society of Jesus (the Jesuits) were the least generous in providing priests for the chaplain corps; the Passionists were among the best—in 1944 more than 40 percent of their number were serving in the U.S. Army and Navy.

7. Letter Walsh to Flynn, October 2, 1942. PHA Record Group 322—Passionist Army Chaplains, Box 3, Folder 7—Fabian Flynn, Army Chaplain, 1942–1945; War Relief Services, 1945–1949 (hereafter 3/7).

8. Crosby, *Battlefield Chaplains*, xvii. Flynn's request marked the beginning of a long and mostly successful partnership with Spellman, which continued during Flynn's postwar activities in War Relief Services.

Two days after sending his letter to Father John Monahan in the War Department, he received a reply. Monahan stated that the medical officers had forwarded the application to the office of the U.S. Surgeon General for final approval but had recommended limited service for Flynn. Monahan politely but firmly informed Flynn that the Surgeon General's office was certain to concur with the recommendation. He told him: "You may be sure that we will find plenty of spots where you can be placed in a position to do an immense amount of work. If you are placed on limited service we could not send you on foreign duty nor into a place where you were likely to see action, but boys in this country, you will agree, need attention just as much as the men overseas."[9] Given Flynn's ambitions, Monahan's letter must have been a crushing disappointment.

Flynn received his temporary appointment from the Adjutant General's Office as a First Lieutenant in the U.S. Army Chaplain Corps on October 21, 1942, his first official day in the U.S. Army, although he had been informed of this development the day before by the Chaplain's Office. Writing to Walsh on October 25, Flynn said, "I am overjoyed at the progress I have made. My one prayer now is that I may be a good Chaplain and bring honor to the Church and the congregation." If there was any lingering disappointment over his designation for limited service, Flynn did not show it to his provincial superior.[10] Having received special permission from Walsh to spend the next week with his family in Boston, Flynn's military career then began on the morning of October 31, 1942, his first day of instruction at the U.S. Army's chaplain school at Harvard University. Unlike many other prospective army chaplains, Flynn did not have to travel far for the first stage of his military career.[11]

Two days later, Brigadier General William Arnold, the Chief of

9. Father John Monahan, Office of the Chief of Military Chaplains to Fabian Flynn, October 19, 1942, NPRC Flynn File.

10. Letter from Flynn to Walsh, October 25, 1942. PHA Record Group 322—3/7. Four weeks later, Flynn was formally commissioned as an officer in the U.S. Army at the conclusion of his chaplain's training at Harvard University.

11. Register of Events, Saint Gabriel's Monastery, Brighton, Massachusetts, October 1942. PHA Records of Saint Gabriel's Monastery, Box 204—7, Folder 6—Arrivals and Departures, 1940–1944.

Chaplains of the U.S. Army sent Flynn his formal welcome letter. Arnold did not mince words; his letter began: "Inconveniences, difficulties, and hardships will be your portion. Your only sure reward will be God's blessing the fruits of your ministrations to the lives of your men. Military life is a life of discipline, and essential military virtues of courage, loyalty, obedience, devotion, and self-sacrifice are also religious virtues." He recommended Flynn prepare a spiritual lesson for the men he would serve for each week of the year. Arnold told him to keep in mind that he might well be a spiritual counselor for men who had strayed far from the Catholic faith, or for men who were not Catholic at all, or even have no religious background: "Many, very many indeed will be hearing these eternal truths for the first time. Your earnest words will establish convictions and train consciences in these men." He concluded by reminding Flynn not to waste time on activities that would take him away from his spiritual or military duties, and not to allow his superior officers to make demands of him beyond his duties as a chaplain.[12]

Flynn completed his four-week chaplain's training on November 28, 1942, graduating with a class of more than 300 new chaplains who were about to be sent to Europe or the Pacific.[13] Flynn wrote to Walsh four days later, tell him the process had been a "real grind," especially since Catholic chaplains woke at 4:45 a.m. to celebrate Mass and still make the first morning assembly. He informed Walsh he was being transferred to Camp Barkeley in Abilene, Texas, one of the largest training facilities for American soldiers during the Second World War. Flynn was assigned to the 120th Station Hospital—a Medical Replacement Training Center (MRTC)—as its official Catholic chaplain. MRTCs trained medical personnel and units for the tasks they would face on the front lines, primarily first aid and evacuation of the wounded to field hospitals.[14] Walsh responded on December 13, 1942, promising

12. Letter from Arnold to Flynn, November 2 1942. NPRC Flynn File.

13. Program for the Commencement Exercises for the Chaplain School at Harvard University, November 28, 1942. Harvard University Archives-4.1542, hereafter HUA.

14. Letter from Fabian Flynn to Edmund Walsh, December 2, 1942. PHA Record Group 322—3/7.

Flynn the Passionist order would provide financial assistance to his mother Julia, who had fallen ill. He marveled at how Flynn's health had held up through his military training at Harvard: "I need hardly tell you that I'm happy your health is so much better. It's really wonderful how well and strong you've become. I am sure you will be able to do much for the men in the service."[15]

Service in Army Medical Hospitals,
December 1942 to June 1943

During his first full month in Texas in December 1942, Fr. Flynn offered six Sunday masses, as well as eighteen morning services, and three on Christmas Day. He also heard confessions eleven times, visited the training hospital to see patients twice, and also met with soldiers from the Army's Ninetieth Infantry Regiment, which was attached to Camp Barkeley and had no Catholic chaplain.

For Flynn, a life-long Bostonian, the five months in west Texas proved to be a culture shock. His first letter, written on January 9, 1943, expressed his struggles to adjust to living in a largely Protestant section of the United States, and out of the 368 soldiers in Camp Barkeley, there were only sixty-one Catholic soldiers and two officers. He mentioned how the Catholics of the 120th Station Hospital came from all over the country; how his altar server came from Tacoma, Washington, and drove a beer truck before his entrance into the army; and that the choir soloist was from Chicago and worked in a Walgreens pharmacy. The organist was a former medical student at the University of Pennsylvania, and an Episcopalian. Fifteen of the Catholics in his unit were "full-blooded Indians from Santa Fe." He mentioned the beauty of the Christmas Eve and Christmas Day services, which reminded him of services in Boston, and he felt back at home.[16] Five days later, Walsh's assistant, John Lam-

15. Letter from Edmund Walsh to Fabian Flynn, December 13, 1942. PHA Record Group 322—3/7.

16. Letter from Flynn to Walsh, January 9, 1943. PHA Record Group 322—3/7 MRTCs trained medics and medical units in preparation for their deployment to Europe or the Pacific. The 120th Station Hospital at Camp Barkeley was established in November 1941. Others were later established in Illinois, Pennsylvania, Virginia, and Arkansas.

bert, sent Flynn a response thanking him for letting the Passionist order know how he was doing and discussing the death of his mother, Julia, who had recently passed away. The Passionists had sent a sympathetic telegram to his relatives and offered several masses in her memory.[17]

With his mother's death from cancer, Flynn was, in his own words to a superior officer a few months later, "all alone in the world," his father having died of a heart attack six years earlier. Flynn made the train journey from Abilene to Boston to attend her funeral in early January 1943. Condolence letters sent to him from his fellow Passionists note his deep love for his parents, and that their passing was a great loss. Now without immediate family, Flynn would form consistent ties with his various cousins. He would also form close friendships with military personnel and later with officials from the WRS/CRS.

Flynn's service with the 120th Station Hospital continued for the next three months. Monthly reports he sent to the Office of the Chief of Chaplains show that he offered between 25 and 30 religious services each month, combined with hospital visits and individual meetings with soldiers, including confessions. He accompanied them on all their hikes, marches, and formations, and met with his commanding officers concerning the morale of the men. He also found time to supervise athletic competitions every Saturday, direct three retreats, and even perform a handful of weddings. The clerk assigned to him, Private Thomas Morgan, assisted him throughout the week.[18]

A bulletin Flynn printed out for the Catholic soldiers of the 120th Station Hospital provides an illustration of a typical week of religious activities. On Sunday, Mass was offered twice, at 7:30 and 10 a.m.; weekday masses were offered at 6:15 a.m. every day but Wednesday, when Flynn offered an evening mass at 6:15 p.m. He heard confessions before every Sunday mass and on Saturday nights from 6 to 7:30 p.m.[19] Flynn produced these bulletins each month and had them posted throughout the camp. They usually ended with this statement: "To serve God and

17. Letter from Wilson to Flynn, January 14 1943. PHA Record Group 322—3/7

18. Monthly Chaplain's Report, December 1942 to March 1943. NPRC Flynn File.

19. Ibid. The bulletin also discussed how pleased Flynn was with the men for their regular attendance at Mass and their religious observance in general, especially their requests for prayer books and rosaries, and their respectful treatment of him.

in serving Him, to serve our beloved Country, should be your constant endeavor. Be good, be intelligent, be loyal, be practical, be model Catholic men and soldiers. Our real work lies ahead. May God grant us strength and His grace when that time comes."[20]

In his second letter to Walsh, on February 6, 1943, Flynn announced he was disregarding advice of the Military Ordinariate, which recommended that each chaplain should write to his bishop or provincial each month, but he promised to write regularly. He mentioned attendance at the weekly evening masses was satisfactory, with one-third of the Catholics in attendance. Ensuring the soldiers received Holy Communion was more difficult; "big-city men" from Chicago, San Francisco, and St. Louis participated, but Catholic soldiers from "southwestern hill-billy towns" and those of Italian and Mexican ancestry were "terribly dumb and ill-instructed" in their faith. He concluded by claiming: "It is increasingly borne in on me as these days pass what noble, decent, brave men these Catholic soldiers are. I can only pray that as a priest I may be worthy of them."[21]

Flynn asked Walsh to waive any further financial obligations he had toward Saint Gabriel's, most of which was related to the purchase of two chaplain's uniforms, which cost the monastery $750. He mentioned he had spent $350 traveling from Texas to Massachusetts for his mother Julia's funeral and had spent his military salary on vestments for his chapel at Camp Barkeley, as well as dining occasionally in Abilene, as he often missed meals in the camp mess due to the scheduling of religious services. He admitted to having a "monk's foolishness" with money and and mentioned that having his debts written off would be a great assistance. In his response, written on March 3, 1943, Walsh flatly refused, telling Flynn the vow of poverty meant he had to act more conservatively with money, and Saint Gabriel's would expect to be reimbursed for the uniforms "in due time." Walsh went on to suggest that Flynn appeal to his relatives to pay off his debts to Saint Gabriel's.[22]

20. Ibid.

21. Letter from Flynn to Walsh, February 6, 1943. PHA Record Group 322—3/7. Flynn's tendency to disregard official protocols would soon lead to considerable conflict with other members of the Passionists, and occasionally with CRS officials.

22. Ibid.

This was the beginning of a two-decade battle between Flynn and his order over his financial expenses.

On March 2, 1943, Flynn wrote to the Office of the Chief of Chaplains, again requesting a transfer to either the European or the Pacific theatre of the war, and specifically referencing a promise made by Father John Monahan, that he would place him in an overseas assignment if one opened. Flynn noted that Camp Barkeley had recently received two more Catholic chaplains and his own services were now extraneous. He explicitly pointed out that, since his parents were dead, he was an excellent candidate to be sent abroad, in contrast to a chaplain with "dependents or reasons for staying here in the United States."[23] Two days later, Brigadier General Arnold telegrammed Lieutenant Colonel A. S. Goodyear, the Executive Officer of Camp Barkeley, informing him Flynn was needed to fill a replacement in an overseas assignment and would be transferred soon.[24]

Flynn spent two more weeks at Camp Barkeley before he traveled back to the East Coast, then boarded an ocean liner to take him across the Atlantic Ocean and into the Mediterranean Sea, ultimately landing in Tlemcen, Algeria, in early April 1943. He spent the months of April and May as the Catholic chaplain of the 32nd Station Hospital, a temporary assignment until his permanent appointment to the 26th Infantry Regiment in June came through. The 32nd Station Hospital was originally founded in Camp Rucker, Alabama on August 13, 1942. Over the next three months, it was transferred from Camp Rucker to Fort Benning, Georgia, then to Camp Kilmer, New Jersey, whence it departed for North Africa in mid-January 1943, arriving in Algeria ten days later. Unlike the 120th Station Hospital in Camp Barkeley, which was always intended to remain in the United States to train medical teams, the 32nd Station Hospital was formed explicitly to accompany American soldiers overseas.[25]

23. Letter from Flynn to the Office of the Chief of Chaplains March 2, 1943. NPRC Flynn File.

24. Telegram from Brigadier General William Arnold to Lieutenant Colonel A.S. Goodyear, March 4, 1943. NPRC Flynn File.

25. WWII Military Hospitals European Theatre of Operations https://www.med -dept.com/articles/ww2-military-hospitals-european-theater-of-operations/

Although Algeria was a long way from Texas, Flynn's first two months with the 32nd Station Hospital in Tlemcen appear similar in their routine to his time at Camp Barkeley. He said Mass between 25 and 30 times, with a total attendance of two thousand soldiers for all the services put together. Much of the rest of his time was taken up by individual meetings with soldiers and frequent hospital visits, numbering 11 in April and 77 in June. Flynn also had time in month of June to conduct a baptism of a PFC (Private First Class) William Oscar Larson; at the end of May, he personally organized and supervised the unit's Memorial Day services. According to his monthly report, Flynn directed a parade of soldiers, including Military Policemen (MPs) and wounded men, the medical staff, and the officers. Mass at the local Church of Saint Michael's followed the parade. Flynn's report stated the event had a "deep effect" on the native population. Sensitive to French sensibilities, Flynn made sure the band played "La Marseilles" before the "Star Spangled Banner." It would not be the last time in Flynn's life that he would perform tasks that balanced the interests of different countries.[26]

The World in 1943

The Soviet victory at the Battle of Moscow in December 1941 fatally disrupted Hitler's entire military strategy, which had been predicated on defeating the Russians in a six-month campaign. Yet for much of 1942 the war still went Germany's way. An ill-advised Soviet offensive in the spring of 1942 conducted under Stalin's orders as an attempt to drive the Germans out of all their territorial conquests from the year before, ended in a disastrous defeat for the Red Army that allowed the Germans to take back the initiative on the battlefield. Rejecting the advice of most of his military advisers to strike at Moscow again, Hitler ordered the bulk of the Axis forces to move into the southeast of the USSR in the summer of 1942, to control the Volga River and then the Caucasus region, with its massive oil reserves. In the meantime, the Afrika Korps, under the command of Field Marshal Erwin Rommel (the

26. Monthly Chaplain's Report, April to May 1943. NPRC Flynn File.

"Desert Fox") and augmented by significant numbers of Italian forces, advanced steadily across North Africa, pushing the British forces eastward, taking the key Tunisian city of Tobruk in July 1942.

Beginning in the fall of 1942, and continuing in the summer of 1943, the initiative in the war swung away from Germany and the other Axis powers and toward the Grand Alliance of the United States, Britain, and the USSR, where it remained until the end of war. In North Africa, the Afrika Korps were finally checked by the British Army under Field Marshal Bernard Montgomery at the Battle of El Alamein in November 1942, and German access to the oil resources of the Middle East was cut off. In combination with successful landings of the U.S. Army in northwest Morocco, these Allied victories meant the German and Italian forces were caught between British forces to their east and American forces to the west. The forces of the Axis powers were overrun in Tunisia in May of 1943, where they suffered the loss of more than half a million men.

The disaster in North Africa was overshadowed by even greater defeats in Russia. The attempt by the German forces and their Romanian and Hungarian allies to take the city of Stalingrad, pivotal to controlling the Volga River, led to the encirclement and annihilation of the Axis forces by the Red Army from November 1942 to February 1943; Axis loses totaled almost a million men. Not only were the resource-rich Caucasus closed off forever to the Axis, but the loss of men and material could not be easily replaced, especially since Germany had only just mobilized its industrial economy on a total war footing, and the defeats in North Africa and Russia closed off the oil resources it desperately needed. Rome, Budapest, Helsinki, and Bucharest began to look for ways to extricate themselves from their ties with Hitler. The Germans kept control the battlefield initiative until the final turning point in the East at the Battle of Kursk in July 1943, but the material advances of the Allies gradually ground down those of Germany.

Preparing to launch invasions of Sicily and then Italy, the Americans continued to pour resources into North Africa. American and British military leaders, emphasizing the need to eliminate Italy from the war, demurred on Soviet demands that a "second front" be launched in Western Europe in 1943, but they acquiesced to a cross-channel invasion in the summer of 1944. Despite the major differences between the democratic governments of America and Britain and the totalitarian Soviet Union—especially over the fate of Eastern Europe in general and Poland in particular—the Americans, British, and Soviets remained in agreement that none would seek a separate peace with Germany, and, further, that Germany would be forced to surrender unconditionally. Germany's fate may have been sealed in the face of the unity of the Grand Alliance and its massive advantage in resources; Allied soldiers, though, still had to defeat a wounded but nonetheless formidable war machine that occupied most of Europe.

The 26th Infantry Regiment from Sicily to Normandy, June 1943 to June 1944

In June 1943, Flynn's service at the 32nd Station Hospital came to an end and he was appointed chaplain for the "Blue Spaders." They were the men of the 26th Infantry Regiment, one of three regiments composing the legendary "Big Red One," the U.S. Army's First Infantry Division. The "Fighting First" as it was also known, formed in May 1917, shortly after America's entry into the First World War. It saw almost continuous combat following its arrival in Europe in July of 1917 until the official armistice sixteen months later.[27]

In the spring of 1942, the Joint Chiefs of Staff made the decision to send the First Infantry Division into combat in Europe. Commanded by Major General Terry Allen and his subordinate, Brigadier General Theodore Roosevelt, Jr., the First Infantry Division landed in North Africa in November 1942, and spent the next five months campaigning against the Afrika Korps. In May 1943, as Tunisia and Algeria were secured by the British and American forces, the First Infantry Division was then assigned to spearhead Operation Husky, the Allied invasion of Sicily. Flynn arrived in Tunisia on June 11, one month before the Sicilian landings, and began his work as a chaplain with the Blue Spaders.[28]

27. Flint Whitlock, *The Fighting First: The Untold Story of the Big Red One on D-Day* (Boulder, Colo.: Westview Press, 2004), 10. The nickname of the 26th Infantry Regiment came from the Blue Spade that was the regiment's official emblem.

28. Whitlock, *The Fighting First*, 15–19. Because the 1st Infantry Division was usually

He said Mass at least once on the boat heading across the Atlantic; a photo of him celebrating Mass with dozens of American soldiers in life preservers, captioned "A Solemn Moment at Sea," was published in the *Washington Post,* the *New York Times,* and the *New York Sun* in late June 1943. An anonymous Passionist, commenting on the photo in a chronicle of the Province of Saint Paul in 1943, wrote: "Flynn, who had done so well with *The Sign* and as a retreat leader, had to have much of his stomach removed and appeared to be a chronic invalid. Look at him now!"[29]

This three-week period, from June 11 to the end of the month, was the last period in Flynn's career before he became a true "battlefield chaplain." He conducted fewer religious services and engaged in the usual activities of chaplains at the front line, such as helping transport wounded soldiers to medical stations, visiting them when time permitted, conducting the removal of dead soldiers from both sides, and presiding over funerals. During this month for the First Infantry Division, Flynn offered Mass 33 times and heard more than 400 confessions. Twice during the month Flynn was put in charge of distributing books, games, and sports equipment that had been donated by the American Red Cross to more than 950 soldiers. Unlike the 120th Station Hospital, where Catholic personnel were a minority, the 26th Infantry Regiment was almost 60 percent Catholic, nearly 40 percent Protestant, and slightly above 1 percent Jewish.[30]

By the beginning of July, Flynn was with the rest of the Blue Spaders on ships destined for the Sicilian coast as part of the spearhead for Operation Husky, the second of the four amphibious invasions undertaken by the U.S. Army during the Second World War in Europe. During this time, the 26th Infantry Regiment had three chaplains: the regimental chaplain was Captain Richard Chase, who also served as chaplain for the Third Battalion; Captain Alfred Jorgenson served

---

the first to engage in combat against the enemy, it usually had the highest casualties. Other, more cynical nicknames for the division soon emerged, such as the "Big Dead One" and "The Bloody First."

29. Photograph collection from Flynn's Military Service. PHA Record Group 322—3/7.

30. Monthly Chaplain's Report, June 1943. NPRC Flynn File.

as chaplain of the Second Battalion; while Flynn served as chaplain of the First Battalion, which consisted of about 1,000 soldiers. The Blue Spaders in total numbered about 3,000 soldiers and the First Infantry Division, slightly over 10,000.[31] The First Infantry Division was part of the American, British, and Canadian invasion force, consisting of the American Seventh Army and the British Eighth Army, which together numbered over 100,000 men. They landed on the southern coast of Sicily on July 10, 1943. The campaign continued until the Axis forces evacuated the island on August 17, following the triumphal entry of the American forces into Messina seven days earlier.[32]

The Blue Spaders, much like the other regiments of the Big Red One, were at the tip of the spear of U.S. Seventh Army's attack on the Italian and German positions. Both the commander of the Seventh Army, Lieutenant General George S. Patton, and his deputy, Major General Omar Bradley, commander of II Corps—which was composed of the First Infantry Division and the Forty-Fifth Infantry Division— specifically asked Generals Terry Allen and Theodore Roosevelt that the First Infantry Division, specifically the 16th and the 26th infantry regiments, should lead the American assault. Patton informed Eisenhower he needed "those sons of bitches in the Big Red One" to open the path to Sicily after their success with the African landings the year before.[33]

Following the landings on July 10 at 2:45 am at the beachhead near Gela in the southwestern corner of Sicily, the First Infantry Division would be in near continuous combat for the next twenty-eight days against the Italian Sixth Army, which consisted of more than 200,000 Italian and 50,000 German soldiers, including the tank units of the elite Hermann Goering Panzer division. The landings themselves went off successfully, as the Italian defenders were taken by surprise, but

31. General Information Record of the First Infantry Division July 15, 1943, National Archives at College Park, Maryland Record Group 407—Records of the Adjutant General's Office Entry 427—WWII Operating Reports, 1940–1948, 1st Infantry Division (hereafter NARA Record Group 407 Entry 427).

32. Crosby, *Battlefield Chaplains*, 95–96.

33. James Scott Wheeler, *The Big Red One: America's Legendary 1st Infantry Division* (Lawrence: University of Kansas Press, 2007), 227–28.

the German and Italian forces launched a brutal counteroffensive on July 11 and 12, attempting to drive the American and British forces into the Mediterranean. The First Infantry Division was crucial in repelling this assault; it spent the next week pushing the Germans and Italians back from the beachheads. From July 23 onwards, the Big Red One was at the front of the Allied assault across the island of Sicily, engaging the Axis forces in Niscemi, Villa Rosa, Alimena, Bompietro, Petralia, Nicosia, and the Ponte Clivo Airport.[34]

Flynn personally distinguished himself at the landings at Gela on July 10, administering last rites to a number of mortally wounded soldiers from the 26th Infantry Regiment while under continuous enemy fire from Italian forces. On April 3, 1945, the Army awarded Flynn the Bronze Star for his actions on that day.[35] On July 22, at the Battle of Bompietro: "In total disregard for his own personal safety, Flynn moved fearlessly about the danger area, giving first aid and comfort to the wounded and administered to the dying, while his battalion was subjected to devastating mortar and artillery fire," which earned him the Silver Star for bravery, which he was formally awarded on January 25, 1945.[36]

During the battle of the Gela beachhead, Flynn had sustained his one major combat injury: in late July, shrapnel from a grenade hit him. It incapacitated him for only a handful of days before he was back in action, although his right eye was permanently damaged. He would gradually lose sight in it until the eye was completely useless by the early 1950s.[37] For this injury, Flynn was later awarded the Purple Heart.

The decisive battle during Operation Husky was Troina, located in north central Sicily and fought from August 1 to August 6, 1943. Casualties for the Blue Spaders, along with the other regiments of the First Infantry Division, were high, but this battle broke the back of

34. Final Letter from Major General Terry Allen to the First Infantry Division, August 7, 1943. NARA Record Group 407, Entry 427.

35. General Orders—Award Citation by Command of Brigadier General Burton Andrus, April 3, 1945. NPRC Flynn File.

36. General Orders—Award Citation by Command of Brigadier General Burton Andrus, January 25, 1945. NPRC Flynn File.

37. Military Record and Report of Separation/Certificate of Service. PHA Record Group 322—3/7.

the Axis resistance in Sicily. The German panzer divisions took heavy casualties during repeated attacks from American infantry and tank assaults. Over the next week, the remaining German and Italian forces evacuated Sicily at the southeastern port of Messina. It was a fairly orderly evacuation, as the American and British forces did not reach the city, their ultimate destination, until August 18, the day after the Axis withdrawal was completed. Still, the campaign had been successful for the Allies, as they had moved one step closer to Italy, Hitler's main European ally; indeed, the failure to repel the Allied invaders led directly to the fall of Mussolini's government in Rome.[38] Morale remained high among the Blue Spaders, according to a report from their senior officer, Colonel John Bowen, to the Big Red One's new commanding officer, Major General Clarence Huebner, who replaced Terry Allen following the battle of Troina. The men of the Big Red One would spend the next two months in Sicily, returning to Britain in mid-October. Bowen noted he was glad his regiment would not be used in the planned invasion of Italy in September, since the loss of so many veteran soldiers to injuries, illnesses, or death had left the remaining men with a lack of enthusiasm for engaging in further combat with the new replacements to the regiment.[39]

By Flynn's own account, serving in a regiment attached to the First Infantry Division meant that he and his fellow soldiers encountered the stiffest resistance from Axis forces. "The Chaplains work various tasks and their job is by turns encouraging and depressing, thrilling and heart-rending. Such is War, I suppose," Flynn wrote to his provincial in late July. The duties of the military chaplain, which often involved identifying and helping to bury the dead, as well as the constant disruptions that came with the military campaign, usually left little time for religious services. Flynn admitted he had been able to celebrate a full Mass only three times in as many weeks, often using the hood of his jeep as an altar. On a positive note, he proudly reported Mass attendance by Catholic soldiers of the 26th Infantry Regiment was nearly

38. James Scott Wheeler, *The Big Red One*, 249–53.
39. Letter from Bowen to Huebner, August 10 1943. NARA Record Group 407, Entry 427. Other correspondence also attests to the combat weariness of the men in the 26th Infantry, and appreciation that they were being sent back to England.

100 percent, excluding men engaged in combat during service times. Amazingly, the dispute over military uniform costs between Flynn and Saint Gabriel's Monastery was still going on, as Flynn remarked to Walsh he did not appreciate the "negative publicity" this financial dispute had attracted back in Boston. He promised he would pay the $700 due for the uniforms as soon as he could.[40]

Flynn remained impressed by the spiritual devotion of the American soldiers in the 26th Infantry Regiment but had little positive to say about spiritual conditions in Sicily. He frequently described the societies as "priest-ridden, yet most are terribly ignorant about their own faith. Many of the people are braggarts and cowards, thieves and forever whining." The local population's looting of dead bodies—including gold fillings out of teeth, watches, shoes, and boots, as well as theft of American soldiers' property—helped create an environment of "moral anarchy" which made the already difficult atmosphere of war even more taxing for the spiritual health of the average soldier. Flynn noted he had more than $50 of personal property stolen, and no one left anything unguarded; Flynn had to keep two men watching over the chaplain jeep at all times.[41]

Perhaps most disturbing was the terrible state of disrepair of many churches, reflecting the "damaged spirituality" of a continent ravaged by its second war in three decades. The clergy were "dirty, unshaven, omnipresent, yet lazy at the same time." He noted that many Catholic soldiers of the 26th Infantry Regiment expressed to Flynn their poor impressions not only of Sicily but also of similar conditions in the "nominally Catholic" French colonies in North Africa. He bitterly noted "centuries of exposure to Catholicism have led to absolutely nothing." He went on to say that, if was exposed to Sicilian religious culture for much longer, he would be on his way to becoming a "hardcore anticlerical" and only now could he understand why Catholic countries in Europe had developed an anticlerical political tradition. The only positive as-

40. Letter from Flynn to Walsh, July 29, 1943. PHA Record Group 322—3/7 It was also during this time Flynn formed a close friendship with the beloved deputy commander of the 26th Infantry Regiment, General Theodore Roosevelt Jr., who was, interestingly enough, a staunch Calvinist.

41. Ibid.

pect he could note was the moral example that American Catholic soldiers provided for the local population; he hoped that example might
help them rebuild their religious life once the war had ended.[42]

Flynn's reports from July to September manifest the dramatic
change in his duties, with fewer religious services, numbering between
15 and 20 during the combat months of July and August, then a slight
increase to 25 during the month of September. By this point, because
of the influx of replacements to compensate for the losses experienced
by the Blue Spaders during the Sicilian campaign, Protestants had become the majority (55 percent) of the 26th Infantry Regiment, the pro-
portion of Catholics having dropped to 38 percent. Flynn also made
time for hospital visits, morality lectures, and, since the Blue Spaders
lacked a Jewish chaplain, he sponsored two religious services a month
for the Jewish soldiers in the regiment.[43]

At the beginning of October, shortly before the Blue Spaders began
their journey back to Britain, Flynn served as co-celebrant of a special
"field mass" to celebrate the Allied victory in Sicily. In attendance were
commander of the First Infantry Division, Major General Clarence
Huebner, his deputy, Brigadier General John Wyman, the commander
of the 26th Infantry Regiment, Colonel John Bowen, and his executive
officer, Lieutenant Colonel John Corley. Ironically, the other celebrant
with Flynn was the bishop of Agrigento, the Passionist John Peruzzo.
Flynn later noted his view of the spiritual condition of the Sicily had
slightly improved when he viewed the work of his Italian Passionist
brethren. The trials and tribulations of the Sicilian campaign had been
worth it: "On that day of the field mass I was certainly proud to be a
Passionist that day and proud to be an American. We are a great and a
wonderful and a lovable people."[44]

By the third week of October, the First Infantry Division were on
their way back to Britain, departing on four British transports between
October 18 and October 21. After brief stops in Algiers and Gibral-
tar, they docked in Liverpool on November 5. A week later, they had

42. Ibid.
43. Monthly Chaplain's Reports, July–September 1943. NPRC Flynn File.
44. Letter from Fabian Flynn to Edmund Walsh, November 9, 1943. PHA Record
Group 322—3/7.

arrived at Camp Piddlehinton, outside the southern English city of Dorchester; it would be their home for the next seven months.[45] Much of their time there was spent on intensive training in preparation for their spearheading an Allied invasion force. This was Operation Overlord, the invasion of northern France—the launching of the long-planned "second front." The First Infantry Division was among the most battle-hardened of all divisions, so, along with the Fourth and Twenty-Ninth Infantry Divisions, it was to launch the American thrust on the Utah and Omaha Beaches.[46]

The men of the Blue Spaders followed a busy schedule during their time in Britain. There were often periods of three or four days during which soldiers were "in the field," engaged in military maneuvers to simulate the upcoming campaign in France. When they were on maneuver, soldiers slept in tents or in the open field, and they were usually accompanied by their chaplains. According to their monthly reports, the average day, except for Sunday, began at 5:50 a.m. with First Call, followed by reveille and march at 5:55 a.m. and assembly at 6 a.m. Breakfast mess followed, then drills from 7:30 a.m. to noon, an hour for lunch, followed by more drills and training from 1 p.m. until 4 p.m. An evening assembly and a mess call for dinner was at 5 p.m.; soldiers were sent back to their quarters at 9:45 p.m., and lights out, announced by the playing of "Taps" on a bugle, was at 10 p.m. There were exceptions to this schedule: soldiers did not have to rise until 7:20 a.m. on Sunday and then often their mornings or afternoons were free from training exercises, in part so that the men could attend either Protestant or Catholic religious services. Soldiers occasionally received passes to visit Dorchester or, on rarer occasions, London.[47]

There were also times for recreation at Camp Piddlehinton, such as visits from the USO, including movie stars of the time, such as Adolphe Menjou and Cesar Romero (he posed for pictures with both of

45. Wheeler, *The Big Red One*, 262–63.

46. Flint Whitlock, *The Fighting First*, 60–61. Gold, Juno, and Sword Beaches were designated for the British Second Army, consisting of the British Fiftieth and Third Infantry Divisions and the Canadian Third Infantry Division.

47. Monthly Reports for the 26th Infantry Regiment, October 1943. NARA Record Group 407, Entry 427.

these). There were also dances, concerts, and sporting events. For most of the soldiers and officers, living in Britain meant a "return to civilization," as they received regular mail, and living conditions as whole were much better than they had been in Sicily or North Africa. Some of the men of the Blue Spaders attended day-long sessions offered at Cambridge, Bristol, and Leeds universities—they were offered a few times a month and included courses on everything from English history and constitutional law to the natural sciences.[48]

On December 22, 1943, Clarence Huebner wrote an open letter to the soldiers of the First Infantry Division, wherein he praised the fighting ability they had demonstrated in North Africa and Sicily, upholding the "glorious heritage of the Big Red One." General Huebner also gave a vague hint at what was to come, telling them the First Infantry Division would make sure the next year would bring "total victory" to the Allied cause.[49] As Huebner was aware, one month earlier, at the Iranian capital of Tehran, the leaders of the "Big Three" had met for the first time, and the American President Franklin Roosevelt and British Prime Minister Winston Churchill had promised Communist Party of Soviet Union's General Secretary Josef Stalin that the second front would begin in the summer of 1944, and it would be launched in northwest France. This essentially meant Western Europe would be liberated from Nazi rule by the Allied Expeditionary Force (AEF), while the eastern half of the continent would await the arrival of the Red Army. This would have profound consequences for Europe's future, and for Flynn's.

During this long sojourn at Camp Piddlehinton, the Blue Spaders again experienced a turnover in leadership, for Bowen's health problems led to his replacement as regimental commander by Colonel John F. Seitz; Lieutenant Colonel John Corley was his executive officer. For Flynn, the fall of 1943 was a certainly a mixed bag, as he spent much of late October and early November in the camp hospital, suffering from a case of malaria.[50] Eventually recovering from yet another bout

48. Monthly Reports for the 26th Infantry Regiment, November and December 1943. NARA Record Group 407, Entry 427.

49. Letter from Major General Clarence Huebner to all members of the First Infantry Division, December 22, 1943. NARA Record Group 407, Entry 427.

50. Photograph collection from Flynn's Military Service. PHA Record Group 322—3/7.

of malaria, Flynn received word he was to be promoted to the rank of captain, effective on New Years' Day 1944.[51]

Flynn's records indicate that his level of specifically ministerial activity was similar to that of his time in Texas: an average of 25 religious services, 8 to 10 hospital visits, and somewhere between 60 and 100 confessions per month.[52] He had the asset of a personal assistant from the First Battalion, Private Charles Mason, who also worked as an altar server during celebrations of the Mass. Mason served in this capacity until September 1944. At least once a month, Flynn arranged to have a rabbi in Dorchester come to Camp Piddlehinton to offer a service to the Jewish soldiers in the 26th Infantry Regiment, who composed 2 percent of the regiment's men.[53]

During the spring of 1944, the same pattern of religious services continued. Since a significant percentage of the men of the Blue Spaders were stationed in local homes away from Camp Piddlehinton, Flynn would often use nearby recreational facilities, meetings halls, and local churches to celebrate Mass. When he met the soldiers in the field during training exercises, he used a trusty Ford GPW Jeep as a makeshift altar.[54] The combination of the replacement of the beloved Terry Allen by Clarence Huebner, as well as the lingering effects of the brutality of the Sicilian campaign, led to a light training regimen and a corresponding lack of discipline among many of the soldiers. After the new year, the length and realism of the training intensified, as it did for the thousands of American, British, French, Canadian, Dutch, Belgian, Czech, and Polish soldiers who would take part in the launching of the second front. By mid-May 1944, both Huebner and his regimental commander, Seitz, were convinced their men were ready to take part in what would be the largest amphibious landing in history.[55]

51. Promotion Order, December 12, 1943. NPRC Flynn File.

52. John Votaw, *Blue Spaders: The 26th Infantry Regiment 1917–1967* (Wheaton, Ill.: Cantigny First Division Foundation, 1996), 54–55. During the time in Britain, the Blue Spaders numbered 871 men, with 35 officers, 178 NCOs, 40 technicians, and 618 privates; the Catholic membership of the unit fluctuated between 35 and 40 percent.

53. Chaplain's Reports, October–December 1943. NPRC Flynn File.

54. Monthly Chaplain's Reports, January–May 1944. NPRC Flynn File. Many of these training exercises went on for days at a time, sometimes as many as ten.

55. Votaw, *Blue Spaders*, 49–52.

*The 26th Infantry Regiment from D-Day to the Battles of Aachen
and the Huertgen Forest, June to November 1944*

The field marshals Hitler placed in defense of northwestern
France—Gerd von Rundstedt and his deputy, Erwin Rommel—gam-
bled everything on being able to halt the invasion on the beaches,
wherever it came, and that was seen as likely either Normandy or Calais. Both men correctly believed if the Allied Expeditionary Force established an impregnable beachhead within the first few days of the
invasion, even if it initially was contained close to the English Channel,
the enormous advantages in Allied manpower and material resources
would turn the tide in the West. As Rommel put it: "We beat them on
the beaches or not at all."[56]

Consequently, the northwest coastline of France was peppered with
mines and with pillboxes armed with artillery and machine gun emplacements, which were designed to bog down any potential invasion
on the coastline, until elite tank regiments could move in and drive
the Allied invasion back into the channel. The task for the Supreme
Commander of the AEF, Dwight Eisenhower, and his deputies Bernard Law Montgomery, Omar Bradley, and Walter Bedell Smith, was
to launch a broad assault that could weaken the German defenders to
the point that an Allied amphibious invasion could come off successfully. Their strategy was three-pronged; the first—in one of the most
successful examples of counterintelligence in military history—was to
convince Hitler that the landings at Normandy were a sham and that
the main invasion force, led by George S. Patton, would land at Calais,
to the northeast of Normandy. This feint, which they hoped would
keep the Germans from immediately bringing their heavy armor into
battle, succeeded: indeed, Hitler refused to consider the requests of
both Rundstedt and Rommel to commit the German panzers to battle,
as he continued to believe—for more than a month after D-Day—that
the Normandy landings were just a diversion.[57]

The second step was to launch a massive parachute drop, led by

56. John C. McManus, *The Dead and Those about to Die. D-Day: The Big Red One at
Omaha Beach* (New York: Penguin Group, 2014), 48–49.
57. Ibid., 23–25.

the American 82nd and 101st Airborne Divisions and the British 6th Airborne Division, the night before the invasion, to attack and destroy various German defensive positions. The third and final phase was the landing of more than 150,000 Allied soldiers beginning at 6 a.m. on the morning of June 6, 1944, following one of the largest collection of naval and aerial bombardments in history. The Allies would attack five beaches—Sword, Juno, Gold, Utah, and Omaha (the destination of the 29th and 1st Infantry Divisions).[58]

The Allied landings in Normandy on D-Day, June 6, 1944, are rivaled only by the battle of Iwo Jima in the Pacific theatre as the Americans' most famous and memorialized event of the war. Omaha Beach was the center of the bloodiest combat of the day, partially because the bombing raid the night before had completely missed the German positions and also because the German units were conducting a training exercise with live ammunition when the American soldiers arrived. Consequently, the combat at Omaha Beach has dominated popular perception of the amphibious landings D-Day; by comparison, the landings at the other beaches are not nearly as well remembered outside the realm of professional military historians.[59]

The invasion points at Omaha Beach itself were divided into eight different landing zones: Charlie, Dog Green, Dog White, Dog Red, Easy Green, Easy Red, Fox Green, and Fox Red. The first five were attacked by the 116th Infantry Regiment, which was part of the 29th Infantry Division; the latter three were designated for the 18th and 16th Infantry Regiments of the Big Red One. The 26th Infantry Regiment was kept in initial reserve when the day began, the plan being for its forces to land on beaches where the Allied forces were most in need of reinforcements.[60] The landing craft containing the Blue Spaders, including Captain Fabian Flynn, arrived at 1 p.m. at the Normandy

58. Cornelius Ryan, *The Longest Day* (New York: Simon and Schuster, 1959), 12.

59. Whitlock, *The Fighting First*, 182–83. Interestingly, Steven Spielberg's famous 1998 World War II film *Saving Private Ryan* has a brief moment during the Omaha Beach battle scene, depicting soldiers from the 29th Infantry Division at the Dog Green landing zone, with an army chaplain ducking under fire while giving last rites to a dying American soldier. Although the chaplain does not physically resemble Flynn, it captures his duties on that "day of days."

60. Wheeler, *The Big Red One*, 268–69.

beaches and spent the next four hours waiting for their orders to land on Omaha Beach; permission was finally granted shortly after 5 p.m. When the Blue Spaders arrived at the Fox Green and East Red beaches, they encountered hundreds of dead and wounded men from the 16th and 18th Infantry Regiments, which had taken high casualties in their own landings. The beach was still under German artillery and machine gun fire, despite the success of the initial waves of the invasion force in destroying a number of the German pillboxes.[61]

The Blue Spaders, by the early morning of June 7, moved off the beaches with the rest of the First Infantry Division, as more men and supplies arrived. The First Battalion of the 26th Infantry Regiment, where Flynn served as the chaplain, was temporarily attached to the shattered 16th Infantry Regiment. They next day the soldiers of the 1st and 29th Infantry Divisions began to inch inland to take the surrounding towns and villages. As Rommel had predicted, the success of the Allied Expeditionary Force in the landings at the Normandy beaches meant Germany's military hopes, already poor, were doomed. At this time, though, there began nearly three months of continuous combat for the men of the Big Red One, combat all along the route from the beaches of Normandy to the medieval city of Aachen, which became the first German city to be taken by the Allied Expeditionary Force.[62]

A week after D-Day, the First Infantry Division connected with British forces to the east of the Normandy landing zones, near the city of Caen. Throughout the month of June and into July, the AEF operated in a relatively small theater of operations near the English Channel; the Big Red One was focused on taking the key towns of Caumont and Cherbourg. They spearheaded Operation Cobra, Omar Bradley's successful plan to break out of northwestern France, in late July and early August, using the city of Saint Lô as their starting point and pushing on to the Seine and Marne Rivers. By the end of the month, Paris had been liberated and the AEF was nearing the German border.[63] Eisenhower decided that the Allied forces should push through the

61. Report After Action, the 26th Infantry Regiment 1 June 1044 to 30 June 1944. NARA Record Group 407, Entry 427.
62. Ibid.
63. Wheeler, *The Big Red One*, 305–7.

Siegfried Line, a series of military fortresses and pillboxes that guard-ed Germany's western border, and then take the Rhine River bridges and subsequently pour into the Ruhr Valley, Germany's main industrial heartland in the West. Following the disastrous defeats Germany had suffered since D-Day, and more than half a million German soldiers having been lost, it seemed Eisenhower's strategy could possibly lead to the end of the war by 1944. The first obstacle was Aachen, the ancient city on the Belgian-German border where Charlemagne had founded the Holy Roman Empire in AD 800. The city had been constantly con-tested between French and German speakers since medieval times, and it was known as well by its French name, Aix-la-Chapelle. It also held great recent symbolic significance, as no west German city had fallen to an invader since the Napoleonic era.[64]

The September 1944 issue of *The Sign* (for which Flynn was still writing articles when he could) was published shortly before the battle of Aachen commenced. In his contributed article, Flynn described his role in the lead-up to the invasion, D-Day itself, and the days and weeks that followed. Thought to have been written in late July or early August of 1944, it is probably the best article Flynn ever wrote, filled with vivid detail and revealing the passion of a man of God who had literally seen hell on earth.

Flynn began by informing his readers that he said Mass each night in the weeks leading up to the invasion, and both attendance at religious services and the spiritual fervor that American Catholic soldiers showed were "not merely gratifying, they were inspiring." He dismissed notions by "secular scoffers" who claimed this was the product of fearful super-stition on the eve of battle, noting, "Scoffers rarely make it to the front lines." American soldiers on the eve of D-Day were, according to Flynn, motivated by the "hope that only their religion could give them."[65]

As Flynn put it, "H-Hour stands for hell let loose!" Although he strove to present to his readers in the United States that American soldiers were engaged in a holy war, he made no effort to disguise the murderous nature of combat on Omaha Beach on D-Day:

64. Robert Baumer, *Aachen: The U.S. Army's Battle for Charlemagne's City in World War II* (Mechanicsburg, Penn.: Stackpole Books, 2015), v.

65. Fabian Flynn, "D-Day and After," *The Sign*, September 1944, 61.

No figures can estimate or suggest the terrific physical and mental strain, the awful draining of a man's powers and faculties, the racking tension, the moments of fright, the pounding hearts, the shock, the labored breathings, the sobs, the sighs, the groans, the fearful toll of lives, the painful wounds, and the heroism of the smoking, flaming, bloody cauldron that is a beach battle. There are no words that can even remotely picture the thundering roar of shore batteries vomiting destruction, the vicious crack of the 88s, the billowing smoke of air bursts, their rain of searing fragmentation, the crashing sound of a direct hit, the absurd attempts of a man to make himself shrink, the deafening din as a landing craft is blown up as it heads to shore, the dead bodies that float by amid oil and wreckage on the receding waves, the mortar shells which come from nowhere and feather down in an eerie rush of wind to shake the earth as they hit.[66]

Given the sheer number of the dead and wounded from the 18th and 16th Infantry Regiments at Omaha Beach when the Blue Spaders arrived in the late afternoon, Flynn and the other chaplains spent much of their time under fire performing last rites for the thousands of American casualties on the beach. For their actions at Omaha Beach, the members of the 26th Infantry Regiment were collectively awarded the Bronze Star, Flynn's second time receiving this honor.[67]

After discussing all the odd places where he had celebrated Mass—including a goat pasture, the courtyard of a medieval castle in Sicily, the ruins of a casino, a cow barn, and numerous prisoner-of-war stockades—Flynn wrote that the "manly piety" and "intelligent practical faith" of Catholic soldiers served them well throughout the hardships of war, creating a "happy mixture" of healthy Americanism and vibrant, unashamed Catholicism.[68]

He admitted that "too many" Catholic soldiers neglected their spir-

66. Ibid, 62. "H-Hour" stood for the exact hour when the American landing craft began landing on the shores of Omaha beach.

67. Military Record and Report of Separation/Certificate of Service. PHA Record Group 322—3/7.

68. Flynn, "D-Day and After," 63–64. Flynn's providing religious services to German POWs foreshadowed his work after the war as the official Catholic chaplain to the International War Crimes Tribunal in Nuremberg, and as confessor to several of the Catholic defendants.

itual welfare and were "lax and indifferent" to the teachings of the Church, but he mentioned that in the 26th Infantry Regiment and in the First Infantry Division more broadly, such men were rare. He argued American soldiers' display of "genuine Catholicism" shocked the native Catholic Italian, French, and Belgian populations out of their "spiritual torpor and indifference." He pointed to specific acts, such as American soldiers repairing churches damaged by war, and he recounted how both Catholic and non-Catholic soldiers provided a French bishop with enough money to repair his damaged seminary; in another instance, and many had donated their salaries to pay off the entire debts of a convent and orphanage in Belgium. This, Flynn concluded, was just the beginning of a spiritual renewal in Europe that an Allied victory would bring.[69]

However, Flynn described the life of average soldier in the 26th Infantry Regiment, and the physical conditions under which they lived, in nothing but the roughest language:

> These men have endured the hell of the landing and for twenty-nine days now they have fought without rest or relief. In twenty-nine days they have had one issue of clean clothing—one pair of socks per man. A miserable, steady drizzle is now in its second week and has soaked everything. Fox holes are slimy with mulch. The night wind is chill and whips about to reach one's very marrow. A quick fire to brew a cup of coffee is out of the question. Night and day, a constant vigil must be kept for the least enemy move. It is a wearing, nerve-taxing, punishing kind of warfare. Yet there he is, badly needing a shave and a bath, growling at cold coffee and spurning perpetual stew, but determined and defiant, still dishing it out, your Infantry man, G.I. Joe, the great unsung hero of the war! The old foot solider there in the rain and the mud, breasting the spray of bullets, sweating over the earth-shaking artillery barrage, fighting, hiking, patrolling, digging in, holding. The first guy to draw fire, the last to be relieved. He's the guy you can't win wars without![70]

69. Ibid., 64. By acknowledging that some American soldiers had shirked their spiritual duties, Flynn may have been referring obliquely to several incidents involving the 26th Infantry Regiment while it was located at Camp Piddlehinton. There was at least one violent encounter between some of the Blue Spaders and black soldiers from a support unit; a few soldiers engaged in petty thefts at local businesses.

70. Ibid.

Flynn concluded his article, the last he would contribute to *The Sign* for the next year, by writing that the average American soldier, for all his faults, was a great guy, and "I am mighty proud and happy to be with him!"[71] Flynn was personally present at the liberation of Paris at the end of August with a number of other members of the 26th Infantry Regiment, remarking to a reporter from *The Boston Globe* it was an amazing thing to watch the capital returning to life now that the Germans had gone. He noted the Wehrmacht tried to loot everything of value from the city before they fled, describing his discovery of an abandoned freight train outside Paris that was weighted down with all kinds of goods from every department store the Germans could find.[72]

By the time the September 1944 edition of *The Sign* appeared in the United States, the Battle of Aachen was about to begin. The Blue Spaders, along with the rest of the men of the First Infantry Division—more than 70 percent now were replacements—had just undergone three weeks of field training in recently liberated Belgium. Training having come to an end, the siege of Aachen commenced. The battle lasted more than four weeks, from the last week of September to the third week of October. Following skirmishes in the suburbs, the city was the site of a tortuous three-week siege between the First Infantry Division and a number of elite SS units that had been transferred from the eastern front to keep the city from falling into the hands of the Allies.[73]

The Blue Spaders and the remainder of the American soldiers spent the first three weeks of October fighting street-to-street and house-to-house against determined, and occasionally fanatical, German resistance from elements of the 1st, 2d, and 12th SS Panzer divisions. About 4,000 civilians remained in the city; the rest had been forcibly evacuated under the orders of Colonel Gerhard Wilck, commander of the Aachen garrison. Those who remained tried to keep their heads down for much of the battle, but a few engaged in active resistance against the American forces. On October 21, Wilck, bowing

71. Ibid.

72. Carlyle Holt, "Archbishop Spellman's Belgian Visit Has Tragic Sequel," *The Boston Globe*, September 27, 1944, 8.

73. Headquarters 26th Infantry Regiment Action Report September 1944. NARA Record Group 407, Entry 427.

to the inevitable—since the German forces had no remaining food, water, or ammunition—issued the surrender order, stating that any further loss of life was useless, and German soldiers should prefer Allied captivity to death, as they would be needed one day to "rebuild Germany." By the evening of the 21st, according to the regimental report, the "American flag was waving over the first captured German city."[74]

The fall of Aachen was viewed by many of the city's inhabitants not as a day of occupation but as one of liberation from an increasingly oppressive Nazi regime. Casualties on both sides were high; the Americans and the Germans each lost almost 5,000 men as casualties. Seventy-five Blue Spaders had been killed. The members of the 26th Infantry Regiment were awarded the Distinguished Unit Citation for their actions during the Battle of Aachen. Yet the ability of the Germans to mount such a stout defense, when combined with similar delays along the German border with Belgium and France, meant that an end of the war in 1944 was out of the question, especially following the massive failure of Operation Market Garden the previous month.[75]

Flynn's war records reveal the same kind of pattern as for Operation Husky in Sicily. The number of religious services sharply dropped during the combat conditions of June through September, averaging between 15 and 20 per month, and about 40 to 50 confessions; celebrating daily mass was, in Flynn's words, "simply impossible."[76] Since the Blue Spaders' movements during this time period took them from France to Belgium and then to Germany, he occasionally had the chance to hold services in Catholic churches and cathedrals in liberated towns. The usual visits to military hospitals and conducting last rites for military casualties, which included 23 for the month of July,

74. Headquarters 26th Infantry Regiment Action Report October 1944. NARA Record Group 407, Entry 427.

75. Votaw, *Blue Spaders*, 84–85. The largest air drop after D-Day, Operation Market Garden was personally designed by Montgomery to end the war by December 1944. Tens of thousands of American and British paratroopers were dropped into German-occupied Netherlands, where they were to seize and hold key bridges over the Rhine until Allied infantry and tanks could reach them. A combination of poor planning, faulty intelligence, and a strong counter-offensive by elite German units recently transferred from the eastern front led to Market Garden's failure.

76. Monthly Chaplain's Report, June 1944. NPRC Flynn File.

27 for the month of August, and 36 for the month of September, were also part of his routine.[77]

On September 19, Flynn served as co-celebrant with Archbishop Francis Spellman in a special Thanksgiving victory Mass held outside Aachen on the Belgian side of the border in the village of Kelmis. The Mass was well-attended, but it had a dark denouement, as one of the military policemen from the 26th Infantry Regiment died in a car accident on his way back from the service. Flynn conducted the funeral Mass for the soldier in the same Catholic church in Kelmis where Spellman had offered the Thanksgiving Mass, the Neuapostolische Kirche. Flynn informed the *Boston Globe* reporter Carlyle Holt that the 26th Infantry Regiment greatly impressed the noncombatants in the area. Dozens of civilians from Kelmis, most of whom were German speakers, decorated the church for the funeral and attended it as well, honoring a soldier whom the Nazi regime had proclaimed a deadly enemy of all Germans. Despite this optimistic note of a future reconciliation between the Americans and Germans, Flynn also impressed on Holt the horrors of the war and what the Blue Spaders had seen over the previous sixteen months: "Africa was a novelty, Italy was the first crack in Fortress Europe, and this is a horrible hellish grind. Those who have not seen action cannot possibly imagine what it is like. I urge you all to pray for the quick end to this horrible war."[78]

The Big Red One and the other ten divisions that composed the U.S. First Army would spend the next two months after Aachen engaged in a violent stalemate with a roughly equally sized German force of composed of eleven divisions; most of those forces were hardened veterans of the eastern front. The Battle of the Huertgen Forest was fought in the region south and southeast of Aachen. Huebner and the other American commanders hoped that the First Army would quickly break through the Huertgen Forest and then seize the major German city of Cologne. The German divisions, under the command of one of Hitler's most ruthless and capable officers, Field Marshal Walther Model, put up a dogged defense, slowing the Allied advance and engaging both infantry and armored regiments in close-quarters

---

77. Monthly Chaplain's Reports, July–September 1944. NPRC Flynn File.
78. Carlyle Holt, "Archbishop Spellman's Belgian Visit," 8.

combat on an almost daily basis. The battle led to more than 28,000 casualties on the German side and 30,000 casualties for the Americans; more than 100 in the 26th Infantry Regiment alone died, many in the desperate attempt to take the Belgian village of Merode in late November 1944.[79] At the end of the battle, Major General Clarence Huebner, who had the commander of the Big Red One since the end of the Sicilian campaign, was removed from command and replaced by Major General Clift Andrus, who remained as commander of the First Infantry Division through the end of the war. During this extremely difficult autumn, meanwhile, Flynn followed his established pattern of field masses, confessions, and burials.[80]

From Boston to Le Havre to Nuremberg,
December 1944 to July 1945

The inability of the American forces to achieve a significant breakthrough in the fall of 1944 led the Germans to attempt a grand offensive of their own in mid-December: the Ardennes Offensive, also known as the Battle of the Bulge, was Hitler's last gamble to win the war. Flynn, however, was no longer with the Blue Spaders when the Battle of the Bulge commenced. His role as a field chaplain during the Battles of Aachen and the Huertgen Forest devastated his still-fragile health. The suffering endured through months on the battlefield, combined with complications from his stomach surgery and the lingering effects of his injury in Sicily the year before, led to his transfer from the 26th Infantry Regiment in early December 1944. Eventually he was sent back to the Lovell General Hospital in Fort Devens, Massachusetts, the first time in his home state since his mother's funeral two years before. He would not return to the 26th Infantry Regiment until the end of the war in June 1945.[81]

Throughout the spring of 1945, as Flynn recovered from a combination of pneumonia and malaria, he wrote numerous letters to the

79. Charles MacDonald, *The Battle of the Huertgen Forest* (Philadelphia: University of Pennsylvania Press, 1963), 170–72.
80. Votaw, *Blue Spaders*, 90–91.
81. Monthly Chaplain's Reports, November 1944–March 1945. NPRC Flynn File.

U.S. military's Office of the Chief of Chaplains, as well as to officers in the 26th Infantry Regiment such as its executive officer, Lieutenant Colonel John Corley, and to Major General Clift Andrus. In a letter to Captain Thomas Parker, dated March 9, 1945, he thanked Parker for his efforts to return him to "his men" in the 26th Infantry Regiment, but expressed disappointment it had not happened yet. Flynn wrote: "My plea still awaits you. I am ready and anxious to go. Matter of fact, I even hope that somebody will succumb to, as you call it, 'gangplank fever' so that I may go in his place and would not have to wait for another shipment."[82]

In another letter to Parker, written on April 2, 1945, Flynn offered an interesting sort of apology when he told Parker he had not meant to high-pressure anyone at the Office of Chaplains when he had some officers from the First Infantry Division contact them and request Flynn be sent back to the 26th Infantry Regiment. Flynn wrote that he would persist in these tactics until he returned to Europe: "I must confess I am far from blameless myself. Matter of fact, I have lost all sense of shame and propriety in my attempts to return to my men. I haven't yet spoken with General Marshall or the President, yet. I know that you appreciate my great anxiety."[83] Just a couple of weeks later, in mid-April, Flynn's wish was partially granted: he was sent back to Europe—not to Germany, where the Blue Spaders were located, but to the U.S. Army's 16th Major Port in Le Havre, in northwest France, one of the main ports from which men and material meant for the AEF disembarked.

It was also during this time Flynn received a full efficiency report from his commanding officer at the 16th Major Port in Le Havre, Colonel T. J. Weed. Weed based his evaluation, written on July 15, 1945, on the previous six months, during which time he had served with Flynn at Fort Devens, Massachusetts, and then both had come to the 16th

82. Letter from Flynn to Parker, March 9, 1945. NPRC Flynn File. This letter was written on stationery from Saint Gabriel's Monastery in Brighton, indicating Flynn would at least occasionally leave Fort Devers to return to his old home before he enlisted in the U.S. Armed Forces.

83. Letter from Flynn to Parker, March 9, 1945. NPRC Flynn File. The "General Marshall" to whom Flynn refers was General George C. Marshall, Head of the Joint Chiefs of Staff and President Franklin Roosevelt's primary military adviser, as well as a future U.S. Secretary of State.

Major Port as replacements. Weed gave Flynn either an "Excellent" or the highest ranking, "Superior," on the various success metrics listed in the report. Among them were "Stability under Pressure," "Initiative," "Intelligence," "Judgment and Common Sense," "Ability to Obtain Results," and, appropriately, "Physical Activity and Endurance," where Flynn received a "Superior" rating. Flynn's overall ranking placed him in the "Superior" category, the highest possible ranking. Weed's commentary on Flynn's suitability as an army officer said: "An intelligent, dignified, loyal, hard-working, capable officer. Has the ability to gain confidence of officers and men. Very conscientious; accomplished all duties exceedingly well." Given Flynn's later success with the Catholic Relief Services, Weed's evaluation appears to have hit the target closely. He did note Flynn's fiercely independent, even volatile streak.[84]

Flynn's two and a half months at Le Havre, in the upper Normandy region, from mid-April to late June 1945 were, per his reports, generally uneventful, with the usual routines of numerous celebrations of Mass, confessions, and hospital visits. Flynn saw the end of the war in Europe during this time, and he took part in the offering of special memorial masses following V-E Day on May 7, 1945.[85] While Flynn continued his chaplain's work at Le Havre with his usual energy and dedication, he was determined to return to the Blue Spaders as soon as possible, and he continued to petition his superiors to allow him to return. By the end of the June, Flynn's persistence had finally paid off, and he was again sent to serve with the 26th Infantry Regiment. This time, though, rather than serving as the chaplain of the 1st Battalion, Flynn was now the regimental chaplain, a role he would continue to occupy until the end of his military career a year later.[86]

During his six-month absence, the Blue Spaders, like the rest of the men who composed the Big Red One, withstood and pushed back the last German offensive during the Battle of Bulge from mid-December 1944 to early February 1945. They crossed the Rhine and closed the Ruhr pocket from late February to early April, and then took part in

84. U.S. Military Efficiency Report written by Colonel T. J. Weed for Captain Fabian Flynn, July 15, 1945. NPRC Flynn File.

85. Monthly Chaplain's Reports, April–June 1945. NPRC Flynn File.

86. Ibid.

the drive across Germany. That drive took them through the towns of Bonn, Remagen, Siegen, Halle, and, at the beginning of May, into the city of Karlsbad (soon to be renamed Karlovy Vary) in Czechoslova-kia.[87] This would be the last battle of the Second World War for these men. With Berlin surrounded by the Red Army, Adolf Hitler killed himself on May 1; his successor, Grand Admiral Karl Dönitz, agreed to Germany's unconditional surrender a week later. When Flynn rejoined the Blue Spaders, they were settling into a new task, occupation duty in a defeated Germany, which had been divided into four zones by the vic-torious Allied powers. On June 11, 1945, slightly more than one month after Germany's surrender, the *Stars and Stripes*, a newspaper published by and for members of the U.S. military, announced that the American Third and Seventh Armies would engage in the military occupation of Germany. This meant the Blue Spaders would take part, as they had been members of the Third Army since D-Day.[88]

There remained the question about what should be done regarding the German population after the fall of the Nazi regime. The training materials disseminated to the soldiers and officers of the 26th Infantry Regiment left little doubt about the U.S. Army's official perspective on the Germans. In September 1944, as the Blue Spaders fought the Battle of Aachen, they received a pamphlet informing them of how to approach the local population:

> For most of the past century, Germany has sought to attain world domi-nation by conquest. To many Germans, this defeat will only be an inter-lude, a time to prepare for the next war. The Germans have no regrets for the havoc they have wrought in the world, except for loss of life and property they themselves have suffered. The German has been taught that the national goal of domination must be obtained regardless of the depths of treachery, murder and destruction necessary. Defeat will not erase that idea. Each American soldier must watch every action of him-self and of his comrades. The German will be watching constantly, even though you may not see him. Let him see a good American soldier.[89]

87. Wheeler, *The Big Red One*, 377–81.

88. "3rd and 7th Will Occupy Germany," *Stars and Stripes*, Southern Germany Edition, June 11, 1945, 1.

89. Special Orders for American-German Relations, issued by the U.S. Army,

The pamphlet also ordered its readers to keep contact with Germans to an absolute minimum; though most of the population were not members of the Nazi party, even so they could not be trusted.

Flynn's perspectives on the Germans were more complex. His letters to his family and to his provincial superiors reveal a full awareness of and great dislike for the Nazi regime's crimes; on the other hand, he admired the organizational abilities of the German people that were displayed in their taking the initiative to rebuild their homes and cities after the war's conclusion. Nor did Flynn denounce the Germans for spiritual and mental "primitiveness" in the manner he had spoken about the Sicilians. Clearly, Flynn's later charitable work on behalf of the German and Austrian people had its roots in this benevolent perspective, which he held at a time when few Americans in or out of military uniform had little positive to say about the Germans.

Many of Flynn's letters to Walsh discussed the downward trajectory of moral standards of the soldiers of the 26th Infantry Regiment when combat was exchanged for occupation duty in the summer of 1945. Still, he proudly noted that American soldiers in Germany—especially in the heavily Catholic areas of the Rhineland and Bavaria—continued the work they had begun in Sicily, Italy, and France, helping to rebuild churches, donating their salaries to fight the effects of the war, and using their own "sterling moral example" to revive Catholicism in a devastated and defeated nation. In a letter dated July 2, 1945, Flynn admitted despite the noble work that continued to be done by the Blue Spaders, he looked with a sense of "wistful envy" upon ships, filled with GIs, departing for America. He also admitted during the heady weeks following his transfer in late June of 1945—weeks that took the 26th Infantry from the Rhineland to Czechoslovakia and finally to Bavaria, supervising the surrender and disarmament of thousands of German and Austrian soldiers—he was "so punchy I scarcely knew what I did." Nevertheless, the men with whom he served had accomplished their mission, and could be satisfied they had done "God and their country's work."[90]

September 1944. The U.S. Army History Institute and Education Center, Carlisle Barracks, Pennsylvania, the Burton Andrus Collection, Box 30, Folder 15 (hereafter USAHEC, Andrus Collection—30/15).

90. Letter from Fabian Flynn to Edmund Walsh, July 2, 1945. PHA Record Group 322—3/7.

Flynn's time in the U.S. Army had taken him from Massachusetts to Texas, then to Tunisia, Sicily, Britain, France, Belgium, and Germany. One of the most decorated chaplains of the Second World War, he had received the Silver Star, two Bronze Stars, the Purple Heart, the European, African, and Middle Eastern campaign medals, the World War II Victory Medal, and the Distinguished United Citation.[91]

A Chaplain to the International War Crimes Tribunal, Nuremberg, August 1945 to April 1946

Nuremberg, the second largest city of American-occupied Bavaria, became the home for the most famous war crimes trial in history, the trial of the surviving political and military leaders of the Third Reich. The remaining members of the 26th Infantry Regiment who had not been mustered out of service were assigned to serve as the guards in the Nuremberg Palace of Justice; Flynn was appointed by the chief American prosecutor, Robert Jackson, as the official chaplain of the international tribunal. Flynn provided spiritual guidance not only to the American guards of the trial, but also to a handful of Catholic defendants and to many of the prosecution witnesses and relatives of defendants. These witnesses and relatives were housed in a small villa on the city's outskirts. His duties moved far beyond just those of a chaplain. For a few of the Nazi defendants at the trial, many of their family members, and some of the witnesses for the prosecution, Flynn was, from the fall of 1945 into the spring of 1946, their official U.S. Armed Forces representative.

As the occupation began, American soldiers were instructed to have minimal contacts with German civilians and to maintain a policy of strict nonfraternization. Of course, it was one thing to issue these commands to a force that occupied a substantial portion of a nation of 60 million people, and another to enforce it. The policies of strict nonfraternization with Germans and the removal of Nazi Party members from all public duties, were eventually abandoned by the American au-

91. Army Military Record and Report of Separation, Certificate of Service, July 15, 1946. PHA Record Group 329—29/C.

thorities.[92] The first easing of fraternization rules between American soldiers and German civilians was announced by Dwight Eisenhower on July 13, 1945; over the period of the four-year occupation, the rules were gradually loosened to a greater extent.[93] Following the surrender of Germany and the beginning of the Allied occupation, certain American soldiers and officers—Flynn among them—had more dealings with the Germans, especially former Nazis, than did others.

The 26th Infantry Regiment had been assigned to occupation duties in Bavaria, which made up the bulk of the American occupation zone. The regiment's headquarters was in the city of Grafenwöhr, while its 1st Battalion was stationed in Ludwigsburg and the 3rd Battalion in Nuremberg. The bulk of the Blue Spaders' work during the first six weeks of the occupation involved processing and disarming tens of thousands of German POWs, most of whom were coming across the nearby German-Czech border. In early June, this work ended and the entire First Infantry Division redeployed to regular occupation duty.[94]

Flynn spent the first few months of occupation with his usual routine of religious services, confessions, and hospital visits, taking time as well to give a number of lectures on sexual morality and sexually transmitted diseases. Flynn also took the time to visit and supervise religious services in both Displaced Persons' (DP) camps and in German prisoner of war camps, usually a few times each month. Displaced Persons included liberated prisoners from German concentration camps, slave laborers from all over Europe, and refugees who had been expelled from their countries of origin because of their religious or ethnic background. What they all had in common was they had neither the ability nor the desire to return to their homes. The DP camps in Nuremberg contained more than 11,000 people. Flynn appointed Polish priests or rabbis, to lead the worship, while at the German prisoner stockades, which included more than 6,000 men from the Waffen-SS, German Catholic priests

---

92. Ian Buruma, *Year Zero: A History of 1945* (New York: Penguin Press, 2013), 241.

93. "Ike Eases Non-Fraternization Rule," *Stars and Stripes*, Southern Germany Edition, July 13, 1945, 1.

94. Wheeler, *The Big Red One*, 387–89. Thousands of German soldiers were soon followed by thousands of German civilians who had been expelled by the restored Czechoslovak government.

or Lutheran ministers, most of whom were former chaplains in the German military and consequently POWs as well, led religious services.[95]

In all likelihood Flynn wrote the letter signed "from a Chaplain" to the southern German edition of *Stars and Stripes* published on September 13, 1945. In it, he complained that although fraternization rules had been relaxed regarding American military interactions with German civilians, and German POWs were commonly used as laborers to help rebuild shattered cities, continuing regulations prohibited Germans from taking part in religious services led by American military servicemen. The author wrote that the mutual participation of Germans and Americans in religious services could only have a positive effect, especially when compared to black-marketeering and prostitution that characterized other American-German encounters. The "Chaplain" wrote: "Regardless of who wrote this stupidity, I will avail myself of the services of German civilian organists, in the absence of an organist of my own and shall refuse to order any German who may drift into my service to leave the church. I have a higher commanding officer than even a two-star general, Jesus Christ."[96]

While the Blue Spaders conducted their complex duty in a defeated and ruined country, the leaders of the victorious Allied powers proceeded with their plans for the surviving leaders of the Nazi regime. The decision to create an international military tribunal was a long and complicated one, especially since the former leaders of the Third Reich were being tried for crimes defined by a curious merger of the 1907 Hague and 1928 Geneva Conventions; these laws were used to justify arrest warrants issued for German war criminals.[97] There was also the question of whether the defendants, many clearly guilty of horrific crimes, deserved any kind of trial at all; some argued that execution upon capture should be the preferred method. This had been the stat-

95. Monthly Chaplain's Reports, July–August 1945. NPRC Flynn File. Some of the rabbis were Holocaust survivors, others were U.S. military chaplains.

96. "Where Stars Are Plentiful," *Stars and Stripes,* Southern Germany Edition, September 13, 1945, 6. Although signed "A Chaplain," the tone of the writing, especially its impatience with those in authority who made foolish decisions, is a perfect match for Flynn's.

97. Giles MacDonogh, *After the Reich: The Brutal History of the Allied Occupation* (New York: Basic Books, 2007), 430.

ed preference of both U.S. President Franklin Roosevelt and British Prime Minister Winston Churchill until late in the war.[98]

Eventually, the leaders of the occupying powers agreed to a Four-Power tribunal to decide the fate of the leading Nazi war criminals. The London Charter of August 1945 formalized this agreement, although only after considerable wrangling over the trial's structure and format, given the widely divergent styles of criminal justice among the United States, Great Britain, France, and especially the Soviet Union.[99] The initial sessions of the International Military Tribunal (IMT) took place in Berlin in October 1945, per Soviet preference, with both the Soviet military leaders in Germany and the Soviet government desiring a trial in the symbolic former capital of Nazi Germany. At the urging of the French, British, and eventually American governments, the Soviets agreed the IMT would move to the Bavarian city of Nuremberg, not only because of the practical value of having a large courtroom and prison facility that had survived Allied bombing, but also for its own symbolic significance: Nuremberg had been the location for the major Nazi Party rallies during Hitler's dictatorship.[100]

This decision brought Flynn into the history of the IMT. Since the governing of the Nuremberg prison and its Palace of Justice were under the jurisdiction of American military authorities, the geographic proximity of the Blue Spaders to Nuremberg made them the obvious choice to serve as the guards of the courtroom and prison facilities, although ultimately the 26th Infantry Regiment and the 18th Infantry Regiment shared the job. Combined, the soldiers were referred to as the 6850 International Security Detachment of the International Military Tribunal.[101]

98. Leon Goldensohn. *The Nuremberg Interviews: An American Psychiatrist's Conversations with the Defendants and Witnesses* (New York: Vintage Books, 2004), xii.

99. Norman J. W. Goda, *Tales from Spandau: Nazi Criminals and the Cold War* (New York: Cambridge University Press, 2007), 20.

100. Goldensohn, *The Nuremberg Interviews*, xvii. The fact that the Western powers had far more of the chief Nazi war criminals in their custody than the Soviets did also influenced the decision.

101. General Instructions, December 1945, USAHEC Andrus Collection—39/38. The specific battalions assigned to guard duty were the 1st Battalion of the 18th Infantry Regiment and the 3rd Battalion of the 26th Infantry Regiment.

During the war, Flynn became close friends with Colonel Joseph Corley, executive officer of the Blue Spaders. Corley was also friends with Thomas Dodd, a former lawyer and Connecticut Senator who was the chief deputy of the main American prosecutor, Robert H. Jackson. Robert Kempner, another one of Jackson's deputies, Dodd, Corley, and Flynn often dined together in the late summer and early fall of 1945 as the groundwork for the IMT was being established in Nuremberg. Flynn made an extremely favorable impression on Dodd, and this convinced both him and Jackson that Flynn would be an excellent Catholic chaplain for the IMT, and thereby the spiritual counselor for the Catholic defendants and witnesses for the IMT. He was officially appointed Catholic chaplain of the IMT on August 25, 1945.[102]

Throughout September and October, Flynn worked in his new task as the Catholic chaplain for the IMT. According to his reports, in September he conducted in excess of 21 spiritual interviews with prisoners in the Nuremberg jail, defendants as well as witnesses for the prosecution, some of whom were being held for trial on later occasions. On seven different occasions in October, he visited the Nuremberg jail to meet with many defendants, and he offered Mass in the guardhouse three times. He also had time to conduct his first wedding as an army chaplain on October 22 when, at the Antoniuskirche, Flynn witnessed the nuptials of Jeannine Sesier, a German civilian, and Sergeant Joseph Morvan, who belonged to the 26th Infantry Regiment.[103]

There was another and unique task that occupied Flynn's attention during this period. On August 15, shortly before his appointment as the Catholic chaplain of the IMT, Flynn met a Hungarian countess of German origin named Ingeborg Kálnoky, who, having fled to Germany after Budapest fell to the Soviets, was in a Nuremberg hospital following the birth of her fourth child. Accompanied by several other

102. Christopher Dodd, *Letters from Nuremberg: My Father's Narrative of a Quest for Justice* (New York: Crown Publishers, 2007), 97–99. Captain Henry Gerecke, from the 98th Station Hospital, attached to the American Third Army, was the Protestant chaplain for the trial; later, another Catholic chaplain would be appointed to the IMT, Father Sixtus O'Connor; his service overlapped with Flynn's for a few months in 1946.

103. Monthly Chaplain's Reports, September–October 1945. NPRC Flynn File. This was in addition to his regular duties on behalf of the men of the 26th Infantry Regiment.

U.S. Army officers, Flynn spoke with Kálnoky about her husband—who was in the custody of the Red Army—and her children, who were in Czechoslovakia with relatives, trying to rejoin their mother in the American zone of Germany. Born in Thuringia as Ingeborg von Breiten, she had married the Hungarian Count Hugo Kálnoky in 1934 and lived until 1945 in Transylvania. Kálnoky became separated from her husband and sons, and she was now desperate for a home and an occupation while she was attempting to reunite her family.[104] With the authorization of both Colonel Joseph Corley and Thomas Dodd, Flynn asked Kálnoky if she desired to work with the U.S. Army authorities on an important mission. She agreed and, following a series of interviews, including one with U.S. Army intelligence officers, she was cleared for the assignment.[105]

A month after Flynn began his work in Nuremberg, he wrote another lengthy article for *The Sign*. Entitled "Report from Nuremberg," it discussed the arrival of many of the major German defendants in Nuremberg for the beginning of the IMT, including Hermann Goering, Joachim von Ribbentrop, Arthur Seyss-Inquart, and Franz von Papen. Flynn referred to them as a "sorry lot" and argued that the sight of these former leaders huddling and shivering under a torrential downpour was a "dismal and ironically graphic picture of Germany and the Germans today, beaten, broken, bewildered, thoroughly cowed, spiritless, and facing the bleakest of futures." Neither was the city of Nuremberg in any better condition, as 91 percent of it had been reduced to rubble; only a handful of buildings remained standing in a scene of "total ruin."[106]

Flynn criticized the decision to have the trial in Nuremberg, in spite of his recent appointment. The ruined city was filled with destitute German civilians scavenging each day, and even-worse-off dis-

104. Christiane Kohl, *The Witness House: Nazis and Holocaust Survivors Sharing a Villa during the Nuremberg Trials* (Boston: Other Books, 2010), 18. Kálnoky's three older children were reunited with her in November, after leaving Czechoslovakia and spending a few weeks in a displaced persons camp in Bavaria. Her husband did not rejoin the family for another two years.

105. Ibid., 17. Flynn baptized Ingeborg's daughter, who shared her mother's name.

106. Fabian Flynn, "Report from Nuremberg" *The Sign*, October 1945, 31.

placed persons (DPs) from all over Europe, who were crowded into the same barracks that had housed them as slave laborers during the war. Each day trains left the city filled with former slave laborers trying to make their way back home, while other trains arrived filled with ethnic Germans who were being expelled from their homes by the Polish, Czech, and Soviet authorities: "Every freight train today is a crawling disorderly mass of humans. Sometimes it seems as if all of Europe is on the road moving, moving constantly, painfully, abjectly."[107]

The American occupying forces, Flynn implied, barely preserved order. The reason for moving the war crimes trials to Nuremberg, therefore, was purely symbolic, with little consideration of practical realities:

> This, then, is Nuremberg in Bavaria, the site of the trials of the Axis war criminals. Whoever decided upon holding the trails here must have done so sight unseen. Quite evidently, they were men urged by a desire for the fulfillment of some sort of public poetic justice or possessed of a flair for theatricals. Probably, they reasoned that since it was here the Nazi leaders rode to power and glory, it is here that they must stand condemned before all the world. Whatever the reason the selectors were certainly not guided by practicality.[108]

Flynn's description of the physical environment of the Nuremberg Palace of Justice—where, along with other members of the 26th Infantry Regiment, he had lived for several weeks in the summer of 1945—spoke of a "rambling trio of buildings." He also mentioned how he had taken over the only remaining Catholic church standing in the city, the Antoniuskirche (Church of Saint Anthony), to offer religious services for civilian and military personnel, but only after American soldiers and German POWs repaired the church from extensive bombing damage.[109]

Flynn revealed some sympathy for the Nazi prisoners, who "languished in the local jails in durance vile and solitary," and were not

107. Ibid., 32. Caring for these ethnic Germans would occupy much of Flynn's first ten years with War Relief Services.

108. Ibid. Although Flynn did not mention this, Luxembourg (where many of the Nazi war criminals were initially held) and also Mainz and Berlin were considered as possible locales for the IMT.

109. Ibid. The idea of American soldiers rebuilding the physical and more importantly the spiritual foundations of Europe was a common theme in Flynn's articles for *The Sign*, as was Flynn's belief in the possibility of redemption for the Germans.

allowed to meet with news reporters, or their lawyers, or even to speak with each other. Nor were they able to see any family members. He mentioned that, since secrecy surrounding the prisoners was so tight, often the guards and prison staff were not sure who their prisoners were: Colonel-General Alfred Jodl's wife came to prison to give him a few eggs and an orange, and the first lieutenant in charge at the entrance emphatically stated that Jodl was not in prison or even in Nuremberg. Jodl's wife insisted she knew her husband was there; she had read so in the U.S. military newspaper *Stars and Stripes*.[110]

Despite his criticisms, Flynn concluded the article on an optimistic note, assuring his American readers that the men associated with the trial were "men of honor and integrity" who understood the importance of the trial as "the eye of the world and the searchlight of history are upon them." He pointed out that Andrus had acted wisely and judiciously in dealing with the German prisoners and had helped Hermann Goering, whom Flynn referred to as a "strange man," finally to break his addiction to morphine. Given the terrible crimes of the Third Reich, a reckoning of some kind was necessary regarding its surviving leaders. The last words of the article convey a sense of Flynn's hope despite the difficulty circumstances: "This will be a fair trial. Of that I am convinced."[111]

During the next few months, Flynn was extraordinarily busy, for his role as a spiritual leader was not to be limited solely to the German defendants. He also ministered at the Antoniuskirche to Catholic soldiers and personnel associated with the trial, which meant that, for all intents and purposes, the Antoniuskirche was his church for the duration of his time in Nuremberg. Working with other officers from the 26th Infantry Regiment, Flynn also helped to set up accommodations for witnesses and family members of the defendants in a medium-sized villa located at 24 Novalistrasse, which was a thirty-minute walk from the Palace of Justice. He frequently visited the house, befriending many of its inhabitants, including Countess Kálnoky.[112] Among those who lived at

110. Ibid., 33.

111. Ibid. It is doubtful that Flynn viewed the Soviet participants in the trial as "men of honor and integrity."

112. Christiane Kohl, *The Witness House,* 18.

the Witness House during the time period, besides Kálnoky's children, were Heinrich Hoffmann, Hitler's personal photographer; Hoffmann's daughter Henriette von Schirach, who was the wife of Baldur von Schirach, former *Gauleiter* of Vienna and Hitler Youth Leader; and Rudolf Diels, the first head of the Gestapo. There were also numerous former prisoners from various Nazi concentration camps, who were witnesses for the prosecution during the trial.[113]

During Flynn's time in Nuremberg, he visited the Witness House a few times each week. By all accounts, Kálnoky and Flynn became close friends during his time in Nuremberg. Flynn regularly brought gifts for Kálnoky and her children, everything from a typewriter for the countess to handcrafted toys for her children. One person who did not arrive at the Witness House until 1947, after Flynn had left Nuremberg, was Ingeborg's husband, Count Hugo Kálnoky, who fortunately had been released by Soviet authorities.[114]

According to Elise Krülle and her son Gerhard—the former owners of the Witness House, who were allowed to stay on condition that they work as its domestic staff—the relationship between Flynn and the countess may have been more than just a simple friendship. Mother and son, though, may have had an axe to grind, and there is little evidence, beyond Flynn's frequent trips to the Witness House and occasional solitary meetings with Kálnoky, of anything resembling a physical relationship. None of the Passionist records concerning Flynn during this time or afterwards reflect a fear that he had violated his vow of celibacy, with Countess Kálnoky or anyone else. The Passionist order certainly had other issues with Flynn, but this aspect of his life as Passionist was not one they believed he had ever violated. Whatever the character of their relationship, Kálnoky's contacts with Flynn paid her considerable dividends, as he expedited her and her family's immigration to the United States in 1949.[115]

113. Ibid., 208–12.

114. Ibid., 88–89. Giving German toys and other handcrafted goods as presents would be a regular habit of Flynn's. Years later his numerous relatives would recall Flynn bringing these gifts from Germany and Austria every time he returned home to Boston.

115. Ibid., 213. It is possible the Krülles spread this story as they were resentful for the loss of their home on the orders of the American military authorities, of which

The visitor log of Colonel Burton Andrus—the commandant of the Nuremberg prison and the jailer of most of the Nazi war criminals since their detainment in Luxembourg—reveals Flynn was a frequent visitor to the prison and often consulted with Colonel Andrus regarding his work with the German prisoners. Among the prisoners with whom Flynn met were Hitler's former lawyer and the governor-general of Poland, Hans Frank; Hitler Youth leader Baldur von Schirach; former Reichsbank president and Hitler's finance minister, Hjalmar Schacht; and Hitler's first—and, as it would turn out, last—vice-chancellor, Franz von Papen.[116]

While Flynn had occasional visits with both Frank and Schacht, according to his chaplain's reports and the records of the Nuremberg prison, the two Nazi defendants with whom he interacted to the greatest extent were Franz von Papen and Baldur von Schirach. A tall man with a prominent mustache and an aristocratic air, von Papen served as a general staff officer in the German military during the First World War, including a term as military attaché in the German embassy in Washington, D.C. During the Weimar era, he became a prominent member of the Catholic Center Party and the leader of its most conservative faction. He occupied a variety of positions in various governments in the Weimar Republic. After an unsuccessful term as chancellor of Germany throughout much of 1932, he was appointed by President Paul von Hindenburg to serve as vice-chancellor. In early 1933, he fatally persuaded the aging, borderline-senile president to appoint Hitler as chancellor, arguing that Hitler would be "controlled," since the Nazis would hold only a minority of ministries in the cabinet. During his October 12, 1945, interview with U.S. Army interrogators, thirteen years later, von Papen rationalized his support for Hitler as

---

Flynn was the primary representative with whom they had contact. Also, Elise had lost her husband, Walter, who had volunteered to serve in the German army in the last months of the war, despite being more than fifty years old. The facts remain shrouded in mystery. In the author's opinion, it is unlikely but not impossible that their relationship was a romantic one.

116. Visitor Log, September 1945 to February 1946, USAHEC Andrus Collection—39/32. Flynn was not the only U.S. Army chaplain at the Nuremberg prison; since most of the German prisoners were Lutheran, the Lutheran chaplain Major Henry Gerecke also ministered to the prisoners.

having been a way of preventing Germany from slipping into a civil war. He protested loyalty to his country as the justification for his later service as Germany's ambassador to Austria, from 1934 to 1938, and Turkey, from 1938 to 1944. Von Papen expressed regrets to Thomas Dodd over the atrocities committed by the Nazis, but he pled ignorance of them.[117]

If Franz von Papen—who was, in the words of German historian Fritz Stern, one of the "grave-diggers of German democracy"—could be excused as a misguided conservative who fatally underestimated Hitler (and he was not alone in this), Baldur von Schirach was an altogether different and more sinister character. He was son of an aristocratic family, a large man with dark hair and sharp features. Many of his family members emigrated back from the state of Pennsylvania to Germany in the early twentieth century. Joining the Nazi Party in 1925, von Schirach was appointed by Hitler in 1933 to lead the Hitler Youth, following his success as the leader of the National Socialist German Students Bund (National sozialistischer Studentenbund), the Nazi organization for German university students. Von Schirach informed his U.S. Army interrogators on September 11, 1945, about the ease with which the Hitler Youth absorbed Catholic, Protestant, and secular youth organizations in the early years of the Nazi regime.[118] By 1938, more than eight million German children were part of the Hitler Youth, and von Schirach's image was almost as omnipresent to them as Hitler's. Following the German invasion of France in May 1940, von Schirach volunteered in the Wehrmacht and served with distinction, winning two medals for bravery. Hitler rewarded him with the post of *Gauleiter* of Vienna in August 1940.[119]

During this time from 1940 to 1945, von Schirach oversaw the deportation of more than 65,000 Viennese Jews to various death camps

117. Interrogation Record, Franz von Papen. NARA Record Group 238—World War II War Crimes Records, Roll 14—Papen, Franz von—Puhl, Emil.

118. Interrogation Record of Baldur von Schirach. NARA Record Group 238—World War II War Crimes Records, Roll 19—Schilling, Claus-Seldte, Franz.

119. Ibid. The position of *Gauleiter* could be roughly described as the head of the Nazi Party administration in a particular city or district, but usually the authority of the *Gauleiter* went far beyond party matters.

in the General Government of Poland. During his postwar interrogation, von Schirach denied he had played any role in this process, until
his American military interrogators produced a speech he had given to
assembled Nazi Party leaders in Vienna on September 15, 1942; in this
speech, he referred to the removal of the city's Jewish population as a
"great contribution of European culture." He attempted to walk back
this statement during his interrogation, and then in his next session
he tried to contextualize it, unconvincingly. He did, however, obliquely
and occasionally criticize Nazi extermination policies from 1943 onwards, and he was one of the handful of defendants at the Nuremberg
trial who openly criticized Hitler and his regime.[120]

The German prisoners with whom Flynn interacted had nothing
but praise for his spiritual work. Franz von Papen complimented Flynn
in his memoirs written in the early 1950s. He wrote Flynn helped ar-
range transportation and living arrangements in Nuremberg for his
wife and daughter and had notified him of this after it had been completed. He also wrote that Flynn and his eventual replacement as the
Catholic chaplain, Father Sixtus O'Connor, were a "great solace" to
him during this trying period, and he was grateful for their spiritual
assistance.[121]

Another defendant who strongly praised Flynn was Baldur von
Schirach. In a letter that von Schirach wrote to Flynn's superior in the
Passionist order, he said, "[Flynn] did far more than preach religion,
he lives it." Much as von Papen had done, von Schirach emphasized
that Flynn looked after his wife, another Hitler Youth leader who was
briefly imprisoned before her transfer to the Witness House, and their
four children during the trial. Distressed when he was informed that
Flynn was leaving his military service to take a position in War Relief
Services, von Schirach wrote: "Losing this dear friend of mine makes

---

120. Ibid. Von Schirach was also at least enough of a realist to be aghast at Goering's statement in May 1945 to a group of Nazi leaders that the end of the war would
resemble the end of a soccer match, with everyone shaking hands and going home
afterward.

121. Franz von Papen, *Memoirs,* trans. Brian Connell (New York: E. P. Dutton,
1953), 546–47. Von Papen was also complimentary of Thomas Dodd, Robert Jackson's
chief deputy for the American prosecution. He was among the three defendants acquitted at the trial.

the rest of this modern torture called a trial (in the name of humanity) a very lonesome journey."[122]

Schacht and von Papen were acquitted of all charges at the end of the Nuremberg trial, whereas von Schirach and Frank received guilty verdicts. Found guilty of crimes against humanity for his role in deporting Viennese Jews to Poland, von Schirach served twenty years in Spandau Prison. Frank, found guilty of war crimes and crimes against humanity for his role in the murderous Nazi occupation of Poland, was among the twelve defendants who were sentenced to death. He was executed on October 16, 1946, along with nine other condemned German defendants—the eleventh condemned Nazi, Hermann Goering, having committed suicide the night before.[123]

The role of Flynn and Gerecke at the Nuremberg prison became an issue of contention between Colonel Andrus and the defense lawyers for the accused. Andrus received numerous letters during the trial from lawyers who represented the defendants, from the defendants themselves, and from other prisoners, including Albert Speer, Joachim von Ribbentrop, Albert Kesselring, Franz Halder, and Theodore Westphal. These letters complained about the living conditions of the prison, the lack of privacy for the prisoners, "boisterous guards" who made too much noise at night, an inability to meet with or receive parcels from family members, and the lack of German chaplains for the prisoners. Many of the letters pointed out that since numerous German POWs were performing custodial and maintenance tasks at the prison, and since the prisoners were allowed to meet with their German lawyers, there was no reason prisoners shouldn't also have German spiritual counselors.[124]

Andrus refused to accept the validity of these complaints, noting

122. "The Priest Who Put Europe Back Together," *Catholic Herald*, December 22, 1972, 7. Von Schirach's wife, Henriette, divorced him in 1949, three years into his twenty-year sentence at Spandau Prison.

123. Giles MacDonogh, *After the Reich*, 449–50. Goering had convinced his American guard to smuggle cyanide to him a few days earlier. The twelfth condemned major war criminal, Martin Bormann, had been tried and condemned in absentia, even though he was generally thought to be dead already.

124. Letter from Colonel Andrus to Colonel Joseph Corley, May 11, 1946. USAHEC Andrus Collection—33/81.

that prisoners were not allowed to visit with family members, but they were certainly free to write to them, and he had personally appealed to British, French, and Soviet authorities in their respective zones to ensure that mail from and to prisoners was delivered. Regarding the question of German clergymen for the prisoners, Andrus noted the two Catholic chaplains, Flynn and Father Sixtus O'Connor (a Franciscan priest from New York who had served as chaplain to the 11th Armored Division of General George Patton's Third Army) and the Protestant chaplain Ralph Gerecke were "quite competent" and fluent in German, and therefore were more than capable of providing spiritual counseling to prisoners. Andrus wrote that, apart from their lawyers, no Germans could meet with prisoners while they were in the Nuremberg jail. He pointedly noted that the German prisoners were "permitted much greater freedom of movement and spiritual guidance than were ever permitted prisoners held by the Nazis." Former Waffen-SS General Erich von dem Bach-Zewelski, who had distinguished himself by brutally crushing the Warsaw Uprising in 1944, wrote a letter to Andrus's superiors in the early summer of 1946 claiming he represented most of the prisoners, who were generally happy with the treatment they received at the hands of the U.S. military, including their spiritual counseling.[125]

Flynn wrote an article for the December 1945 issue of *The Sign* that paid tribute to the memory of the troops with whom he had served. It was perhaps the most heartfelt of his writings. Entitled "November Soldiers," the three-page memorial recounted Flynn's recent return to a small Belgian town the Blue Spaders had liberated shortly before the Battle of Aachen. He wrote that returning to the town—he did not mention its name, but it was almost certainly located near the Henri-Chapelle cemetery for American soldiers—revealed how the scars of the war were still visible, six months after its conclusion. Most of the shops remained closed because of the damage they had suffered in the fighting; those still open had little to sell to customers, who had little money with which to buy. Flynn noted mordantly: "One store featured in its window an assortment of religious articles, cheap rosaries, garish

---

125. Ibid. Andrus's only small concession was that he looked into the complaints that the guards were acting inappropriately, especially about their being too noisy at night.

miniature statues, and in their midst, a copy of the daily paper of the French communist party. All Europe is like that today, somehow. Mixed up. Confused."[126]

He recalled the difficulty he had encountered, during the period of combat, trying to find churches where he could celebrate Mass; although the hood of his jeep could function as a suitable altar, he always investigated standing churches when they came across them. Flynn wrote that the soldiers with whom he served eagerly took advantage of a Mass in an actual church, as it offered physical, mental, and spiritual support. He offered up a series of anecdotes about the men who attended these services, and then described their fate. There was John, who played the organ during services, and was found shot dead in his foxhole, still gripping his walkie-talkie. There was Ray, who, holding onto Flynn's hand and the only prayer book the regiment had (the *Christian Brothers Hymnal*), died on an ambulance truck as there was no more plasma to give him to save his life. Finally, there was Leo, who was the lead singer in the church choir for the 26th Infantry Regiment, and who, like Ray, died in Flynn's presence following a mortal injury from a German artillery barrage. Among his last words, according to Flynn, were a repetition of a sermon Flynn had given: "I remembered the sermon you gave. You said, no matter what was dropping around us, God was there all the time." Flynn wrote that all these men died as brave Christian soldiers in a noble cause.[127]

In what was probably his most honest expression of his feelings about the war and what he had seen, Flynn concluded: "There were others, all good men, God rest them, many of them only boys. Men with whom I lived and laughed, whom I loved and who so loved me. I miss them terribly. Their like I will not know again on this earth." He urged his readers to oppose "those little, hate-filled minds planning the next war." The best tribute to the fallen Christian soldiers of the 26th Infantry Regiment, and of the all the other men who fought for freedom and peace, was to fight to restore Europe and the world to a stable, Christian

126. Fabian Flynn, "November Soldiers," *The Sign,* December 1945, 29. Flynn explicitly referred to having buried several soldiers during his time at the Henri-Chapelle cemetery.

127. Ibid., 30.

order and to help those surviving the horrible war to recover physically and spiritually. Flynn, like so many others who came through the Second World War, suffered from "survivor's guilt," especially since he served in a regiment where casualties were so high. It almost certainly helped motivate him to succeed in the trials to come.[128]

Flynn's work outside the Nuremberg prison eventually became as demanding as his work inside, as he frequented the Witness House on the Novalistrasse on the outskirts of Nuremberg almost daily in the winter and spring of 1946. In November 1945, he arranged to have the three children of Ingeborg Kálnoky—who, having fled Czechoslovakia, were living in a displaced persons camp in Bavaria—returned to her.[129] Flynn's duties as the priest in charge of the Antoniuskirche also occupied much of his time. He usually offered Mass there daily during the week and twice on Sundays. On Christmas 1945, his congregation numbered in excess of 1,400 people.[130]

According to the final series of his chaplain's reports, from November 1945 to March 1946, Flynn visited the Nuremberg prison an average of seven times per month and the hospital three times a month. He offered twenty masses monthly, as well as the usual lectures on sexual morality and the occasional marriage ceremony—he performed three in December, all between American servicemen and German women.

The complexities of the relations between American servicemen and German civilians, especially young women, were the subject of regular discussion in the *Stars and Stripes*. In one particularly memorable letter from February 4, 1946, a soldier from the 26th Infantry Regiment admitted he had gotten a German girl pregnant, that he had forgiven her other affairs since "an American soldier is always willing to take advantage of a poor German girl," and now he badly desired to marry her, and he hoped the restrictions on this practice would be lifted. Perhaps this man and his German bride were among the weddings Flynn witnessed at the Antoniuskirche.[131]

128. Ibid., 31

129. Kohl, *The Witness House*, 35.

130. Ibid., 89.

131. "Pro and Con on Marrying Frauleins," *Stars and Stripes, Southern Germany Edition*, February 14 1946, 8.

In addition to these other duties, Flynn was also already transitioning into his later work with War Relief Services, usually visiting the various DP camps and POW camps in and around Nuremberg to conduct religious services, both for the victims of Nazi crimes and those who had perpetuated them, although not at the same time.[132] Flynn rarely talked openly about his military service, but he did say to his relatives years later that his work as a chaplain in occupied Germany was to provide spiritual assistance to anyone who needed it.[133]

His reports also gave evidence of a critical attitude toward some military authorities. His January 1946 report expressed aggravation at his superiors in the 26th Infantry Regiment for refusing to consider his request that several rabbis who were located in DP camps in Nuremberg should be appointed as chaplains to Jewish personnel working as part of the IMT. Flynn noted there were numerous Jewish personnel involved in the IMT as interrogators and translators, and they were not able to celebrate the Sabbath on a regular basis since the Jewish chaplains stationed in Nuremberg were already hopelessly busy administering to the needs of the Jewish American soldiers. Flynn also went on to complain that, since he had returned to the Blue Spaders seven months before, he had been forced to requisition all of his supplies from the various battalions that composed the 26th Infantry Regiment, as none of his requests had been granted. He emphasized that "not a single item" had been sent to him from the Office of the Chaplains.[134]

Because Flynn's time was stretched thin, the role of spiritual counselor to many of the German defendants during the IMT at Nuremberg was taken over by Father Sixtus O'Connor, OFM. This transition began in February 1946, when Flynn traveled to Rome to meet with Pius XII as well as his former acquaintance, the soon-to-be Cardinal Francis Spellman, and also a priest who would have an enormous impact on the rest of his life, Father Edward Swanstrom, the newly appointed director of the National Catholic Welfare Conference's War Relief Services (WRS). This meeting was ostensibly to discuss the return of several former Italian army chaplains, who were in American custody in

132. Monthly Chaplain's Reports, November 1945–January 1946. NPRC Flynn File.
133. Suzanne Birdsall, Interview, February 12, 2015.
134. Monthly Chaplain's Report, February 1946. NPRC Flynn File.

Germany, to their homes in Italy, and to attend the consistory at which Archbishop Spellman was created cardinal, on February 18, 1946.[135]

During their time in Rome, Spellman and Swanstrom discussed with Flynn the role they had envisioned for him after his military service was over: director of WRS activities in the French occupation zone of Germany. After the meeting, Flynn returned to Nuremberg to resume his army duties. In early March, Flynn was promoted to major in the U.S. Army, and a month later, on April 14, 1946, he was placed on terminal leave and sent home to the United States for his honorable discharge and decommissioning, which occurred on July 16, 1946, at Fort Dix, New Jersey. Flynn would be a part of the U.S. Army reserve until September 1952, but since he was serving in Europe for the WRS, he was not called to serve in the Korean War. After a few months back at home in Saint Gabriel's Monastery, Flynn returned to Europe for the task that would consume the next sixteen years of his life, working as director of the WRS in various parts of Central Europe.[136]

Flynn's prose may strike one reading it almost seventy years later as somewhat dramatic and even overwrought. There remains the question of how much of Flynn's writings expresses his genuine sentiments rather than his desire to appear in a good light to his provincial superiors. One might wonder, as well, about just how many Catholic soldiers of the 26th Infantry Division shared Flynn's belief that their moral example would help rebuild European Christian foundations. There can be no doubt of his own personal courage and the strength of his religious convictions, and it is plain that they served him well during the Second World War. Indeed, these traits would continue to be of vital importance as Flynn continued his spiritual work.

Flynn's task as the first Catholic chaplain of the IMT had been a difficult but successful one. In some ways, it mirrored the trial itself. The trial began in difficult circumstances, in an environment of questionable legality and historical precedent, just as many questioned whether the German defendants could be convicted of acts that were not against the law at the time and place they occurred. Some involved

135. Kohl, *The Witness House,* 122.
136. U.S. Army Military Record and Report of Separation, Certificate of Service, July 15, 1946. PHA Record Group 379—29/C.

in the trial at the time questioned whether Nazi war criminals deserved a chaplain at all, given how few of the victims of the Third Reich had had any type of spiritual assistance before their deaths or during their imprisonment.

Flynn never questioned the need to provide his services as a confessor to the Catholic defendants of the IMT, much as he never questioned the need to hear the confessions of American soldiers and officers or, eventually, German civilians. He dedicated himself to this task without hesitation or reservation, just as he dedicated himself to acting for the inhabitants of the Witness House on the Novalistrasse. Despite his misgivings about whether the trial should be held in the ruined city of Nuremberg, he never questioned its legality or the need to bring the German war criminals to justice. In this sense, Flynn's work as Catholic chaplain of the 26th Infantry Regiment was a prominent chapter of his nineteen years in Europe, during which he worked at restoring a Christian order in a continent plagued by war, genocide, and dictatorship.

The World in 1946

As Flynn's military service came to an end and he re-entered civilian life, the diplomatic environment of the Second World War, characterized by the Grand Alliance of the Western democracies and the Soviet Union, was also coming to an end. The Nuremberg trial was among the last events in which the Soviets and Western Allies worked together. As Hitler had predicted shortly before his suicide, the defeat of Germany would be followed by a long rivalry in the areas of politics, economics, and military competition between the United States and the Soviet Union. Although the Cold War would not emerge in earnest for another year, events were clearly moving in this direction in 1946, with controversies such as the Italian/Yugoslavian dispute over the city of Trieste, the Greek civil war, and the Iranian and Turkish crisis—all were marked by the Soviets on one side of the issue and their former allies on the other.

The agreements made at Yalta and Potsdam in 1945 promised that although Germany and Austria, as well as their capitals of Berlin and Vienna, would be divided into four zones/sectors, they would still be governed as a united country through the Four-Power administration set up at the end of the war, the Allied Control Council. Sixteen months later, these administrations were beginning to break down, especially in Germany. Disputes over Soviet demands for immediate reparations payments from the industrial sectors in the western occupation zones of Germany, combined with American and British fear that these demands would plunge the economy of their zones into chaos, was undoubtedly the largest issue poisoning the well between the former allies. Soviet refusal to allow the three Western powers any role in the administration of the Soviet zone of Germany was met with a determination on the part of the Western powers to remake their zones as they saw fit. While the French authorities in their zone were initially reluctant to cooperate too closely with the Americans and British, they ultimately would join them in treating the three occupation zones as one administrative unit.

Both Western and Soviet sides in Germany traded insults over political activities in the other zones; the Soviets accused the Americans and British of allowing former Nazis back into positions of administrative prominence, while the Soviets' "friends," the Socialist Unity Party of Germany, formed in April, were viewed by London and Washington as puppets of Moscow. Austria did not have the same prominence as Germany, but similar divisions had also taken root there between the Soviets and the West. In neither country did it appear the military occupation would end anytime soon.

In the Soviet zones of Germany and to a lesser extent in Austria, as well as in the various other countries of Europe, the foundations were being laid for the establishment of communist dictatorships on the Soviet model. Stalin did not immediately impose communism on the countries liberated from Nazi rule, but from the first day after liberation things were moving in this direction. Communist parties, with the support of the Soviet military authorities, were forcing Socialist or Social Democratic parties to merge with them to create "united Left" parties that were dominated by communist leaders. These included the Socialist Unity Part of Germany (SED—Socialistische Einheitspartei Deutschlands), the Hungarian Workers' Party (MDP—Magyar Dolgozók Pártja) and the Polish United Workers' Party (PZPR—Polska

Zjednoczona Partia Robotnicza). While the governments of Hungary and Poland were popular front governments consisting of Communists, Liberals, and representatives from Peasant Parties, the members of MDP and PZPR controlled key ministries such as transportation, defense, and the interior, which meant they would control all the necessary levers of power when it came time to seize control of the government.

Within a few years, worsening tensions between the Soviets and the West, when combined with Stalin's open split with Yugoslavia's Josip Broz Tito, led the Soviet leadership to give the green light to their various puppets in Eastern Europe to construct Stalinist communism. Flynn would see this firsthand during a few months in Hungary in 1948, as the MDP, under its leader Mátyás Rákosi, purged the country of his most prominent opponents, including the most visible, Cardinal József Mindszenty, the primate of the Catholic Church in Hungary. By the formation of the German Democratic Republic in October 1949, this process would be largely be completed in the Soviet sphere of influence. Austria was among a handful of European countries whose position between the democratic West and the communist East was unclear.

The Cold War, as it came to be known, lasted for over forty years, with Europe as its primary battleground. Now as a key official in the NCWC's War Relief Services, first in the French zone of Germany, then in Hungary, then in the American zone of Germany, and, finally and most significantly, in Austria, Flynn found himself at the center of an ideological struggle between atheist communism and Christian democracy and freedom.

Figure 1. The staff of the Boston Latin School *Register* for the year 1920–1921; Flynn is in the top row, far right

Figure 2. Yearbook photo of Flynn from his final year at the Boston Latin School, 1922–1923; the photo was taken shortly before his entry into the Passionist order

Figure 3. Flynn at Saint Ann's Monastery in 1927, with two of his seminary classmates on the right, Jerome O'Grady and Andrew Ansbro (man in the center unidentified)

Figure 4. Flynn with actors Dick Haymes and Cesar Romero, who were on a USO tour in 1943

Figure 5. Flynn in his chaplain's Jeep outside Aachen, Germany, in 1944

∞4

CATHOLIC RELIEF SERVICES, GERMANY
AND HUNGARY, 1946–1949

God evidently meant Austria to be one of the happiest lands of Europe, and probably this was true throughout the eighteenth and nineteenth centuries. But Austria today is a land of scars, so deep that many of them can never be healed. In the years before the *Anschluss*, there were twenty years of mass unemployment and violent political hatreds. More recently, there have been reprisals and assassinations, concentration camps, hordes of refugees and deportees from every quarter of Europe, and devastating air raids in every important city. The immediate future of Austria is dark. There is the vital question of food. The daily ration in the American zone is 1800 calories per day. There are the questions of work, of overpopulation, of refugees. Austria itself is probably destined to be the buffer between the Western powers and the Russian zone of influence.[1]

So wrote Thomas Kernan, a former official with the American military government in Austria, in the November 1945 issue of *The Sign*. His article was entitled "Austria—Land of Scars," but the circumstances Kernan described could easily apply to many of the countries in Europe in the years following the Second World War, including three other locations where Flynn served as director of CRS before arriving in Austria in 1949: the French zone of Germany (from 1946 to 1948);

---

1. Thomas Kernan, "Austria, Land of Scars," *The Sign*, November 1945, 5–9.

Hungary (in 1948); and the American zone of Germany (from 1948 to 1949). All three countries played an important role in the early decades of the forty-year conflict known as the Cold War, which would define the remainder of Flynn's life and career.[2]

Flynn's role as director of the National Catholic Welfare Conference's (NCWC) Catholic Relief Service programs in Germany, Hungary, and Austria was multifaceted. During his sixteen years as one of the chief officials of CRS in Europe, Flynn did everything from helping to reopen the Newman Center at the University of Freiburg in the French zone of Germany, to accompanying Cardinal József Mindszenty throughout Hungary to rally opposition to its Stalinist regime, to assisting hundreds of thousands of refugees from communism who had fled to Austria. Flynn negotiated with secular and clerical leaders, and also with government officials in the United States, Hungary, Germany, and Austria, not to mention authorities from various other charitable agencies and the United Nations High Commissioner for Refugees (UNHCR). Although based in Salzburg, Austria's second largest city, Flynn frequently traveled to CRS's European headquarters in Geneva and to the United States to coordinate relief efforts, as well as to raise funds and public awareness of the humanitarian crisis in Europe.

The primary task of Catholic Relief Services was to provide aid to those who needed it, especially refugees. This aid took many forms: medical supplies, surplus food, and clothing donations; the arrangement of transit to, and employment in, a new homeland. CRS's mission statement asserted that its aid programs were for all people fleeing religious, political, or ethnic persecution, regardless of their religious, racial, or social background. CRS operated all over the world, but during its first two decades most of its activity took place in Europe and East Asia, and to a lesser extent in South America. It distributed tens of millions of dollars in aid to refugees and the impoverished and helped hundreds of thousands of them build a new life in different parts of the world.

2. For readability, I use the designation Catholic Relief Services (CRS) to refer to the organization except in direct quotations; the organization was founded in 1943 with the name War Relief Services but was renamed Catholic Relief Services in 1954 and has kept that name ever since.

The first two decades of its existence also corresponded with the opening of the Cold War, as the Soviet Union was imposing and maintaining communist rule on the countries the Red Army had liberated at the end of the Second World War. Europe, and soon the world, was split in two—a communist East and a capitalist West, with some parts hotly contested. The Soviets violently suppressed opposition to communism, most famously in East Germany in 1953 and Hungary in 1956. These uprisings created countless refugees, of all economic, religious, and social backgrounds, many of whom fled to countries that bordered the communist bloc, such as West Germany and Austria. CRS was undoubtedly motivated by its Catholic faith to assist these people, but it also saw charitable aid as a weapon, perhaps the best weapon of all, against communism, to which the Catholic Church in America—much as in Austria, Germany, Hungary, and the Vatican—was inextricably opposed. In order to move the impoverished and desperate people of the world away from false utopian promises offered by Stalin and his successor, Nikita Khrushchev, the Church had to demonstrate it could provide for them in a more humane and successful fashion than the communists could.

The principal ally of CRS in this effort was the American government, specifically the State Department. In the first two decades of its existence, CRS devoted a majority of its efforts to Europe, which paralleled the greater commitment of the United States government to Europe, most notably American participation in the North Atlantic Treaty Organization (NATO) and the Marshall Plan. While it would not be accurate to say CRS was basically an American government agency, the State Department during the Truman, Eisenhower, and Kennedy administrations gave CRS between 70 and 80 percent of the aid it distributed. American diplomats and the NCWC had a common interest in containing, and perhaps even rolling back, Soviet influence in Europe. It was not always a perfect partnership, but it was a lasting and effective one. The various leaders of CRS, from Bishop Edward Swanstrom to James Norris, the director of its European branch, to Fabian Flynn, were all devout Catholics but also staunch Cold Warriors, and they saw their work with CRS as fulfilling both functions.

Flynn's career working for CRS in Europe possessed three distinct stages. The first stage, from 1946 to 1948, unfolded in the French zone of Germany, where Flynn's work involved assisting people in Displaced Persons (DP) camps and in Prisoner-of-War (POW) camps, as well helping the German Catholic community rebuild their churches and clerical infrastructure. The second stage was Flynn's three months in Hungary in 1948, where he worked with Hungary's equivalent of CRS, Actio Catholica, and befriended Cardinal József Mindszenty during the final stages of the country's transformation into one of Stalin's satellite regimes. Following his expulsion from Hungary in 1948, Flynn continued his work with CRS in Germany and then in neighboring Austria, where he stayed for the next thirteen years. During the first six, Austria remained under Four-Power occupation, which ended with the State Treaty of 1955, at which point it reemerged as a neutral country in Cold War Europe. Despite its neutrality, the country remained a crucial battleground between the East and West for the next decade.

Flynn's work in Austria has three separate aspects, largely due to the nature of his refugee work at that time. Flynn served as the director of all CRS activities in Austria, but most his time there was spent assisting refugees arriving from various other parts of Europe. From 1949 to 1956, he worked largely with *Volksdeutsche,* ethnic Germans who fled to Austria following the ethnic cleansing in various Soviet bloc countries after the end of the Second World War. In the revolutionary year of 1956, Catholic Relief Services faced a flood of Hungarian refugees from the failed Hungarian attempt to throw off Soviet rule; there were also, to a lesser extent, refugees from Tito's regime in Yugoslavia. Meeting the challenges of this year certainly ranks among CRS's, and Fabian Flynn's, finest hours.

The Origins of Catholic Relief Services

Catholic Relief Services was founded as War Relief Services by the National Catholic Welfare Conference (NCWC) on January 15, 1943, and officially began activities in September of that year. It was head-quartered in the Empire State Building in the heart of Manhattan. From the outset, the Catholic Church in America intended it to provide various forms of aid in response to the ongoing humanitarian catastrophes in both Europe and the Pacific in the aftermath of the Second World War. Its origins went back almost thirty years, with the creation of the National Catholic War Council (NCWC) in 1917 upon the American entry into the First World War. The NCWC coordinated its efforts with other organizations such as the YMCA, the YWCA, the Salvation Army, the Jewish Welfare Board, and Herbert Hoover's American Recovery Administration (ARA). Its activities continued after the end of the war, providing aid for countries sucked into the maelstrom of revolution, such as Mexico and Russia.[3]

In 1922, the organization was renamed the National Catholic Welfare Conference, keeping the same initials, and it maintains the name to the present day. It scaled back its relief efforts during the interwar era, but expanded them again after the United States entered the Second World War. In the fall of 1942, the Catholic Association for International Peace (CAIP) met in Washington, D.C. under the auspices of the NCWC. CAIP created a "World Committee for the Transition from War to Peace." The chairman of this committee was a Brooklyn priest of Swedish and Irish ancestry, Edward Swanstrom. The first report from this committee stated that following the war, the problems of refugees would be tremendous, and long after Germany and Japan had surrendered a massive relief effort by various charitable agencies would still be required: "We must look now to the possibilities of organizing the proper handling of the migration problems. Private social agencies would perform a great service if they would now enquire into their own resources and make their own plans for assisting in the postwar reconstruction. This preparation would consist of planning for an organization which can manage a social program for the destitute for other continents." Swanstrom called for the formation of a new Catholic charitable agency to work overseas, whose primary task would be to assist the poor, especially refugees affected by wars and revolutions.[4]

Given Swanstrom's own impressive record before 1943, it was little surprise he was selected as assistant executive director of CRS and became executive director in 1946, a position he continued to hold until

3. Eileen Egan, *Catholic Relief Services: The Beginning Years* (New York: Catholic Relief Services Press, 1988), 10.

4. Ibid., 13.

1976. For all intents and purposes, Swanstrom was not only the leader of CRS but also the face of American Catholics to the impoverished all over the world. His impact on CRS was incalculable. Along with the long-serving director of CRS activities in Europe, James Norris, Swanstrom also was the most important figure in Flynn's service in CRS. A large, burly, blonde man with pronounced Scandinavian features, Swanstrom was born two years before Flynn, in 1903, in New York City. Swanstrom was a lifelong New Yorker, and in his youth he had been an amateur boxer. His Brooklyn upbringing was as essential to his character as Flynn's childhood in Dorchester. A graduate of Fordham University in 1924, Swanstrom attended Columbia University's School of Social Work and trained for the priesthood in St. John's Seminary in Brooklyn before returning to Fordham to obtain a Ph.D. in social work in 1938. His dissertation, later turned into a book as *The Waterfront Labor Problem*, was an analysis of dock workers in Brooklyn.[5]

Swanstrom based much of his dissertation on personal experience, as his parish, Saint James Pro-Cathedral, was in heart of Brooklyn's dock-worker neighborhoods. He worked extensively with families who lived day-to-day; the lives of entire families were dependent on whether their fathers and sons were fortunate enough to be selected for dock work each day. He also dealt with the corruption of organized crime, which was later dramatically presented in the 1954 film *On the Waterfront*.[6] Swanstrom had a narrow brush with death on July 28, 1945, when, in an infamous incident, a B-52 bomber, lost in a fog, crashed into the 79th floor of the Empire State Building, where the offices of Catholic Relief Services were located. Swanstrom was out for the day at a meeting, but ten CRS employees, including his secretary, died. A few months later, Swanstrom traveled to Rome to meet Cardinal Francis Spellman and Pope Pius XII—and, as it turned out, Fabian Flynn. Their meeting would be the beginning of a long and fruitful partnership and friendship between Swanstrom and Flynn.[7]

---

5. "Bishop Edward Swanstrom Obituary," *The New York Times*, August 14, 1985, 28.

6. Ibid. Some scholars believe Karl Malden's character in the film was at least partially inspired by Swanstrom.

7. Egan, *Catholic Relief Services*, 24. This meeting followed Spellman's appointment as Cardinal.

Another notable figure in the CRS administration was James J. Norris, who served as director of CRS activities in Europe from 1946 to 1958. Since Europe was the main site of activities of CRS throughout much of its first twenty years, few people in the organization rivaled Norris's importance. His own life and career has parallels with Flynn's. Born in 1907 in Roselle Park, New Jersey, Norris attended Battin High School in Elizabeth, New Jersey, and then, like Flynn, he left his secular high school, in 1924, for a seminary education, at St. Joseph's Seminary in Holy Trinity, Alabama. There he was in the novitiate of the Missionary Servants of the Most Holy Trinity, a part of the Missionary Cenacle, which had been founded by Father Thomas Judge in 1912.[8] After realizing he lacked a vocation to the priesthood, he left the Missionary Servants and transferred from the seminary to the Catholic University of America in 1926, where he obtained his bachelor's degree in accounting in 1933. Norris returned to charitable work with the Catholic Church in 1936, and obtained his Master's degree from Fordham University's School of Social Work in 1941.[9]

Following completion of his graduate work, the NCWC appointed Norris director of the National Catholic Community Service (NCCS) agency, designed to coordinate Catholic charitable activity with the American government. He served as director until he was drafted into the U.S. Navy in 1944. After completing training at the Naval Reserve Station in Princeton, New Jersey, Norris spent the next sixteen months serving on the SS *William Windon* as part of an armed guard unit. Norris's service took him to both the Atlantic and the Pacific. Following Norris's honorable discharge in late 1945, Swanstrom offered him a position as one of his assistants, which Norris accepted. Two years later, Swanstrom appointed him director of all European operations of CRS, which resulted in Norris moving in early 1948, with his wife Amanda and their two sons, to the new CRS headquarters in Geneva. A tall,

8. William Portier, *Every Catholic an Apostle: The Life of Thomas A. Judge, CM 1868–1933* (Washington, D.C.: The Catholic University of America Press, 2017), 313.

9. Raymond Krupke, "James J. Norris, An American Catholic Life" (Ph.D. dissertation, Catholic University of America, 1995), 10–15. The enormous roles played by a Bostonian, a New Yorker, and a New Jersey resident in CRS show the still-overwhelming role that was played by northeastern Catholics in the American Church.

lanky man with prematurely white hair and horn-rimmed glasses, Norris, like Swanstrom and Flynn, was a skilled administrator who devoted his entire life to charitable work, with particular interest in refugee affairs. His isolation from activities "on the ground" occasionally led to conflict between himself and Flynn, but theirs also proved to be a lasting partnership and friendship during the height of CRS activity in Europe.[10]

Finally, there was French-Canadian Jean Chenard. Like Norris, Chenard was a layman with a wife and children. He was born in Saint Arsene, in the Canadian province of Quebec, in 1917. His family moved to New Hampshire in 1923, where he attended Manchester High School. Later, he went to American University in Washington, D.C., graduating in 1939 with a degree in advertising. After moving to Maine to work for the Brown and Williamson Tobacco company, Chenard was drafted into the U.S. Army in 1941, in which he served until 1947 as a Foreign Liaison Officer between the American and French armies. Like Flynn, he left the U.S. Army with the rank of major. After working for the U.S. State Department in Germany until late 1957, Chenard replaced Norris as the director of CRS offices in Europe in 1958, a position he then held for twenty years. A clever, patient, strong-willed man, Chenard also developed a durable relationship with Flynn during the latter's final four years in Austria.[11]

For these men, their work with Catholic Relief Services was less a job than a vocation. Their tasks demanded an ability in foreign languages and international relations, and a knack of working with a diverse group of government, military, and religious leaders. It was certainly not a 9-to-5 type of employment: CRS administrators often received phone calls in the middle of the night about incidents in refugee camps or attempted burglaries at food warehouses. For married men like Norris and Chenard, constant absences from their wives and children characterized their time in Geneva; priests such as Swanstrom

10. Ibid. As a married layman, Norris was the exception rather than the rule in the CRS hierarchy at the time. He would later be the only layperson to participate in the debates of the Second Vatican Council.

11. Christian Chenard (son of Jean Chenard), Interview by the author, August 16, 2016, Hopkington, Massachusetts.

and Flynn often had little time for their duties as clergymen. Many of the CRS leaders were military veterans: Flynn and Chenard had been in the Army, Norris in the Navy. Their time in the Second World War had profoundly influenced their organizational and leadership abilities, as well as how they dealt with any problem—namely, one drew up a plan, and then pursued it with every resource one had. They acted under the assumption, following the Allied victory in World War II, that no problem was insurmountable. The rise of the Cold War put these beliefs to the test.[12]

The First Assignment: The French Zone of Germany, 1946–1948

Flynn's appointment to CRS grew out of a variety of factors: the personal bravery and tenacity he showed during the Second World War; his effective administrative abilities in charitable work, which he demonstrated throughout his time in Sicily, France, Belgium, and Germany; his leadership skills as manager of the Witness House during the International Military Tribunal; and his acerbic pen in the pages of *The Sign*. His appointment to CRS, though, came down to a series of meetings in Rome in February with Edward Swanstrom and Francis Spellman. Flynn had impressed Spellman during the then-archbishop's visit to Belgium in September 1944, and Flynn had a number of strong recommendations from the officers under whom he had served, including Lieutenant Colonel Joseph Corley. Ironically—given the difficulties the Passionist congregation would cause for Flynn's association with CRS over the next two decades—his provincial, Carroll Ring, quickly gave permission for Flynn to work for CRS once his military career was completed, but first he had to return for a few months to Saint Gabriel's in Boston.[13]

Following his formal decommissioning at Fort Dix, New Jersey, in July 1946, Flynn returned to Brighton, Massachusetts, and spent the next three months with friends and family members. In preparation for

12. Ibid.

13. Letter from Carroll Ring to Fabian Flynn, April 26, 1946. PHA Record Group 322—3/7.

his return to Europe as a CRS official, he traveled both to the CRS offices in the Empire State Building in New York and to its headquarters in Washington, D.C. During this time, Catholic Relief Services, along with ten other relief agencies, formed the Council of Relief Agencies Licensed for Operation in Germany (CRALOG), which worked with the American, British, and French authorities to coordinate charitable work. Supplies of food, clothing, and medicine from the eleven relief agencies were kept in CRALOG warehouses in major German cities, where civic and religious leaders of German communities assisted with their distribution. On September 12, 1946, Flynn left for Europe on the ocean liner *Queen Mary;* he arrived a week later in Freiburg im Breisgau. Located in Baden, this city served as the headquarters both of CRALOG and of the other relief agencies in the French zone of Germany. Although much of his time was spent in Baden, Flynn would periodically visit other CRALOG representatives in the British and American zones, usually in Frankfurt am Main, Hamburg, or Munich. There were also a few visits to Berlin to meet with Allied military authorities.[14]

During his first month in Germany, Flynn divided his time between Freiburg, Munich, and Frankfurt, undergoing further training for his position in CRS. Interestingly, his career working with CRS almost ended as soon as it began, due to the request from Bishop Aloisius Joseph Muench, the papal nuncio (that is, the personal representative of the Pope) in occupied Germany and the official liaison between the American military authorities in their zone and the Catholic Church. Muench had been the bishop of Fargo, North Dakota since 1935. In 1946, he was made a cardinal by Pope Pius XII, who named him to the post of nuncio to Germany. His own ancestry and German language skills made him well-suited for the position. Muench came to know Flynn during his time in Germany with the 26th Infantry Regiment, as well during his Nuremberg chaplaincy. Impressed with Flynn's abilities, Muench asked both Swanstrom and Norris that Flynn be appointed his personal secretary at his offices in Frankfurt. Flynn was not interested in the job, and both Norris and Swanstrom declined the request: Flynn had spent months training to work for CRS, and while "any American

14. "Passionist to Assist in Relief Abroad," *The Catholic News,* September 14, 1946, 6.

layman would serve as a messenger boy, Flynn has the potential for much more," as Norris wrote to Swanstrom on October 15, 1946.[15]

Freiburg im Breisgau was the administrative center and largest city of the French occupation zone of Germany, located on the western edge of the Black Forest and southern section of the Upper Rhine River. With a population of slightly less than 200,000, Freiburg had been the capital of the German state of Baden for centuries, although it had periodically fallen under French rule as well, its French name being Fribourg in Brisgau. A British bombing run in November 1944 had killed 30,000 people and destroyed much of the city center. Occupied by French troops on April 17, the city was like Nuremberg, Hamburg, Munich, Frankfurt, and Berlin—largely in ruins and under a military occupation of indefinite duration.[16]

The French zone consisted of the German provinces of Baden, Württemberg, the Saarland, Rheinland-Pfalz, and Koblenz. The French government was never intended to take part in the postwar occupation of Germany. Charles de Gaulle envisioned a French zone of Germany that would encompass nearly all of southwestern, southeastern, and half of the western parts of the country, but he was not invited to take part in the Allied war conferences at Tehran, Yalta, or Potsdam. France received a zone only when Franklin Roosevelt and especially Winston Churchill—who feared a quick American exit from Europe and wanted to build up France to counterbalance Soviet power—vocally supported the idea at the Yalta conference in 1945. Stalin agreed to French zones of Germany and Austria, as well as sectors in Berlin and Vienna, but only if these were carved out of the British and American territories. Referencing the French defeat in May 1940, Stalin made it clear he did not view de Gaulle's France as a victorious power alongside the British and Americans.[17] The result was the awkward shape of the French zone, bisected by the American zone.

15. James Norris to Edward Swanstrom October 15 1946, University of Notre Dame Archives, James Norris Papers Box 42, Folder 2 (hereafter, UND James Norris Papers—42/2).

16. F. Roy Willis, *The French in Germany 1945–1949* (Stanford, Calif.: Stanford University Press, 1962), 17.

17. Ibid., 9–15.

The major priorities of the French military authorities were to exploit the considerable economic resources of their zone to assist France to recover from the war and to punish the Germans for the calamity of 1940 to 1944. Consequently, French military rule, while not nearly so harsh as that of the Soviets, was tougher on the German population than the rule experienced in the American and British zones. The military government in Freiburg received clear instructions from Paris their zone was to be used primarily as a resource for raw materials, as well as for goods produced by those German factories that remained standing. It therefore fell to CRALOG to assist the German population dealing with the fallout from the French occupation policies. Flynn told Eileen Egan, another official in CRS in Freiburg, of the nickname the Germans gave to the license plates of French military vehicles in the zone: although the letters "TOA" officially stood for *Troupes d'Occupation en Allemagne* (Occupying Troops in Germany), many German civilians joked that they really meant *Tyrannie Ohne Adolf* (Tyranny without Adolf [Hitler]).[18]

Flynn shared another story with Egan concerning the first visit of a group of German civilians to one of the warehouses in Freiburg. He had heard the story from CRALOG chairman Claude Schotts, and it related to the first major arrival of food supplies, in March 1946, six months before Flynn's arrival. Schotts observed that German religious, welfare, and city officials could view the supplies in the warehouse before they were sent to their ultimate destinations throughout the French zone of Germany. Schotts reported that one of the women broke down in tears, as she apparently could not believe there were people throughout the world who would assist the German people after the war. She assumed "that all Germans were so hated that people of the world would simply want us to die."[19]

In a fundraising appeal for CRS that was sent on April 30, 1946, to Catholic parishes, universities, and schools across the country, Bishop Edward Swanstrom, who had toured throughout Europe, told of devastation that existed in Germany, devastation hard to comprehend unless

18. Egan, *Catholic Relief Services*, 197.
19. Ibid., 193

it was seen at first hand. In nearly every city, most buildings and streets were in still ruins, and the roads and railway stations were clogged with Displaced Persons, some trying to make their way home, others merely trying to survive day-to-day. More than a million DPs, many of whom had been slave laborers for the Nazis, remained in the country, both in and outside the various refugee camps. Making a bad situation worse, for every DP from a foreign country who returned home, three or four ethnic Germans—who had been expelled from Poland, Hungary, Romania, and especially the Sudetenland region in Czechoslovakia—arrived. Conditions were deplorable: "The food ration is very, very low, and Germany has a population of women, children, and old men. All young fathers are either dead, missing, or still prisoners. The lack of food, clothing, and medical care is reflected in the faces of the children in particular." Swanstrom offered the slightly optimistic assessment that CRS and other charitable agencies, working with the Allied authorities, were making the best effort to alleviate the situation.[20]

Things had not improved in any great measure six months later, according to an article written by Dr. Max Jordan for the February 1, 1947, issue of *The Catholic News*, which also contained an interview with Fabian Flynn. Jordan detailed how the devastating winter of 1946–47 led to a meager harvest, even in the parts of Germany where normal agricultural production was possible. He then described how supplies to be distributed by CRALOG arrived at the north German port of Bremen, then were transferred to barges on the Rhine River, before their arrival in the cities of Mainz and Freiburg. CRS, so Flynn informed Jordan, had six trucks with which to distribute charitable aid, and though they received several hundred tons of supplies each month, the demand in the French zone of Germany was so great they ran out almost immediately. The average calorie intake for the inhabitants of the cities in the French zone was a mere 1,100 a day.[21]

20. Edward Swanstrom, "Food for the Children Report," April 30, 1946. Catholic University of America Archives, NCWC International Affairs: Relief CRS 1942–1949 Box 48 Folder 16. (hereafter CUA—48/16). Swanstrom also emphasized that charitable aid sent from America would help the population resist turning to communism out of sheer desperation.

21. Max Jordan, "Father Flynn, C.P. Union City Describes Hunger on the Continent," *The Catholic News*, February 1, 1949, 5.

"Little children come to their kindergartens in the morning without having any bread at all and only a bit of skimmed milk. The people have received barely any sugar or cereals in the morning. Of the 550 babies on whom we kept a check, only 15 percent were able to receive any mother's milk. Some children come to school through the snow wearing wooden sandals"—this was how Flynn described the daunting conditions CRALOG faced in the French zone. He optimistically pointed to efforts by CRS to establish food canteens at the train stations of Freiburg and Offenburg, as well as attempts to purchase fats from Denmark and supplies from Sweden to print catechisms. Closing the interview with a reminder that the ravages of the Second World War were still everywhere in Germany, Flynn noted the clock on the main building of the University of Freiburg had been stuck on 7:49 for three years, the time when British bombs struck the city on the morning of November 14, 1944.[22]

The next month, March 1947, Flynn returned to the pages of *The Sign* magazine with a new article, this one concerning the one group of people worse off than German civilians living in the French zone: the Displaced Persons (DPs). They lived in refugee camps containing people from all parts of Europe, camps that, for the most part, had been used by Nazis before 1945. "They Are People" outlined the conditions in the DP camps, as well as the kind of people who inhabited them. The DP was, according to Flynn, among "the world's most pressing postwar problems." In many ways, like Flynn's article "November Soldiers" from the December 1945 issue, it used descriptions of certain figures he encountered as microcosms of the broader population. He also provided some general comments about the refugees in the camps throughout the French zone of Germany. He wrote bitterly: "The great crime of the refugee was that he and his family and his home stood innocently in the path of onrushing conquering armies in the maddest, the most cruel, most brutally mechanistic, and soulless war in all human history."[23]

Flynn then discussed the odd parallel with prisoners liberated from

22. Ibid.
23. Fabian Flynn, "They Are People," *The Sign*, March 1947, 39–40.

the Nazis. There were now thousands of Jews sharing former concentration camps with ethnic Germans who had been expelled from Poland, Hungary, and Czechoslovakia, "the victims of a vicious and satanically planned program of wholesale mass exile wherein entire populations are uprooted and driven forth from homes and lands inhabited for hundreds of years. This horrid social and economic immorality is candied even by our own United States Government." At best, DPs were viewed by Germany's occupying powers as a nuisance.[24]

While referring on a number of occasions to the nasty irony of using of Nazi concentration camps to house the refugee population, Flynn conceded there were as well substantial differences between the situations. The camps remained dirty, overcrowded places, but the machine gun emplacements were gone, the food was better, and it was in greater supply. The refugees created their own local committees and governments, turned a warehouse into a chapel, and started a school for the children in the camp. Some left the camps for daily work in various jobs for the French military authorities. Still, many of those who stayed suffered depression and despair. Flynn wrote of a young German woman who was a *Volksdeutsche*, formerly from Prussia, which had just been dissolved as a territorial entity on the orders of the Allied Control Authority. The woman—whose picture shows her looking out sadly from a window—was featured on the first page of the story; the Gestapo had sent her from her home in Prussia to work as a laborer in a munitions factory in the Ruhr Valley. Her father had been killed by Russian soldiers, and she had no knowledge of the fate of her mother and sister.[25]

He informed his readers that the refugees such as ethnic Germans who had been expelled from Poland or, ironically, ethnic Poles who refused to return to Poland now that it was under Soviet domination would need help until some other country could take them in. Many of them could not return "home," as their native lands were now under the rule of totalitarian despots who were certain to sentence them to

24. Ibid. One senses Flynn was glad to be no longer serving the U.S. government and to be thus free to speak his mind about American policies—with many of which, as we will see, he disagreed.

25. Ibid.

imprisonment, exile, or death. "Would you go back?" Concluding optimistically, Flynn noted that most of the refugees regularly attended Catholic, Protestant, or Jewish religious services, and thus were establishing the foundations for a "Europe and a world where charity, peace, and justice will reign."[26]

A few months after the article was published, on July 10, 1947, Flynn joined with other prominent religious, government, and military leaders from Britain, France, and the United States at the Hôtel du Louvre in Paris for the founding conference of the Vatican Migration Bureau in Germany and Austria. Designed to work as liaison between the Western military authorities in Germany and Austria and the various nationality committees for the refugee populations in both countries, the Vatican Migration Bureau, consisting of numerous Catholic relief agencies, including CRS, would help with refugees' material needs in the DP camps and, if possible, help them emigrate.[27]

Flynn's published his next article for *The Sign,* "The Valiant Woman," in the July 1948 issue, after he had left the French zone of Germany for Hungary. He told of a meeting with a female official from Caritas, the federation of German charitable agencies. The meeting had happened in March 1948, shortly before Flynn was transferred out of the French zone of Germany to Hungary, and Flynn referred to the woman as "Fraulein Doktor L," a professor of social sciences at the University of Freiburg who held graduate degrees from the University of Manchester and the Sorbonne. Flynn wrote how he had encountered the woman on several earlier occasions, at a number of charitable functions, but on this particular occasion, his inquiries about her life during the Third Reich led to a fascinating story of heroism.[28]

Flynn wrote how Fraulein L was part of the German resistance against Hitler, assisting German Jews, as well as Jewish converts to Catholicism. Flynn, to a greater extent than in any of his previous public writings, outlined the parameters of the Holocaust: "Before the ultimate collapse of the Nazi terror, six million Jews would be foully

26. Ibid.

27. James Norris to Edward Swanstrom, July 16, 1947. UND, James Norris Papers, Box 2 Folder 5.

28. Fabian Flynn, "The Valiant Woman," *The Sign,* July 1948, 13–14.

murdered by sadistic madmen for the sole crime of being Jews. Had it not been for the actions of Fraulein L and her spiritual leader, the Archbishop of Freiburg Conrad Gröber, the carnage would have been even greater."[29] Gröber was a controversial figure—mostly because of his attempts to reach an accommodation with the Nazi regime in 1933—but he stands with Bishop August von Galen of Münster and Bishop Konrad von Preysing of Berlin as among the most prominent high-ranking Catholic clergymen who actively resisted Hitler's dictatorship. According to Flynn, Gröber met with Fraulein L and gave her a secret mission for the Archdiocese of Freiburg in late 1933—to do what she could to assist Jews and Jewish converts targeted by the Gestapo.[30]

Over the next decade, Fraulein L helped hide German Jews, providing them food and medicine, and in some cases she helped them flee the country. Her luck in dodging the Gestapo finally ran out in 1943, when she was arrested on a train from Berlin to Karlsruhe, cruelly interrogated by the Gestapo, and then sent to the Ravensbrück concentration camp, with "50,000 women of over twenty different nationalities, including 10,000 German women." Sentenced to forced labor, Fraulein L described how she was fortunate to survive when many of the other prisoners did not. Flynn concluded by writing that Fraulein L continued her work assisting Jews in the refugee camps in Germany, and her message of Christian renewal was close to Flynn's own writings: "We as a nation must do penance, we must rebuild, this time on firmer foundations. If there is battle, we must conquer by the Charity of Christ."[31]

Before the rise of the Nazis, the University of Freiburg, Germany's fifth-oldest university, had been a center of intellectual and religious life in southwestern Germany for young men and women. Flynn determined to restore its former position, especially since the Jesuit church

29. Ibid., 13. The name "Fraulein Doktor L" Flynn used for his mystery woman was a reference to another woman named Elsbeth Schragmuller, one of the first German women to receive her PhD in political science at the University of Freiburg. She had worked as a German spy in occupied Belgium during the First World War and her nickname, too, was "Fraulein Doktor."

30. Ibid., 14.

31. Ibid. Flynn's selection of this quote was surely no accident, since it encapsulated the mission of the CRS in postwar Europe.

on the campus had been destroyed during the November 20, 1944, bombing raid. Although much of his time was dedicated to major issues such as refugee and food relief work, during his two years in the French zone Flynn had many smaller projects that improved the spiritual life of the local population. This approach characterized his entire career with Catholic Relief Services. Nearly all of them were his own initiative, with little prodding from Swanstrom, Norris, or anyone else.

In a ten-month effort, from the summer of 1947 to the spring of 1948, Flynn supervised the construction of a Cardinal Newman House on the campus of the University of Freiburg. Flynn traveled to the British and American zones of Germany as well as to Switzerland to obtain building materials for its construction. In the words of a March 6 article in *Catholic News*, Flynn had spent the better part of a year "searching, begging, and buying throughout Germany to make this project a reality."[32]

Flynn arranged for male student volunteers to do most of the wooden building's construction, so the schedule was haphazard, especially in the first few months. Eventually the students completed the small building, which, per Flynn's request, had a library of books, newspapers, and journals in German and English, a small prayer room and chapel, and a continually roaring fire in the winter months. He also requested large amounts of hot chocolate from CRALOG so the young men and women, many of them destitute, could enjoy an "American luxury" for a few moments during the day. It would be, as Flynn informed other CRALOG officials, his personal contribution to peace and understanding for the population of Freiburg, and a first step in helping the university—and, by extension, the city—recover from the calamity of Nazi rule and the Second World War. What he had envisioned as a military chaplain in the darkest days of the war, Flynn now helped to make a reality.[33] He persuaded his superiors in CRS to provide $5,000 to purchase paper and printing supplies from Sweden,

---

32. "Germany Bound," *Catholic News*, March 6, 1948, 8. Newman Centers, named after the nineteenth-century English Catholic cardinal, Blessed John Henry Newman, were common at the secular university campuses across America. They were built explicitly to provide a spiritual home for Catholic students at largely Protestant universities.

33. Egan, *Catholic Relief Services*, 196–98.

much of which was used to publish Bibles, prayer books, hymnals, catechisms, and pamphlets.[34]

Other, more mundane matters were also on Flynn's agenda. As always, his financial situation was complex and problematic. Perhaps reflecting a slight paranoia about the kinds of things on which he could or could not spend money, Flynn wrote to James Norris in December 1946 asking him how much he could spend from the CRS accounts, and expressing in advance his appreciation if might be granted an official budget. Norris promised Flynn he would take care of the matter. A few days later, he advised Swanstrom that he empathized with Flynn's situation, for, unlike Reverend Edward Klaus, the head CRS official in the American zone, Flynn had to spend quite a lot on food and transportation for himself, since he did not have the same cooperative relationship with the French military that Klaus enjoyed with the U.S. Army.[35]

The financial issues between Flynn and the Passionists continued during his service with CRS. In December 1947 he paid $900 to Saint Gabriel's Monastery to cover some of the debts he had accumulated since leaving Boston in December 1942. These funds came from his pay as the director of CRS activities in the French zone of Germany. Flynn begged his provincial, Carroll Ring, that he might retain the remaining $252 in his account to take care of various personal expenses. In a letter written from Freiburg on December 17, 1947, Flynn promised he would provide Ring with the balance of money he still owed by using the $475 in U.S. War Savings Bonds he had obtained during his military career, funds he would access to once he returned to the United States.[36] Nine days later, Ring acknowledged receipt of the $900 check and would discuss the rest of Flynn's financial affairs following his arrival back in the United States.[37]

34. Letter from Patrick O' Boyle to Howard Carroll, April 10, 1947. CUA, NCWC International Affairs: Relief: CRS 1942–1949 Box 48, Folder 18

35. James Norris to Edward Swanstrom, December 6, 1946. UND, James Norris Papers—42/2.

36. Letter from Fabian Flynn to Carroll Ring, December 17, 1947. PHA Record Group 322—3/7.

37. Letter from Carroll Ring to Fabian Flynn, December 26, 1947. PHA Record Group 322—3/7. Later questions regarding Flynn's debts and financial obligations to his order while he worked for CRS were not resolved as amicably.

Flynn arrived in Boston in early January. He spent two months in the United States, visiting with family members and speaking on behalf of CRS fundraising activities before returning to Freiburg in March 1948. By this time, his service in Germany was almost done, for at the end of April he was appointed head of the CRS office in Hungary. During his two years in the French zone of Germany, CRS had distributed more than 4 million pounds of food supplies and 180 thousand pounds of clothes throughout all three of the Western zones, including the Western sectors of Berlin. Donations of $107,000,000 from American Catholics helped pay for this considerable endeavor. Because of its smaller population and geographic area, the French zone received about one fifth of these amounts.[38]

The CRS authorities assisted tens of thousands of refugees make their way out of Germany, and they helped to provide a decent standard of living at the refugee camps. CRS also created organizational structures and methods that could deal with refugee aid as a long-term problem. Two poor harvests and two brutal winters in row, as well as the sweeping expropriations of resources by the French military authorities, meant many of those who were destitute when Flynn arrived in September 1946 were in the same situation when he left in April 1948. Despite these unpleasant realities, CRS was successful—through coordination with other relief agencies and the Allied authorities—in stopping the mass starvation that otherwise would certainly have occurred and in preventing, in the words of Edward Swanstrom, "human suffering becoming a pawn in the hands of the Communists, who, rather than seeking a just solution, prefer to continue this suffering as a means of accomplishing their own ends."[39] The West German *Wirtschaftswunder* (Economic Miracle) was still a long way off, but the German people had weathered the worst of the postwar storm.

38. Report on the Progress of the Campaign, June 28, 1948. CUA, NCWC International Affairs Collection, Relief: CRS 1942–1949, Box 48, Folder 17. A much larger portion of the finances for this aid came from the U.S. State Department, the main partner of CRS throughout Flynn's tenure with the organization.

39. Edward Swanstrom, "The Importance of the Thanksgiving Food Collection," November 19, 1947. CUA, NCWC International Affairs Collection, Relief: CRS 1942–1949 Box 48, Folder 18.

At the Center of the Storm: Hungary and Germany,
April 1948 to April 1949

The only voice of protest against tyranny and terror to be heard behind the Iron Curtain has finally been silenced. Ruthlessly and with satanic efficiency, the last obstacle to the complete suppression of all liberty has been removed. The "bravest man in Europe" has been doomed to a slow and living death. No man in his right senses or the least familiar with Soviet tactics believes for a minute that we have been given the true story of one of history's most infamous travesties of justice.

—Fabian Flynn[40]

With these words in the Catholic diocesan newspaper *The Brooklyn Tablet*, Fabian Flynn described the fate of his friend Cardinal József Mindszenty following his notorious trial under the Hungarian Communist regime in February 1949. Seven months earlier, Flynn's brief tenure as director of Catholic Relief Services in Hungary had come to an end when the Hungarian secret police force, the State Defense Authority (AVH—Államvédelmi Hatóság), expelled him from the country, accusing him of spying for the Vatican and the Central Intelligence Agency (CIA).

In the spring of 1948, CRS consolidated its offices in the three Allied zones of Germany. The American, British, and French zonal authorities had merged their governing agencies into one central authority, a clear step—along with the introduction of a common currency, the Deutschmark—toward the creation of a West German state. The CRS consolidation meant that Flynn could no longer continue his work as the director of CRS in Germany; instead, Edward Swanstrom and James Norris transferred him to the Hungarian capital of Budapest. There Flynn replaced the former director, Tom Fox, who had a poor relationship with the main Hungarian charitable agency, Actio Catholica. Flynn wrote to Norris that the Hungarians were worried he would be "another ogre" like Fox and were "expecting the worst," but he had already alleviated most of their fears.[41]

40. *The Brooklyn Tablet*, February 12, 1949, 1.
41. Letter from Fabian Flynn to James Norris, April 24, 1948. UND, James Norris Papers—42/2.

Flynn spent much of March and the first few days of April waiting in Vienna for permission from Russian military authorities to enter Hungary. In his April 2, 1948, letter to his new provincial, Gabriel
Gorman, Flynn wrote that Vienna was recovering from the effects of
Nazi rule and the Second World War: "This city is beginning to pull
itself out of the defacement and discouragement resultant upon the
war. Shop windows are filling, people walk more briskly, and repairs
are going apace."[42] Flynn passed his time meeting with U.S. military
authorities and conducting numerous religious services for soldiers,
including one mass with Father Flanagan of Boys Town, who had a
long-standing relationship with the U.S. Army. At the end of the letter
Flynn informed Gorman that his next letter would, he hoped, arrive
from Budapest, but, once in Hungary, he would have to be "very cautious in the wording of [his] letters."[43]

Hungary in 1948 was in the later stages of its transformation into a
Stalinist dictatorship, and the Cold War was under way. Before finally
shutting it down altogether, the communist regime frequently impeded
the work of CRS in the country. Flynn's observation of the imposition
of communist rule and creation of an atheist regime, which he chron-
icled for American Catholics, profoundly affected the remainder of
Flynn's life and career with CRS. While Flynn had written about the
evils of communism for years, his time in Hungary gave him a chance
to observe it firsthand. Mindszenty and Flynn's friendship demonstrated how, for many American Catholic priests who worked in postwar
Europe, this new struggle was a mere continuation against the forces of "godless totalitarianism," a fight in which the Church had been
engaged since the Russian Revolution. In the eyes of both Flynn and
Mindszenty, the communists (whether of the Russian or the Hungarian
variety) resumed their role as the great foe of Western civilization and
Christianity, a role that had been occupied by the Nazis during the
Second World War.

Flynn arrived in Hungary on April 5. The Passionists had never

42. Letter from Flynn to Gorman, April 2, 1948. PHA Record Group 322—3/7.
Flynn was much less optimistic about Germany, referring to it as a "bleak, dreary,
defeated land."

43. Ibid.

established a presence in the country, despite its largely Roman Catholic population. Flynn wrote to Gorman—who had taken over from Carroll Ring as provincial of the Saint Paul of the Cross Province in late 1947—"I have only met one Hungarian who ever saw a Passionist before." To get to his destination, Flynn flew from Vienna to Prague, and then from Prague to Budapest. His living quarters were in one of the local secondary schools run by the Catholic Church, with about 1,500 students. He mentioned he was deeply pleased that the Catholic authorities had provided him with a full-time assistant who woke him in the morning and served mass for him. Budapest was, in Flynn's words "still pretty well beat up," but the spirit of the people was "magnificent." He had an opportunity to visit the CRS and Actio Catholica staff, as well as to view the CRS warehouses and soup kitchens. The need was great, but "wonderful work was being done." Concluding the letter with the news he would meet Cardinal József Mindszenty the next day, he promised Gorman he would write again soon.[44]

Mindszenty was easily among the most prominent Catholic leaders in Central Europe during this era. Born József Pehm in 1892 in the Austro-Hungarian Empire, he was ordained a priest on June 15, 1915. During Bela Kun's short-lived communist regime (1918 to 1919), he was arrested for taking part in rallies against the government. Taking the name Mindszenty in 1941, after his hometown, he was consecrated bishop of Veszprem in March 1944. He was again imprisoned in November 1944, this time because of his opposition to the Fascist Arrow Cross movement, which had overthrown Admiral Miklós Horthy's regime. Following his release at the end of the war, Mindszenty was elevated to the post of primate of Hungary and archbishop of Esztergom (the seat of the Catholic Church in Hungary). Shortly thereafter, Pope Pius XII made him a cardinal. A short man with a prominent forehead, haunted eyes, a regal bearing, and an inflexible manner, the Hungarian cardinal was on a collision course with the Soviet-imposed government after the war.[45]

44. Letter from Flynn to Gorman, April 9, 1948. PHA Record Group 322—3/7.

45. József Mindszenty, *Memoirs,* trans. Richard and Clara Winston (New York: Macmillan Publishing, 1974), x–xiii. Mindszenty's elevation to the post of archbishop of Esztergom occurred in September 1945; he was created a cardinal in February 1946.

The task before Mindszenty as leader of Hungarian Catholics (a majority of the population) was a daunting one. Circumstances in Hungary following the end of the Second World War were, to say the least, dire. Although not agreeing with all of Hitler's ideas, and not a totalitarian dictator, Hungary's military dictator, Admiral Miklos Horthy, had been led, by his fervent fear and hatred of the Soviet Union, to an alliance with Nazi Germany in the late 1930s, especially once the *Anschluss* with Austria and the dismemberment of Czechoslovakia had effectively ended any hope of a regional Central European alliance against either Nazi Germany or the Soviet Union.[46]

The Hungarian government still maintained relative freedom of action in its domestic policies, but its foreign and military policy was sharply limited by its alliance with Germany, an alliance fraught with tension and mistrust. Although Hungary contributed its entire Second Army, numbering almost 100,000 men, to the Axis invasion of the Soviet Union, Horthy had already, as early as the summer of 1942, begun to look for means of distancing himself from Hitler's embrace. Once the Red Army annihilated the Hungarian Second Army in the Don River Basin in early 1943 following the battle of Stalingrad, these efforts took on a much more urgent character.[47]

Horthy's entreaties to the Americans and British that Hungary could form an alliance with them and not their Soviet allies came to naught, as did the hope that British or American soldiers would occupy Hungary once Germany had been defeated. Ultimately, as the military situation worsened for the Axis, Horthy attempted to enter into negotiations with the Soviet government in October 1944. His attempt led to a Nazi-sponsored coup d'état, in which the Arrow Cross Party under Ferenc Szálasi seized power. This change of government moved Hungary from authoritarian to outright Fascist rule, which continued on to the end of the war.[48] The determination of both Szálasi and Hitler

46. László Borhi, *Hungary in the Cold War 1945–1956: Between the United States and the Soviet Union* (Budapest: Central European University Press, 2004), 17.

47. Ibid., 19. One notable exception to this relative freedom of action was the introduction of anti-Semitic legislation in Hungary, although on nothing like the scale that existed in countries ruled by the Nazis.

48. Ibid., 21. Horthy spent the rest of the war under house arrest.

to make a "last stand" in Hungary as the Red Army approached in the winter of 1944–1945 led to terrible suffering on the part of the Hungarian people and massive destruction throughout the entire country, especially in Budapest, where from December 1944 to February 1945 more than 250,000 soldiers and civilians were killed.[49]

With Soviet-occupied Hungary in ruins, its pre-war elite dead, in hiding, in exile, or imprisoned, the ground was fertile for a takeover by the Hungarian Communist Party and its brutal Stalinist leader, Mátyás Rákosi. A fat, bullish, totally bald man with small, piercing eyes, Rákosi looked every inch the cruel dictator he was to become, arguably the worst of the "little Stalins" installed in power by the Soviets in the late 1940s. But, as happened also in the rest of Eastern Europe, the Soviets and their Communist allies did not immediately move to seize power. The Hungarian Communist Party (MKP—Magyar Kommunista Pártja) entered a coalition government with the Smallholders' Party, the Social Democrats, and the National Peasant Party. As with Poland, Czechoslovakia, and elsewhere in Eastern Europe, the communists made sure they controlled the ministries of the interior, transportation, and defense, among others, so that when the time did come to seize power, the communists would have control of all the necessary state institutions to accomplish their power grab. The elections in Hungary in November 1945, though, were a severe disappointment for the communists, as they won only 17 percent of the vote, compared to the 59 percent won by the anticommunist Smallholders' Party, which Mindszenty openly supported.[50]

Two year later, the Hungarian communists under Rákosi's leadership seized power. The two leaders of the Smallholders' Party, Béla Kovács and Ferenc Nagy, were forced out of their party and govern-

49. Ibid., 3. Szálasi would be brought before the newly formed Hungarian People's Tribunal, found guilty of treason and crimes against the Hungarian people, and executed in 1946. Horthy spent the remainder of his life in exile—first in occupied Germany as a witness for the prosecution in the IMT, then in Italy, and finally in Portugal, where he died in 1957.

50. Ferenc Váli, *Rift and Revolt in Hungary: Nationalism versus Communism* (Cambridge, Mass.: Harvard University Press, 1961), 29. The poor results for the communists, in this open and fair election in Hungary, meant that it would be the last genuinely democratic election until the late 1980s.

ment leadership positions in early 1947, and the independence of ministers in the Hungarian government ceased. The following August, new, fraudulent elections were held that crippled the Smallholders' Party. Despite a peace treaty between the Hungarian government and the Soviet government that ended the state of war in September 1947, Soviet soldiers remained in the country to "protect lines of communication" with the Red Army in Austria. The following spring, following a pattern that had been established in the Soviet zone of Germany and in Poland, the Hungarian Social Democratic Party was forcibly merged with the Hungarian Communist Party to create the Hungarian Workers' Party (MDP—Magyar Dolgozók Pártja). This party dominated political life for the next four decades; the remaining political parties were subjugated to the MDP in the "Hungarian People's Independence Front," and within a few years they would be dissolved entirely.[51]

As "Hungary's Stalin," Mátyás Rákosi ably followed his Soviet tutor's lead in establishing a one-party dictatorship in Hungary, complete with frequent purges and the brutal use of state terror through the feared political police, the AVH. He also shared Stalin's hostility to religious faith and religious institutions—he was sharply critical of his Polish colleagues "tolerance" of the Catholic Church in their country.[52] Rákosi was cautious in dealing with a population that was largely Catholic, initially authorizing MKP assistance in rebuilding churches and allowing parish churches to maintain their lands during the land reform. These policies were soon rescinded, and by late 1946 Catholic youth and women's organizations were dissolved; in 1948, monastic orders in Hungary were dissolved as well.[53]

Following the disabling of the Smallholders' Party and the forced merger of the Communist Party with the Social Democrats to create the MDP, the Catholic Church was among the few institutions that was not under Rákosi's direct or indirect control, and Mindszenty was

---

51. Ibid., 32. These "salami tactics" had allowed the relatively small numbers of Hungarian communists, with Soviet support, to come to a position of absolute power in a short amount of time.

52. Ibid., 65.

53. Peter Kenez, "The Hungarian Communist Party and the Catholic Church 1945–1948," *Journal of Modern History* 75, no. 4 (December 2003): 864–89, at 879–81.

certainly among his most active opponents. The cardinal called for the return of the monarchy to govern Hungary after the war; he sharply criticized attempts to create a fully secular education system; and he vocally opposed the ties between the MDP and the Soviet Union. Throughout 1947 and 1948, Mindszenty lead masses and pilgrimages, in which many of his sermons and speeches strongly criticized the communist authorities. Rákosi and the leadership of the MDP viewed the Catholic Church in general, and Mindszenty in particular, as a threat to their monopoly of political power.[54] As Rákosi announced on January 10 1948:

> It is the task of our democracy in the coming year to resolve the issue of the relationship between the church and the People's Republic. We must not allow this impossible situation to continue in which the majority of the enemies of the people hide behind the Cassocks of priests, in particular, those of the Catholic Church.[55]

It was into this extraordinarily tense environment between Church and state that Father Flynn entered in the spring of 1948. He had his first chance to contact Norris during the last week of April, and already he took a less optimistic tone regarding the situation. He had permission from the Hungarian government to stay in the country for only three months, and he had received no news whether he would receive a three-month extension to continue his work with CRS. He asked Norris whether, if the Hungarian government refused to let him stay, he would consider appointing him as assistant director of the CRS offices in Europe. Flynn admitted it was a great relief that CRS now had a headquarters in Geneva, as their officials were just a phone call away. If a transfer to Geneva was not in his future, he expressed a preference to stay in Austria to assist with the considerable refugee problem in that country. He noted that the Hungarian officials in Actio Catholica were glad he did not possess the same personality as his predecessor, Tom Fox, especially that he lacked Fox's tendency toward violent tirades.[56]

In his next letter, sent to Gorman on May 3, 1948, Flynn wrote that

54. Ibid., 884–85.
55. Ibid., 885.
56. Letter from Flynn to Norris, April 24, 1948. UND James Norris Papers—42/2.

the Hungarian government placed roadblocks in the way of CRS's efforts to distribute food, clothing, and medicine to the Hungarian people, who remained destitute three years after the end of the war. The Ministry of Welfare insisted that CRS be allowed to distribute only 20 percent of its total aid material, which numbered over 1,000,000 pounds of food, clothing, and medicine; the rest would be handled by the ministry. Flynn rejected these proposals as "completely outlandish," and they would force CRS to discontinue its operations in the country.[57] He reported that he had met Cardinal Mindszenty, during a pilgrimage next to the Soviet border. Flynn observed that Mindszenty was enthusiastically received anywhere he went, even among Hungary's Greek Catholic minority. Flynn also had enjoyed his two opportunities to visit the Vatican to discuss the distribution of charitable aid in Hungary. These had allowed him to meet with Norris and Swanstrom, as well as numerous Vatican officials and occasional representatives from the U.S. State Department, for strategy meetings regarding the tricky issue of distributing charitable aid behind the Iron Curtain.[58]

His next letter to Gorman, dated June 10, 1948, was written while he was back in Vienna.[59] Flynn admitted "the lid has blown off" in Hungary between the MDP and the Catholic Church, especially over the secularization of the education system. He acknowledged the next few years would greatly test the loyalty and faith of the Hungarian laity. Flynn credited Mindszenty for the cardinal's adamant resistance to the government and even his ability to unite "fractious elements" of the Catholic Church, such as the Society of Jesus.[60]

57. Letter from Flynn to Gorman, May 3, 1948. PHA Record Group 322—3/7. Outlandish these proposals may have been, but they were not unlike demands made upon CRS in other countries under communist control, such as Poland and Czechoslovakia.

58. Ibid. In his response sent a few days later, Gorman wrote that Flynn's observations were similar to those made by Passionists living in Poland or the Soviet zone of Germany, namely that the "Reds were preparing to take over completely."

59. Letter from Flynn to Gorman, June 10, 1948. PHA Record Group 322—3/7 . The National Catholic Welfare Conference—War Relief Services' Austrian Mission encompassed Hungary as well, although "Hungary" did not appear in its official title. During this period, Flynn divided his time between the two old Habsburg capitals of Vienna and Budapest.

60. Ibid. Flynn also recorded the ever-present influence of the Soviet Union throughout Hungary, in the form of thousands of Red Army soldiers. Humorously,

Flynn's ability to travel freely from Austria to Hungary was sharply limited, and each time he left Budapest he assumed he might not return. Flynn's movements—like those of many foreigners living in Hungary, indeed, in any communist country—were shadowed by agents of the political police, in this case, the AVH. The AVH tapped his office and private phones, and Flynn confided to Gorman that he was convinced AVH agents followed him to his hotel in Vienna, as he heard men speaking Hungarian in the neighboring room. With his usual flair, Flynn wrote: "How anyone who has experiences behind the famous Iron Curtain can write about them afterwards is beyond me. I merely want to forget the whole dreary business; it was so nerve wracking. Even in a free Vienna one feels the influence of the Iron Curtain everywhere. Poor old Europe." By this point, Flynn was convinced he would be in Hungary long enough to close out the work of CRS, and little else.[61]

As it turned out, Flynn was not even able to see this happen, since the AVH raided the offices of CRS in Budapest on July 2. The AVH arrested Flynn and many of his staff. They took the Hungarians to the AVH's notorious prison headquarters at 60 Andrassy Street, while they drove Flynn to the Austrian border, literally forcing him out onto the Austrian side, and instructed him, as he later wrote, to "never show my face about again." The technical reason for his arrest was the alleged violation of his work visa in Hungary by his excessive travel to Rome, Vienna, and Munich.[62]

Fifteen trucks used by CRS were left behind, with over one million pounds of charitable aid, which was seized by the Hungarian Ministry of Welfare. Both CRS offices in Hungary and, within two months, Actio Catholica, were completely shut down. Although Flynn succeeded in

---

given that his career in CRS might better have suited a Jesuit than a Passionist, Flynn noted with pleasure that even "rogue elements" of the Church, that is, the Jesuits, united with everyone else in resisting the machinations of the Hungarian communists.

61. Ibid. Flynn confided to Gorman that he would have to leave Vienna the next day, before his entry visa to Hungary expired.

62. Letter from Flynn to Gorman, July 7, 1948. PHA Record Group 322—3/7 . Ironically, the headquarters of the AVH, from which many of its prisoners never returned during the Stalinist period, had also been the headquarters of the Fascist Arrow Cross movement during its rule from 1944 to 1945.

having most of his personal effects mailed to him, he would not return to the other side of the Iron Curtain for the next eight years. His relocation to Vienna gave him no pleasure; he referred to the Austrian capital as "a city I never cared for," which was divided into four pieces, "like pie, and the rulers of each segment hating each other's guts. Poor Old Europe."[63]

The day after the incident, the *New York Times* reported that the communist authorities had arrested a number of high ranking officials in Actio Catholica, including its general secretary, Father Ödön Lénárd, for "inciting against democracy" and for engaging in a plot against the Hungarian regime that was directed by both the American government and the Vatican. The Welfare Minister Károlyi Olt justified these actions by claiming that CRS and Actio Catholica continually refused to comply with the Ministry's orders to distribute eighty percent of their aid under its orders. Olt also proclaimed that much of the aid that CRS and Actio Catholica did distribute went to "enemies of the People's Republic." In his own comments to the newspaper, Flynn wrote that a million pounds of charitable aid was certainly lost, and the attack on religious charitable activity was part of the war directed by the communists against the Catholic Church in Hungary.[64]

By the end of November 1948, Hungary was firmly a Soviet-style state. As one of the leading opponents of communism, not just in Hungary itself but in all Eastern Europe, Mindszenty knew arrest and imprisonment were a foregone conclusion. By late November and early December, nearly all his staff had been arrested on trumped-up charges of treason.[65] On December 26, 1948, the AVH came for Mindszenty. He spent the next three months under "conditioning" by the AVH in preparation for its most ambitious show trial yet. This involved "brainwashing" experiments and physical torture, as Mindszenty was beaten repeatedly by rubber truncheons in the days leading up to his trial until he admitted a series of outlandish charges.[66]

---

63. Ibid. Flynn went on to wax nostalgic about the old Habsburg empire, wishing it had been preserved, given the thirty years of chaos that had followed its collapse.

64. "Budapest Priests Accused of Plot," *New York Times*, July 3, 1948, 2.

65. Mindszenty, *Memoirs*, 83–86.

66. Ibid., 91–98.

The trial lasted from February 3 to February 8, 1949. Mindszenty confessed to various crimes, including currency speculation; attempting to steal the Habsburg crown jewels; working as an informant for the CIA and MI6; and the somewhat contradictory crime of planning to bring the Habsburgs back to power but at the same time seizing political power for himself, following a Third World War between the United States and the Soviet Union. Flynn was named in the trial as one of Mindszenty's "accomplices," as an agent of the CIA and the Vatican, and he was mentioned as having brought messages and funds to Mindszenty from Rome and Washington, D.C.[67] Although Mindszenty later renounced his previous confession, the judges (led by a former Arrow Cross member who had joined the MDP) still found him guilty and sentenced him to life in prison.[68]

Flynn wrote a lengthy article about Mindszenty's trial that was published in both *Sign* magazine and *The Brooklyn Tablet*. Not having seen Mindszenty for months, Flynn noted with concern the disturbing physical transformation the cardinal had undergone during captivity by the AVH. Flynn wrote that Mindszenty, although of short stature, was always a commanding figure wherever he went. Now, he had the "tragic appearance of a broken man, whose bulging eyes and contorted facial lines made him almost unrecognizable." Flynn's description of the trial as an "utter travesty of justice" was shared by Pope Pius XII, who excommunicated all Hungarians associated with it.[69] Mindszenty spent the next seven years in various prisons in Hungary, a fate shared by thousands of Catholic clergy, as well as by many from the Lutheran and Calvinist religious minorities. The cardinal emerged from this ordeal as among the most prominent Christian "martyrs" of communist rule in Central and Eastern Europe.

By August, Flynn was settled in Munich, the Bavarian capital. It was his home for the next few months while he served as the transitional director of CRS in Germany. Norris and Swanstrom were waiting to see whether Flynn could be sent back to Hungary if the political envi-

67. *The Trial of József Mindszenty* (Budapest: The Hungarian State Publishing House, 1949), 145–59.

68. Ibid., 127–37.

69. *The Brooklyn Tablet*, February 12, 1949, 1–3.

ronment changed. A more likely result, as Flynn acknowledged to the Passionists, was that he would be sent to work with the CRS's Displaced Persons program in either Germany or Austria. He believed his service in Austria, if that was where he was assigned, would be brief, once the Marshall Plan started to have influence.[70]

Munich had been one of the "birthplace cities" of National Socialism; it was where the Nazis had launched their first bid for power, the "Beer Hall Putsch" of 1923. One of the largest and most significant of the Nazi concentration camps in Germany, Dachau—which housed several prominent political prisoners of the Third Reich, such as the French President Léon Blum and Kurt von Schuschnigg—was in a Munich suburb. Although Munich was not the site of much actual fighting during the Second World War—the German defenders surrendered the city at the end of April to the U.S. Army without incident—the 71 Allied bombing raids from 1941 to 1945 had destroyed much of the city center and killed tens of thousands. The city's population had dropped to almost half of its pre-1939 number. By 1948, though, the city was gradually being rebuilt and its prewar street layout was being preserved. Munich retained its pre-1933 identity as a city with a large Social Democratic presence in a Bavaria that was dominated by Christian Democratic and other conservative parties. Like West Berlin, it was a hub of the U.S. Army presence in Germany—as well as of CRS, as befitting its role as the capital of "Catholic" Germany.

During Flynn's time in Bavaria, from August 1948 to April 1949, CRS distributed more than $125,000 in aid. There was still no central German government, although certain local and provincial matters were dealt with by "de-Nazified" German officials. Thus the CRS officials had to work with American, British, French, or, rarely, Soviet military authorities. Except for the Soviet authorities, the Allies were usually willing to allow CRS to carry out their work with few restrictions on their activities. Yet at the same time, the humanitarian problems facing the occupation zones of Germany were more daunting than in any other country in which CRS operated. More than 12 million refugees still

70. Letter from Fabian Flynn to Gabriel Gorman, August 5, 1948. PHA Record Group 322—3/7.

lived in the Western zones of Germany: former slave laborers, *Volksdeutsche*, and, by 1947–48, people fleeing oppression in the Soviet bloc.[71]

Shortly before Flynn's arrival in Munich, the United States Congress, at the urging of the Truman administration, passed the Displaced Persons Act, which authorized more than 205,000 DPs to immigrate to the United States from refugee camps in Germany. Officers of CRS would process 35 percent of these persons. This meant CRS had to find for the refugees a home and employment in the United States, or in other countries, such as Switzerland, Canada, Australia, and New Zealand. This was often a painfully slow process, and while it was going on, the material needs of the impoverished population had to be met. From 1945 to 1949, CRS distributed more than 5,000,000 pounds of aid for displaced persons, and 31,000,000 pounds for ethnic German expellees and political refugees from communism in the occupation zones of Germany.[72]

While he was in Munich waiting for events to dictate his next, more permanent posting, Flynn made time to engage in extensive publicity work for CRS back in the United States. In mid-December 1948 in Munich, Bishop Swanstrom and Archbishop John McNicholas of Cincinnati—who was the chairman of the board of trustees for CRS—met with Flynn and asked him to consider returning to the United States to spearhead a public relations campaign for CRS. Its apogee would be the Laetare Sunday (the fourth Sunday in Lent) annual appeal for CRS to Catholics across the United States. The purpose of the campaign would be to highlight the work done by CRS in Europe, and to show both how it related to the global mission of the Catholic Church

71. Headquarters of the European Command, U.S. Army, Chaplain Division "Report on the Activities of War Relief Services in Germany," October 9, 1949. CUA—48/20. By the time of Flynn's appointment as the provisional director of the CRS activities in Germany, cooperation between the agency and the Soviet authorities in their zone had practically ceased, apart from the mailing of supply packages to various dioceses to be distributed by parish priests. (This tactic was used in other communist countries as well, such as Poland and Czechoslovakia; it allowed priests to occasionally distribute small amounts of clothing, medical supplies, and religious literature from Western Europe to their parishioners.)

72. Ibid. Flynn oversaw the distribution of one quarter of this total amount between 1948 and 1949.

in America and how it helped in the fight against communism. The conflict between Flynn's public role as a chief official in CRS and his membership in a monastic order such as the Passionists reared its head again, as Flynn insisted to Gorman that if he returned to the United States, he could not live in any Passionist monastery—even Saint Michael's in Union City, New Jersey—and commute to the Empire State Building to work on the public relations campaign. Flynn offered the possibility of living at Swanstrom's residence until he returned to Europe. His offer to his provincial probably had more to do with the fact Flynn did not want to return to a monastic life than with the commute from New Jersey to Manhattan, possibly believing his order would want him to stay in the monastery permanently once he returned. This was not an unfounded belief, as his provincials had informed him on numerous occasions that his proper place was a Passionist monastery.[73]

It is in the rest of his letter to Gorman that the central conflicts of Flynn's life, between his work for Catholic Relief Services and his status as Passionist, emerged again. He wrote: "I honestly have no fear, much less any objections, about returning to the monastic life and routine. At the same time I am quite convinced that I am doing a good and necessary work here, good and necessary for the Church, although I am by no means an indispensable person. I would be a first class liar if I denied that I am quite happy and fairly successful in this work. It is extraordinary work but these are extraordinary times."[74] Continuing to give an almost oblique warning to Gorman, Flynn wrote that the Passionists would receive pressure from CRS leadership to allow him to remain at his post for the time being, but he hoped this would be only for another year to eighteen months, until after the "European crisis had passed." He concluded by promising Gorman he was not an "ecclesiastical racketeer" and, as a loyal Passionist, he would "do what he was told."[75]

73. Letter from Flynn to Gorman, December 17, 1948. PHA Record Group 322—3/7. When Flynn made his return to the United States in 1962, he would become public relations director for the CRS for the next six years. Once again, Flynn received early training during one job for the next one.

74. Ibid. Flynn was, perhaps inadvertently, mistaken about one thing in his letter. He was becoming rapidly indispensable to the CRS, as events three years later would prove. More than this, he knew it.

75. Ibid.

Eleven days later, Flynn dispatched a brief letter to Gorman, confirming he would be coming back to the United States to assist with the Laetare Sunday appeal and the publicity tour leading up to it. He informed Gorman that, upon returning to Europe, he would take over the CRS offices in Austria, as Dr. Alfred Schneider would take over as the director of CRS activities in Germany. He emphasized that Swanstrom "was loathe" to send Flynn back to the U.S., given the "critical situation" in Germany, with the Berlin Airlift now in in its six month and Europe possibly at the precipice of a Third World War, but Flynn's success in raising awareness in America of the fate of Hungarian Catholics, including that of Cardinal Mindszenty, forced Swanstrom's hand. Flynn was under no illusions about the task in front of him when he returned to Europe: "I am deluged with complaints and pleas from refugees in Austria. Recent Soviet terrorism has forced thousands to flee and camps, once thought ready for closing, are swarming again with poor people sans papers, sans clothing, sans hope and in general in the most pitiable state. The overcrowding is worst around Salzburg and Linz where they at least feel safe with the presence of the US Army."[76] Gorman wrote a response to Flynn on January 7, 1949, assuring him that, when he did return to the United States, the Passionist order would not force him to stay in Saint Michael's Monastery.[77]

Following his arrival back in the United States on January 10, 1949, Flynn divided his time between New York and Boston, where he gave homilies informing parishioners about the fate of Mindszenty. He departed with Swanstrom in early February on a month-long tour for the Bishop's Fund for Victims of War, traveling from Boston to New York, Chicago, New Orleans, Dallas, and Cincinnati before returning to New York at the end of the month. During this time Flynn finally paid off the remainder of his debts to the Passionist order that had accrued during his military service, by using funds from his CRS salary; at the same time he disclosed to Gorman that in November he had suffered a painful kidney attack, necessitating a few days at a Munich hospital, his first health scare since 1945.[78]

76. Letter from Flynn to Gorman, December 28, 1948. PHA Record Group 322—3/7.
77. Letter from Gorman to Flynn, January 7, 1949. PHA Record Group 322—3/7.
78. Letter from Flynn to Gorman, March 3, 1949. PHA Record Group 322—3/7.

At the end of his sojourn in America, Flynn wrote the official appeal letter for the Bishops' Fund for the Victims of War, entitled "The Faith Is at Stake in Europe Today." Dated March 8, 1949, the letter was distributed that month to parishes throughout the country; not since his pamphlets from 1936 and 1937 had his work received such a wide audience. In the appeal letter, Flynn first stated that he was writing on behalf of Archbishop John McNicholas, chairman of the CRS board of trustees. He then began to describe how CRS staff had to console "white-faced, trembling refugees, fleeing terror and persecution," many Catholic clergy among them. He painted a grim picture of the situation in the "safe areas" of Germany and Austria, with overcrowded camps, soup kitchens, and welfare stations that were filled with pitiable and desperate refugees fleeing ethnic, religious, or political persecution.[79]

Since the end of the Second World War, "Three Europes" had emerged. The first behind the Iron Curtain: "The Europe where priests are hounded and persecuted, loyal laity intimidated and religion derided and suppressed, the Europe of heavily guarded borders, of terrorism and threats, of brutal reprisals and satanic tortures, of mock trials and strict control that spell the death of liberty."[80] The second was the Europe preferred by American tourists, the French Riviera, the boulevards of Paris, and the sights of Rome, the Europe that "makes the most noise today." Finally, there was the Europe where CRS was most active, especially Germany and Austria. These were lands of "hulking ruins, broken bridges, gutted churches, hastily rebuilt and ill-equipped hospitals, deserted factories and empty-shop windows. The Europe of soup kitchens and food riots, of Communist kidnappings in Vienna, and Berlin, or droning airlifts bearing meagre emergency rations."[81] Flynn gave a harrowing portrayal of the refugee camps where he had spent much of his time during both of his terms as a CRS director in Germany. They were full of hastily assembled huts, most of which had

79. Fabian Flynn, "The Faith Is at Stake in Europe Today," March 8, 1949. PHA Record Group 322—3/7.

80. Ibid. Flynn also mentioned two of the most prominent Catholic martyrs of communism, Mindszenty and the Croatian Cardinal Stepinac.

81. Ibid. Flynn had little good to say about France or Italy, noting that their elegance and luxury masked the moral corruption and poverty teeming underneath.

no plumbing or electricity, were overcrowded and consequently lacked any privacy, and were filled with beds covered by only what the refugees could bring with them. Even worse than the humanitarian conditions were the spiritual and moral conditions in the camps, a toxic mix of helplessness and hopelessness.[82]

Among the largest groups in the refugee camps were German and Austrian POWs, many returning from Soviet captivity. They had been sent to war by a government "drunk on power and conquest"; heeding the call of duty, they had gone off to war "hating no one, like those from all other lands." Now they returned home, bereft of parades, speeches, or ceremonies, searching for whatever family they had left, receiving a curious sympathy from some American soldiers. He urged his readers to consider that these men, as well as the disaffected youths and orphaned children, if they lost the hope religious faith provided, could turn to "other, darker ideologies." Flynn concluded with the position of Christian believers in the communist countries; he singled out Hungary, where the travails of the early Christians under the Roman Empire were paralleled. They needed CRS, as it was not merely a relief agency, but a "defender of the faith in countries where it was under siege."[83]

One of the main priorities of those in charge of administering the refugee camps in Austria was keeping the refugee population occupied. It was not enough merely to ensure there was a roof over their heads, clothing on their backs, and food on their plates. A constant effort was made to find employment for those willing to work outside the camps, and for those who could not, to find work to keep them busy inside. In other words, tailors, cobblers, and carpenters were occupied with helping to supply the needs of the population, especially children, the elderly, and the ill. Another priority was to establish primary and secondary schools for the children in the camps, not merely for the benefit of the children, but also for the refugee teachers and professors

82. Ibid.

83. Ibid. Flynn later admitted to Gorman and some former colleagues at *The Sign* that some his rhetoric in publicity literature, especially the pamphlets, was slightly overdone, and that writing endless examples of "publicity junk" for the CRS could not match his previous work for *The Sign*.

who arrived. As Flynn frequently mentioned in his writings, fruitful employment was part of the effort to prevent the refugee population falling into despair and hopelessness, the danger of which increased the longer the refugees stayed in the camps.[84]

When space was not available in the camps, refugees were housed in private homes, meeting halls, and even in many of the churches in Austria, such as St. Peter's Cathedral in Salzburg, which from 1945 to 1950 housed more than 6,000 refugees. CRS also provided funds directly to Caritas to provide a stipend for refugees. The poorest refugees received 100 schillings per month, while those slightly better off, meaning those who had some form of paid employment outside the camps, were given 50 schillings per month. Both Caritas and CRS also attempted to provide for the spiritual health and material needs of the refugees, often at the same time. For example, each spring CRS provided new clothes to refugee children who were making their First Holy Communion; extra sets of clothes were given to orphans.[85]

Shortly before returning to Europe, Flynn gave an interview to *The Catholic News*, a national newspaper distributed by the NCWC's Catholic News Agency, about the necessity for Catholic laity to provide private aid for CRS and other charitable agencies. In other words, they should not assume American government's support for the Marshall Plan could solve Europe's problems on its own. He referred to the desperate situation of religious institutions in Europe, especially those in the communist world and those that stood on the borders of the Iron Curtain: "The Church in Europe today is pushed back five centuries in moral and physical injuries. Europe is filled with refugees who have fled because of their religious faith." While he acknowledged the Marshall Plan was an excellent idea, "the man on the street must still look to private charities, and private charities must look to America for aid." There might come a time, he acknowledged, when the Mar-

---

84. "Soziale and Chartative Nothilfsmassnahmen für Volksdeutsche, An die hohe Amerkanische Militarbehörde, June 7 1947," Archiv der Erzdiözese Salzburg (AES—Archive of the Salzburg Archdiocese) Bestand 2.17 Erzbischofliches Ordinariat 18/56 Fluchtlingsseelsorge (hereafter AES Bestand 2.17—18/56).

85. Letter to Minerva Mores to from Josef Hornung, deputy director of the Fluchtlingseelsorge, March 15, 1950. AES Bestand 2.17—18/56.

shall Plan would reach "the child in the orphanage, the family in the DP camps and refugee centers," but that time was still years away. In the meantime, CRS and its partner agencies would do much of work for the impoverished people of Europe. Deliberately, given his target audience, Flynn did not mention that much of the foreign aid budget for CRS came from the U.S. State Department; this policy continued during the next three presidential administrations.[86]

Flynn's appointment as head of the CRS mission in Austria came at the same moment as the broad expansion of CRS's activities in that country. By the spring of 1949, CRS had offices in Vienna, Klagenfurt, and Innsbruck, as well as its headquarters in Salzburg. While it was not the only charitable agency that worked with Caritas, the CRS's collaboration with it was the most extensive, especially when it came to supplying it with clothing, medicine, and surplus food. As a sign of the considerable value that both the Church and the Salzburg city government assigned to the CRS mission in Austria, the request of Minerva Mores, Flynn's executive secretary, was granted: CRS would receive two offices in the prestigious Old Residence building in the heart of the Salzburg medieval center, for centuries the home of the Prince-Bishops.[87]

Many CRS officials saw the Austrian mission as one of its most important, given its proximity to the Iron Curtain and its central position (after Germany) in the battleground of the Cold War in Europe. Flynn's appointment to lead the mission in the country demonstrated the faith Norris and Swanstrom had in his abilities. In neighboring Switzerland, the decision to establish of the European headquarters of CRS in Geneva proved to be a fortuitous one, since the Red Cross, the World Health Organization, and, eventually, the United Nations High Commissioner for Refugees were also based there. Flynn and his superiors were forced by necessity to collaborate with these and other charitable organizations.[88]

86. "Need for Private Aid Abroad Remains Dire, Priest Delegate Says," *Catholic News*, April 23, 1949, 2.

87. Letter from Mores to Landeshauptmann Josef Rehrl, April 6, 1949. Salzburg Landesarchiv Präsidalakten 1949, Karton 49, PRÄ—Personalangelegenheiten for Landeshauptmanns Salzburgs (hereafter SLA—Salzburg Provincial Archive 1949—49).

88. Interview with Christian Chenard, August 16, 2016.

On April 20, 1949, Flynn departed for Europe on the ocean liner *Queen Mary*, heading for his new assignment as director of the CRS mission in Austria. His particular expertise would be working with refugees and screening those who were trying to gain asylum in the United States. The assignment would last for thirteen years and take him through a critical period in Europe's history.[89]

89. "Priest Sent to Austria to Head Catholic Relief Work," *New York Times*, April 21, 1949, 13.

5

THE FATE OF THE *VOLKSDEUTSCHE,* AUSTRIA, 1949–1956

The World in 1949

As Flynn began work in Salzburg, the world had been split in two. The alliances of the Second World War now seemed little more than a distant memory. Hungary, Poland, Romania, Bulgaria, Czechoslovakia, and the last and arguably most important satellite, the German Democratic Republic, were all under the control of various "little Stalins," who attempted to impress their master in Moscow in ruthlessness towards all opponents, real or imagined. With the notable exception of the Soviet dispute with Yugoslavia, Stalin's grip on Eastern Europe appeared tighter than ever.

The Kremlin suffered a defeat in 1949 with the failure of the Berlin Blockade to force the Allies out of West Berlin, as the successful airlift of supplies by British and American planes, when combined with the ingenuity and bravery of the West Berliners, outlasted Stalin's resolve. The end of the blockade in the summer of 1949 led to the formal division of Germany three months later; the French, British, and American zones of Germany formed the Federal Republic of Germany in September 1949, while the Soviet zone became the German Democratic Republic the next month. Its leader, Walter Ulbricht, held the country in an iron grip for most of his twenty-two-year rule. In West Germany, the electorate defied the trend toward Social Democracy that had been happening in most West European countries after World War II, electing the Christian Democratic leader Konrad Adenauer as chancellor. He was a committed anticommunist who firmly believed in tying Germany's destiny to its Western neighbors.

The Berlin Airlift aside, 1949 was an excellent year for the Soviet Union's foreign policy. They successfully tested an atomic bomb in Kazakhstan, thereby breaking the American monopoly on atomic weapons. China had fallen to Mao Zedong's communists, while North Korea's Kim Il-Sung made his case to both of these communist titans to support his efforts to unify the Korean peninsula through military means. Communist parties still played a large role in political life in both France and Italy, and the fate of both West Germany and Austria remained an open question.

In the West, Harry S. Truman was re-elected in November 1948, and together with his new Secretary of State, Dean Acheson, he promoted greater economic, political, and military unity among the various countries of Western Europe, as well as a lasting American commitment to European affairs. The European Coal and Steel Community, created because of Marshall Plan aid in 1947, offered the prospect of a free trade zone throughout Western Europe, with ensuing economic prosperity and political stability. Another 1947 creation was the North Atlantic Treaty Organization (NATO), a military alliance of the United States, Canada, Britain, France, Italy, Belgium, Norway, and the Netherlands. Much like the European Coal and Steel Community, NATO was an alliance with great potential, but it had not yet created great results; it remained more of a paper alliance than a powerful deterrent to Soviet military adventurism.

Where Austria, still under four-power occupation since 1945, fit into this struggle remained unclear in 1949. The Austrian Second Republic was one of the true "grey areas" of the Cold War in Europe. The Moscow Declaration of October 1943 had declared the 1938 unification of Germany and Austria through the *Anschluss* to be null and void, but little else was said on the matter until the end of the war. Following vicious fighting with the Wehrmacht in the spring of 1945, the Red Army liberated most of the country, arriving in Vienna in April. The Soviets immediately set up a provisional government, headed by Karl Renner, who had been the last speaker of the Austrian parliament before its dissolution in 1938. Three political parties were formed under Soviet auspices: the Socialist Party of Austria (SPO—Sozialistische Partei Österreichs), the Austrian Communist Party (KPO—Kommunistische Partei Österreichs), and the Christian Democrats, the Austrian People's Party (OVP—Österreichische Volkspartei).[1]

The three Western allies did not formally recognize the new Austrian Second Republic until October 1945, after which time both Austria and its capital Vienna had been divided into occupation zones and sectors. In November 1945, in the first democratic elections since the early 1930s, Austrian voters narrowly chose a Christian Democratic government, as the OVP won a slender majority of seats to the Austrian Parliament and its leader, Leopold Figl, became the chancellor of a coalition OVP/SPO government. Despite their poor showing in the Austrian elections, the Communist Party held two ministries, by Soviet insistence. With much of its infrastructure destroyed and the country full of refugees, Austria was in a desperate economic situation. It received massive amounts of aid from the United Nations, and, after 1948, from the Marshall Plan; the country received $280 billion in aid in 1949 alone. While this assisted with gradual economic recovery, the Cold War standoff froze the "Austrian question" of when the military occupation would end and independence be restored. Paradoxically, although Austria had its own government by the fall of 1945, the military occupation showed no signs of ending, even after the formations of West and East Germany in the fall of 1949.

The position of the Austrian Catholic Church in the postwar Second Republic was also fraught with ambiguity. Roman Catholicism remained the religion of a vast majority of Austrians. One of Austria's religious minorities, its Jewish population, had been almost entirely exterminated by the Nazis from the 1938 to 1945: more than 65,000 had been killed, leaving only about 10,000. Among the refugee population in Austria, there was a larger number of non-Austrian Jews, as well as of ethnic Germans (*Volksdeutsche*), many of the Protestant faith.

---

1. The name was deliberately chosen to distinguish the Austrian Christian Democrats from their German equivalent.

The leader of the Austrian Catholic Church, Cardinal Archbishop Theodor Innitzer of Vienna, was an extremely controversial figure during the 1930s and 1940s. Like nearly every prominent Austrian Catholic bishop, Innitzer was a strong supporter of Dollfuss's and Schuschnigg's authoritarian regime, whose policies were grounded in early-twentieth-century Catholic economic and social teachings. Innitzer and the other bishops, after the *Anschluss* in 1938, wrote a document expressing their support of unification with Hitler's Germany, which Innitzer signed with the phrase *"Heil Hitler."* An angered Pope Pius XI forced Innitzer to walk back the statement, and while the archbishop demonstrated acts of resistance to other Nazi policies over the next seven years, the damage to his reputation had been done. American military authorities in post-1945 Vienna contemptuously referred to him as the *"Heil Hitler* cardinal." The OVP made only limited attempts to tie together their own ideology with Catholic teaching, a clear break from the history of their predecessor, the Christian Social Party. Even the OVP's name distanced them from the Catholic Church, as the ostensibly Christian Democratic party avoided using the phrase in its name.

Thus, Flynn arrived in Austria to work with a Church that represented most of the religious faithful in the country but one whose reputation had been battered by the tumultuous and tragic events of the 1930s and 1940s. Consequently, its links with the Austrian state and the OVP, had been reduced, as the Austrian Second Republic and its ruling party strove to create a more secular identity. Nevertheless, the responsibility for assisting the hundreds of thousands of refugees in Austria fell largely to the Catholic Church, its charitable arm Caritas, and the various foreign charitable agencies that assisted it, the largest of which was Catholic Relief Services of the United States.

A Successful Beginning in a Divided Country: Flynn's Service in Austria, April 1949 to August 1953

No other country in the world was in the same situation as Austria in 1949. By this point, the Austrian communists (KPO) had been out of the government for a few years and, with minimal support from most

Austrian voters, had little chance of taking power democratically. It remained to be seen whether the Soviet government would authorize the KPO to try to overthrow the government, and what would be the response of the Western Allies if they tried.

The country was wedged between three others that were, by 1949, firmly under communist control—Hungary, Czechoslovakia, and Yugoslavia. At the end of the Second World War, two of them expelled ethnic Germans, who in the Sudetenland region of Czechoslovakia, numbered over 3,000,000 people. While most of these ethnic Germans ended up in West Germany, a minority came into Austria, especially to the "safe zones" under occupation by the Western Allies. At that time the *Volksdeutsche* made up the bulk of the refugees in Austria, but a growing group of refugees in Austria were people from numerous Eastern European countries fleeing communist persecution during the Stalinist period of the late 1940s and early 1950s.

During this time, Flynn and his principle secretary, Minerva Morris, overseeing a staff that averaged 150 members and working out of their offices at both the Alte Residenz palace and at a separate building at 12 Dreifaltigkeitstrasse, developed close partnerships with a number of Austrian state and clerical officials. These included Dr. Josef Klaus, the provincial governor of the Salzburg region; Andreas Rohracher, the archbishop of Salzburg; Monsignor Josef Stefan, head of the Austrian Catholic Church's refugee relief agency; and Father Leopold Ungar, the director of Caritas, the Austrian equivalent of CRS. Although Flynn and his superiors Norris and Swanstrom did not always see eye to eye with these Austrian agencies, they developed lasting partnerships that provided relief for hundreds of thousands of people of different ethnic, religious, and political backgrounds. The relationship between Rohracher and Flynn was particularly close. They both had impeccable antifascist credentials. Unlike Innitzer, whose conduct during the 1938 *Anschluss* had been questionable at best, Rohracher had been a strong supporter of the Antifaschistiche Freiheitsbewegung Österreichs (AFO—Antifascist Freedom Movement of Austria) from 1938 to 1945, and was thus highly esteemed by the American occupation authorities, including their supreme commander Lieutenant General Mark Clark. Rohracher and Flynn were in total agreement concerning the primary mission of CRS in Austria: charitable relief that would be distributed in a partnership between it and Caritas.[2]

For clerical officials in Salzburg, the task before CRS was clear. The city officials in Salzburg had been unable to provide food, clothing, and medicine to the tens of thousands of refugees in the various camps outside the city, especially once the city government of Vienna started to send some its "surplus" refugees to other Austrian cities such as Linz, Graz, and Innsbruck. Salzburg, as Austria's second largest city, received the largest share of them. The hope was that CRS would deliver supplies to the refugee camps, in coordination with Caritas, as no one else in the region had the capacity to handle the problem. Rohracher voiced to his subordinates the hope that CRS could stay until the refugee problem had ended, but with ethnic Germans continuing to arrive, and the Cold War ongoing, that goal was a long way off.[3]

Flynn was still getting his bearings in his new home of Salzburg by summer of 1949. He frequently traveled to Bavaria, either for meetings with CRS officials or with some of his former colleagues among the American military stationed there, or to spend time at the Maria Schutz monastery, the Passionist outpost in West Germany. He even had time for one trip to Paris to conduct the wedding of Lieutenant Colonel Thomas Lancer, a veteran of the Blue Spaders, to Elizabeth Soubiran, who worked in the American embassy in Paris. The wedding, held at the Madeleine Church in the heart of Paris, proved to be a reunion of sorts for many veteran officers from the 26th Infantry Regiment who were still stationed in Europe.[4]

Flynn kept busy celebrating masses in various parishes around Salz-

2. Sabine Veits-Falk, "Fürsorge und Seelsorge der katholischen Kirche für volksdeutsche Flüchtlinge in Salzburg," *Erzbischof Andreas Rohracher: Krieg, Wiederaufbau, Konzil,* ed. Ernst Hintermaier, Alfred Rinnerthaler, and Hans Saptzenegger (Salzburg: Anton Pustet Verlag, 2010), 165–82, at 170. Some of Rohracher's staunch resistance to German rule during the seven years can be attributed to Salzburg's long history of resisting external rule; it had not even been under Vienna's control until 1806; before that for centuries it was an independent city-state under the control of the Prince-Archbishop (*Fürstenbischof*).

3. Letter from Rohracher to Peter Ewald, October 10, 1948. AES- Bestand 2.1 Rohracher 19/6: Fluchtlings Evakuierten Seelsorge.

4. "Miss Soubiran Wed at Church in Paris," *New York Times,* September 11, 1949, 91.

burg, including one whose priest had spent three years in Dachau and was physically unable to celebrate Mass much of the time. He persuaded his provincial, Father Gorman, to provide him with stipends for refugee priests in the American zone of Austria. Flynn reported to Gorman that, since the average refugee priest received 100 Schillings from the Austrian Catholic Church per month, and since this equated to about $4, he suggested the Passionist order could assist them in some fashion. Some of the refugees he had met in the camps outside Salzburg, he related, had been men of power and influence in their home countries, yet were reduced to living with only the clothes on their backs. He decried the presence of "Russian brutes" from the Soviet diplomatic mission in Salzburg, reporting that on a weekly basis they harassed certain refugees at the camps with demands they return to their home countries.[5]

From late September to the middle of October of 1949, Flynn was on the road again, this time on another fundraiser/publicity tour with Swanstrom and Norris through Western and Central Europe. Describing the tour as a "real grind," Flynn was on hand at nearly every meeting Swanstrom had with government and religious figures; he also participated in tours of the "foul" refugee camps in Austria, Germany, and Italy, which, Flynn described, were little different from those he saw on a regular basis. The trip did bring one clear benefit: a private audience with Pope Pius XII at his summer residence of Castel Gandolfo on September 30. The Pope praised the generosity of American Catholics and the impressive work of the National Catholic Welfare Conference during and after the Second World War. Flynn noted that the Pope was an honorable man, even if his staff treated Flynn, in his simple black Passionist habit, with "frequent cold stares and fishy hands." Flynn also had the chance later to meet the Italian prime minister and Christian Democratic leader Alcide De Gasperi, whom he described as a "very impressive individual."[6]

5. Letter from Flynn to Gorman, June 30, 1949. PHA Record Group 322—3/7. In his response, Gorman promised to send money to Flynn through American Express, which he could then distribute to the various refugee priests. Gorman also jokingly referred to the Province of St. Paul of the Cross as "the Kremlin."

6. "Pope Receives Brooklyn Monsignors, N.C.W.C. Officials," *The Brooklyn Tablet,*

Following the hectic activity following the visit by Swanstrom and Norris, things settled into a routine in Austria for the next few months—"routine" being regular conflicts with American, British, and French military authorities in Austria. As Flynn wrote to Gorman, CRS had to deal with endless layers of military bureaucracy, and the American military authorities were proving the most troublesome: "Every day we deal with the dictatorship of petty military functionaries who are afraid to return to civilian life and work for a day's wage." Rumors about a treaty restoring Austrian independence and ending the American military occupation also distressed him, as Austria was "an even better foothold into Europe than our Berlin outpost." He acknowledged at the end of his letter that if he sounded bitter, it was simply because he was so, and he would not bore Gorman with "my own gripes." He did inform Gorman that although he would not be able return home to Boston for Christmas, he would get to visit Ireland for the first time. It proved to be an exciting and memorable experience to connect with his ethnic roots.[7]

Exactly how long Flynn's work with CRS would continue depended on how long the Cold War lasted, and, related to that question, how many ethnic and political refugees would continue to arrive from the communist countries of Hungary, Yugoslavia, Poland, Czechoslovakia, and East Germany. Flynn said openly to Gorman in March 1950 that he was ready to return to the Passionist monasteries in either Brighton or Union City, but he could not do so until "I finish the job here." Yet every time he felt he was almost finished, such as in the fall of 1949, another group of refugees would arrive in Salzburg, or the number of "permanent refugees"—those who, for a variety of reasons, had not been resettled in any other country—would grow rapidly. The other issue was the steadfast refusal of both Norris and especially Swanstrom

---

October 1, 1949, 2. Flynn still had enough of his old Irish-American pride, with its long rivalry with Italians, to note approvingly that the Irish Republic had rejected the last three nominees from Pius XII to serve as papal nuncio to Ireland, because they were all Italians.

7. Letter from Flynn to Gorman, December 8, 1949. PHA Record Group 322—3/7. The rumors about the peace treaty proved to be just that, rumors: since the Soviets refused to agree to Western conditions regarding an end to the occupation, the Austrian Question was frozen in place.

to release him from his position. Every time Flynn raised the matter, Swanstrom let loose "a howl of protest. The NCWC has invested too much money in me, and after three years my experience in this work is too valuable for them to simply go and find another priest with the same experience, because there is none. He is right, I suppose." He went on to tell Gorman he hoped to stay on at least until the late fall of 1950. Given that Flynn believed his work was essential for spiritual and ideological reasons, his appeals to Swanstrom to let him return to America were likely not serious but done out of obligation to his order.[8]

Just as he had in Freiburg, Flynn engaged with the local community and its religious life. He regularly offered Mass at the Holy Cross Church (Heilige Kreuz Kirche) in the small town of Guggenthal, located five kilometers east of the Salzburg city center and near the refugee camps outside the city. Flynn usually offered religious services for the refugee community, as well as for Americans in the city, including many U.S. Army officers and soldiers. He persuaded Archbishop Rohracher to renovate the interior of the Church. Rohracher not only welcomed Flynn's initial involvement in the parish but urged him to continue if he wished. Having been at his post for less than a year, Flynn had already made a favorable impression. Rohracher's letter to Flynn on May 24 opened with the statement: "In a time marked by class and racial hatred, the work of your organization is an example of noble purity, a lofty peace, a godly benediction, and love from the depth of the heart." The archbishop stated that it had been a hard year for the thousands of the refugees in the camps, most of whom lived in harsh poverty, but the work of CRS was giving them not only material aid but spiritual assistance—enough, it was hoped, that they could persevere until a new home could be found for them.[9]

8. Letter from Flynn to Gorman, March 2, 1950. PHA Record Group 322—Passionist Military Chaplains, Box 3, Folder 8—Fr. Fabian Flynn, War Relief Services (hereafter PHA Record Group 322—3/8). The main reason for Flynn's letter was that he was returning in the United States again to help Swanstrom prepare for another round of meetings with American congressmen and also religious and business leaders.

9. Letter from Rohracher to Flynn, May 24, 1950. AES Bestand 2.1 Rohracher 19/2 Korrespondenz.

August of 1950 brought a significant change to Flynn's religious order. Gabriel Gorman had completed his three-year term as provincial of the province of Saint Paul of the Cross and was replaced by Ernest Welch, a classmate of Flynn's from their days in the Passionist seminaries. He would serve as provincial throughout the 1950s, in three consecutive three-year terms. Gorman stayed on as one of Welch's deputy provincials. Welch was somewhat less tolerant than Gorman had been regarding Flynn's special path with CRS; he would eventually make the difference known to Flynn.[10]

Flynn, though, had little time for reflection about what the change in leadership of the province would mean for him personally, for near the end of the next month, the Austrian Communist Party (KPO) attempted to seize power. On September 26, KPO activists traveled from factory to factory throughout the four zones, recruiting factory members for a massive general strike, with the hope of reversing the new wage and price fixes made by the Austrian government. Some of the more ambitious KPO members announced the real goal was to bring down the Austrian Second Republic and replace it with a "People's Republic" in line with the models already established in Central and Eastern Europe. Most of the initial strikes took place in the American zone; the general strike then gradually spread east to the British and Soviet zones. However, the strike was weakened from the outset by two factors. First, the SPO (Austrian Socialist Party) leadership failed to endorse the strike and informed their working-class members not to participate in it. The second was the refusal of the Soviet authorities to provide armed assistance from the Red Army in support of the KPO in their street battles with Austrian police and SPO members.[11]

The KPO decided on the morning of September 28 to stop the strikes, hoping to win the possible support of the SPO and the Austrian

10. Letter from Gorman to Flynn, August 17, 1950. PHA Record Group 322—3/8. In fairness to Welch we should note that, in correspondence with other Catholic clergy, he was effusive in praise of Flynn's work with CRS.

11. Jill Lewis, "Austria 1950: Strikes, 'Putsch' and Their Political Context," *European History Quarterly* 30, no. 4 (October 2000): 533–52, at 540. These street clashes led to many injuries but not deaths. After consulting with British and American authorities, the Austrian government decided not to use massive retaliatory force on the part of their police against the strikers.

Trade Union Federation. This tactic failed, as the leaders of both of these latter groups rejected the strike, regarding it as an illegitimate *putsch* attempt directed at overthrowing the Second Republic. In response, the KPO launched a second strike on October 4. It lasted two days, but ultimately collapsed due to the isolation of the KPO and its supporters from the rest of the Austrian working class, and the failure of the Red Army to intervene actively on their behalf.[12]

What part the Soviet Union played in the general strikes of 1950 is uncertain. Reports sent from Soviet authorities in Austria to the government in Moscow reveal that the Soviets reluctantly but thoroughly collaborated with the KPO leadership in planning the strikes, with the goals of ending the wage and price fixes and possibly disabling the Austrian government. The reports reveal that the KPO leadership, especially its chairman, Johann Koplenig, approached the Soviet authorities with the idea, not the other way around.[13] This was the last gasp of KPO, and as the 1950s continued, the party became increasingly marginalized in Austrian politics. Though the formal division of the country into east and west states like Germany seemed unlikely, whether Austria could join the European Coal and Steel Community and NATO and at the same time end the presence of Soviet soldiers in their country was unclear.

Flynn's first letter to his new provincial, Ernest Welch, told how the communists in both Austria and Germany "had been stirring things up a great deal lately, I wonder if we will have to spend the rest of our lives here living under some kind of tension." He took pleasure in seeing refugees leave the camps for emigration abroad: "The refugees depart for their new land, a new life, but above and before all—Freedom!"[14] In his subsequent letters, Flynn frequently touched on his chronic kid-

---

12. Ibid., 542–44. The Soviet authorities did provide military trucks and Red Army drivers to transport the KPO activists from factory to factory, but that was the extent of their active involvement during the second wave of strikes. At most, about 20 percent of the Austrian working class took part.

13. *Sovetskaia Politika v Avstrii 1945–1955: Sbornik Dokumentov*, 393–420. In essence, the Austrian communists were attempting to replicate what had been done by their Czech comrades in February 1948.

14. Letter from Flynn to Welch, October 3, 1950. PHA Record Group 322—3/8. Flynn's grim prediction turned out to be correct: he would not outlive the Cold War.

ney pain and occasional bouts of malaria, which he believed he had contracted during his time in North Africa or Sicily. Each of Flynn's letters ended with an anecdote about refugees he had encountered; in this one, he recalled meeting a group of Slovak nuns in refugee camps in Bavaria. "I shudder to think the day might come when our own American nuns would undergo the same sort of suffering."[15]

The problem facing CRS officials was an enormous one. Both Austrian and CRS officials struggled to find adequate housing for the refugee population in the cities and towns of Austria, as the existing camps were near bursting. Relocating refugees, especially the ethnic Germans, was frustratingly difficult. Although there had been some success in sending a few hundred to live in Switzerland and in German communities in South America, especially Brazil and Argentina, there was a great reluctance on the part of the American government to take in significant numbers. Josef Stefan, the director of the refugee relief for Caritas—Flühtlingsseelsorge—in a pointed letter to Swanstrom said he understood why many Americans were not sympathetic to the plight of Germans, refugees or otherwise. Still, the United States helped create the problem, since it did not protest the ethnic cleansing engaged in by the Soviet, Polish, Hungarian, and especially the Czech governments after the war ended. All the CRS chief could do in response was ask Stefan for patience and promise that the American government would soon take in more of the *Volksdeutsche*.[16]

As Swanstrom wrote in a press release published out of a conference of NCWC leaders held at the Statler Hotel in Washington, D.C., on November 4, the International Refugee Organization (IRO), of which CRS was a member, resettled 190,000 people in the United States following the passage of the Displaced Persons Act in July 1948. CRS still hoped to resettle 200,000 further refugees in the United States, among whom were 44,744 *Volksdeutsche* currently living in DP camps in Germany and Austria.[17] Swanstrom added that the Potsdam Agreements had led to

15. Letter from Flynn to Welch, November 25, 1950. PHA Record Group 322—3/8.

16. Letter from Stefan to Swanstrom, December 10, 1950. AES Bestand 2.17 Erzbischofliches Ordinariat 18/56 Fluchtlingsseelsorge.

17. Edward Swanstrom, "Displaced Persons and Surplus Populations," Press Release, November 4, 1950. Center for Migration Studies Archive, New York City Record

the arrival of 11 million ethnic Germans in West Germany and Austria; only 1.5 million of them could be reabsorbed into the local economies. By 1950, one million remained living in refugee camps in West Germany and 300,000 living in Austria, many of whom were agricultural workers. If a home for them could not be found in either country, they would have to be sent abroad. Many CRS officials supported Swanstrom's argument that the United States had a special obligation to the *Volksdeutsche*, given that President Harry Truman had acquiesced in the population transfers at Potsdam five years before, and those transfers had created a massive humanitarian crisis with no end in sight.[18]

As 1951 began, Flynn wrote a resignation letter to Swanstrom. The letter expressed his desire to return to Saint Michael's Monastery in Union City and perhaps resume editorial duties with *The Sign*: "It [the prospect of leaving CRS] is something that has been in my mind for some time and really torturing in me. Never have I been so unable to make up my mind about something." For a variety of reasons, Flynn could not bring himself to mail the letter, especially as Welch had permitted him to stay a few months longer at his post in Salzburg. Flynn acknowledged he had come to enjoy having a car, a driver, a respectable apartment in Salzburg, a decent salary from CRS, and being "his own boss." He still felt a pull, as a Passionist, to return to "the monastery and the consolations of pastoral work." All this was perhaps idle speculation, Flynn admitted, since Swanstrom, Norris, McNicholas, and the rest of the CRS board of trustees would view this as "quitting under fire." The Korean War—which saw U.N. and Chinese forces fighting along the 38th parallel and American and Soviet fighter planes engaged in the skies over the Sea of Japan—threatened to turn into a third world war at any moment and, in the meantime, ethnic Germans and political refugees from Stalinism continued to stream into the refugee camps.[19]

Group 26—War Relief Services, National Catholic Welfare Conference, Box 2 (hereafter CMS Record Group 26—2). Other groups composing the IRO included the Tolstoy Foundation, the Lutheran World Federation, the YMCA, the World Council of Churches, and the Salvation Army.

18. Ibid.

19. Letter from Flynn to Welch, January 14, 1951. PHA Record Group 322—3/8

His statements to Welch marked the beginning of a year-long process that culminated in Flynn's removal in December 1951 as the head of CRS in Austria. He returned to work on *The Sign* magazine, although this would prove to be only a temporary end of his work in Austria. High on the list of Flynn's concerns was the real threat, the first in a long time, of an institutional schism in the Catholic nations of Central and Eastern Europe, between those who chose to collaborate with the communist authorities and those who strove to resist them. Flynn urged Welch that the Catholic Church in America had to make everyone aware of this problem and to impress on them why communism had to be resisted and ultimately defeated.[20]

Despite the pressure that his congregation was exerting on Flynn to leave CRS and return to Saint Michael's Monastery in Union City, his year as director of CRS in Austria turned out to be his most active yet: his office helped 5,892 refugees—3,860 of whom were *Volksdeutsche*—emigrate from Austria to the United States under the Displaced Persons Act. During the previous year, 1950, there had been 5,172 refugees who immigrated to the United States, nearly 4,000 of whom were ethnic Germans. The process required painstaking effort: the identity of each ethnic German was verified; their past associations, most importantly with the Nazi Party, were investigated; and a sponsoring family or institution as well as a full-time job was found in the United States for each of them. All of this was done by CRS in coordination with Allied occupation authorities and UN officials.[21]

Soon after Flynn returned to New Jersey to resume work with *The Sign*, a significant change occurred in the management of the refugee crisis in Europe. The IRO was formally dissolved in January 1952, after having resettled more than a million refugees. Its mission was transferred to the United Nations High Commissioner for Refugees

20. Letter from Flynn to Welch, July 17, 1951. PHA Record Group 322—3/8. One positive that Flynn could take from the continual arrival of Catholic clergy from Hungary and Czechoslovakia was that those who spoke German could fill shortages in various Austrian dioceses, especially in Vienna.

21. Letter from Norris to Dr. G. J. Goedhart, February 2, 1952. United Nations High Commissioner for Refugees Archive, Geneva, Switzerland (UNHCR) Fond 11—Records of the Central Registry, Series 1 Classified Subject Files 1951–1970, Section 4/39—Voluntary Agencies—National Catholic Welfare Conference, Box 102.

(UNHCR), which had been set up two years before in 1950, and was headed by the Dutch medical administrator Dr. G. J. van Heuven Goedhart. On July 28, 1951, the United Nations passed its first Refugee Convention, which was signed by most of its member states, including Austria and the United States. Per the convention, officials from the UNHCR—which, like the CRS's European branch, was headquartered in Geneva, Switzerland—ensured that signatories followed the convention with regard to the treatment of refugees. It was UNHCR officials who conducted the initial meetings and interviews to ascertain the refugee status of those who arrived in the camps. They would discover whether the refugees were fleeing persecution, and what kind of persecution they were avoiding, whether political, ethnic, or religious. The administration of the refugee camps in Austria in the early 1950s was a bureaucratic nightmare of overlapping claims, divided between the UNHCR, the Austrian government, the Allied military governments, and various charitable agencies.[22]

The formation of the UNHCR was a recognition by the United Nations that the refugee problem was likely to continue indefinitely. The Truman administration made the same calculation and so created the United States Escape Program (USEP) in March 1952. Built under a provision of the Mutual Security Act of 1951, it promised considerable American financial aid through the State Department to aid agencies assisting refugee populations in Europe. Over the next year, CRS agencies in Italy, Trieste, Greece, Turkey, West Germany, and Austria made successful applications to join the USEP, from which they went on to receive millions in aid, both financial grants and surplus food, medical supplies, and clothing.[23]

Flynn's tenure with *The Sign* editorial board, where he once again served as an associate editor, was short lived, lasting only from March to September 1952. During this time, he did not write any articles, al-

22. "The Status of the Refugee within the Meaning of Article 1 of the Refugee Convention of July 28 1951, with reference to the German Indemnification Acts," UNHCR Fond 17—Records of the Office in Vienna, Series 1 Central File 1951–1970, Section 8/15—Eligibility, Box 2.

23. George Warren, "United States Escape Program," *The National Catholic Resettlement Council News Bulletin*, Spring 1953, 5, 19–20.

though he composed a few shorter editorials for the "Current Fact and Comment" section at the beginning of each issue. These editorials were often on the themes of anticommunism and the fate of the Church under totalitarian regimes. One notable essay from the April 1952 issue, "Comrades, Lay Me Down to Sleep," detailed the final years of a Czech politician named Alois Petr, who left the People's Party following the communist seizure of power in February 1948 and joined the Communist Party. He then helped forge an organization that took the name Catholic Action, which had been used by lay Catholics in many European countries to promote greater Catholic influence over society. This Czechoslovak version during the Stalinist period was a simply a front organization for the communists that was designed to infiltrate various Catholic organizations, including religious orders. On his deathbed in December 1951, Petr asked for last rites and a priest-member of Catholic Action arrived. Petr sent him away and screamed for a "real" Catholic priest, but he died before one could be found. Flynn warned his readers all would face the same temptation at some point in their lives, to abandon the Church for political convenience or careerism, and they must not make the same decision as Alois Petr.[24]

Another editorial, from the July 1952 issue, was "The Soviet Blockade of Religion in Germany." It detailed how the communist regime in the German Democratic Republic, rather than simply trying to suppress religious faith entirely and immediately, was gradually chipping away at its free exercise. "Religion is not actually being suppressed, it is merely regulated for the best interests of the people's democracy." This took the form of co-opting certain clergymen who wished to collaborate with Walter Ulbricht's government, while at the same time refusing to allow those seminarians trained in West Berlin to return to the eastern half of the city to engage in pastoral work. Flynn urged his readers to support the Catholic Church in America's efforts to assist their threatened brethren in a divided Germany to continue to operate clandestinely on the eastern side.[25]

Always a critic of foolish bureaucrats, Flynn returned to this theme

24. Fabian Flynn, "Comrades, Lay Me Down to Sleep," *The Sign*, April 1952, 7.

25. Fabian Flynn, "The Soviet Blockade of Religion in Germany," *The Sign*, July 1952, 5.

in his last editorial of significance, "How Silly Can Our State Department Get?" in the September 1952 issue. It discussed how, since 1945, the U.S. Army and the State Department had attempted to "rain democracy" down on Germany with one program after another exposing them to American culture. Among the most successful programs, according to Flynn, were the exchange programs allowing Germans of various ages and professions to visit the United States to see how everyday Americans lived and worked, and offering some German students the opportunity to attend American schools. The program had been recently thrown into controversy when it was revealed that one of the German students who received a scholarship to the United States was Hilde Speer, the daughter of Albert Speer, who was currently serving a 20-year sentence at Spandau Prison for war crimes. Hilde subsequently had her scholarship revoked. Besides noting the obvious injustice of judging a daughter for the sins of her father, Flynn pointed out that a week after her scholarship was revoked, it was revealed that a former Hitler Youth leader had spent two years at an American university without anyone complaining. Such "bureaucratic foolishness," Flynn argued, only strengthened the hands of those in Germany who rejected close ties between Washington, D.C. and Bonn, ties that were crucial to achieve victory in the Cold War.[26]

The problems faced by the CRS officials in Austria and Germany only increased during Flynn's absence. On May 2, Swanstrom testified before the House Judiciary Committee in support of the passage of H.R. 7376, which would have authorized the issuance of 300,000 immigration visas to ethnic German refugees living in Western and Central Europe. Swanstrom stated that somewhere between 4,000 and 5,000 refugees arrived each month in both the American zones of Germany and in Austria, which had been the case since 1945. Leaving out the small number of "hardcore" refugees, people who, for a variety of reasons, proved impossible to resettle anywhere else, the DP camps consisted of at least 250,000 people. He urged Congress to pass the bill, with

26. Fabian Flynn, "How Silly Can Our State Department Get?" *The Sign*, September 1952, 7. Flynn had plenty of first-hand observation of this process, both during his time as a U.S. Army officer and then later during his time as a CRS official in occupied Germany.

the hope it would inspire other countries in the Western hemisphere to follow the example of the United States. Moreover, with "every migrant we move we save ourselves something in relief investments."[27]

By July 1952, Norris, Swanstrom, Spellman, and Archbishop Francis Keough of Baltimore (who was a prominent member of the CRS board of trustees), were putting considerable pressure on the Passionist order, and on Ernest Welch personally, to release Flynn from *The Sign* and allow him to return to duty as head of CRS in Austria. Carrol Ring, one of Welch's deputies as provincial, on July 11 received a letter from Archbishop Keough passing on a request from Swanstrom that Flynn be released immediately and allowed to return to Austria. Keough stated the American government was planning to initiate a massive aid program for refugees in Europe, valued at $4,300,000, and CRS's assistance was needed in its implementation. The refugees who poured into Austria each month from eastern side of the Iron Curtain, as well as the 30,000 *Volksdeutsche* still living in the camps, needed a capable, experienced individual to look after their needs. Furthermore, the Austrian CRS equivalent, Caritas continued to suffer from financial problems, and Flynn had demonstrated a valuable knack for channeling government funds into the Austrian agencies that needed them. Finally, Flynn's extensive experience in working with religious, government, and military figures from various countries and, most importantly, the fact he had lived in a communist country for several months, made him an indispensable individual for Catholic Relief Services: "I realize Father Flynn is now holding an important post in your own Community and that his release may mean a sacrifice to you and to him personally. However, all of us realize how dear this work is to the heart of our Holy Father and to the welfare of Holy Mother Church."[28]

After Ring informed Welch of Keough's request, Welch replied

27. "Statement of Reverend Edward Swanstrom, National Catholic Welfare Conference, May 22, 1952," Center for Legislative Archives, National Archives, Washington DC (CLA) Record Group 287—Publications of the Federal Government. Eighty-Second Congress, Hearings Before Subcommittee Number 1, House of Representatives Judiciary Committee Second Session on HR 7376. Swanstrom's unspoken message in his final statement to Congress was that much of the money that CRS spent on refugee programs came directly from the U.S. federal government, through the State Department.

28. Letter from Keough to Ring, July 11, 1952. PHA Record Group 322—3/8.

to Keough in a terse letter dated July 29, 1952, that he was willing to
release Flynn for five months to resume work in Austria, and, if the
superior general of the Passionist order in the Rome agreed, Flynn
might get another five-month extension, but they could not count on
him being allowed to live outside the monastery indefinitely.[29] Welch
was clearly unhappy, writing that same day to the Passionist superi-
or general Alberto Deane that they had already allowed Flynn to live
outside the Passionist monasteries since 1943, and now, having "got
him back to where he was supposed to be," Welch had to release him
again. Welch went on say that Flynn had not, in any sense of the word,
followed full monastic observance for nine years, and "I don't think it
will help him spiritually for him to be on the loose in Austria for an indefinite period." He encouraged Deane to place whatever restrictions
on Flynn's movements and activities that he deemed necessary; such an
act would be "the best solution to our problem."[30]

A few days later, Welch informed Keough that Flynn would be released from his responsibilities at *The Sign* and be allowed to return to
Austria on September 3. He informed Flynn he would be replaced as
associate editor of *The Sign* by another Passionist, Jude Mead. Shortly
before Flynn left Union City for Salzburg, Welch informed him that
the Passionist order, from Superior General Deane to Welch himself,
was deeply disappointed in Flynn's inability to follow his vows as a Passionist, and he was under "strict obedience to live in conformity with
the Passionist vows and Rules" from this point onward. A month later
Welch received an anguished letter from Flynn in defense of his conduct. He conceded the "heavy burdens" placed on Welch by his role
as provincial, which included ensuring that all of the Passionists in
the Province of Saint Paul of the Cross followed the rules of the order.
Flynn strongly denied he had been lax in his observation of the monastic rules: "In those nigh-on thirty years, years not indeed without
faults and failings and moments of human frailty, I am, nevertheless,
not conscious of having wavered in my regard for or my fidelity to the
duties imposed by those vows and the Holy Rule."[31]

29. Letter from Welch to Keough, July 29, 1952. PHA Record Group 322—3/8.
30. Letter from Welch to Deane, July 29, 1952. PHA Record Group 322—3/8.
31. Letter from Flynn to Welch, September 27, 1952. PHA Record Group 322—3/8.

Flynn was shocked to be under an "extra mandate" or any type of particular restriction, for he had never been engaged in any kind of scandal or betrayal, nor had he—going back to 1923—even so much as received a disciplinary letter from a provincial. He declared he would continue to live in conformity with his vows as a Passionist, as he had always done. To justify his continued absence from Saint Michael's Monastery, Flynn recounted a private audience he had recently had with Pope Pius XII, in early September. The Pope told Flynn he was overjoyed an American Passionist was engaged in "a work of charity so dear to the heart of the Vicar of Christ. It was a wonderful experience and a memory that I will long carry with me." In a response dated October 8, Welch apologized if his letter had upset Flynn, but informed him that all the criticisms he had made of Flynn's failures still stood.[32]

Throughout his career with CRS, in addition to his fundraising trips and conferences back in the United States, Flynn usually spent at least two to three weeks in his beloved Boston, visiting various cousins from his mother's side, always bringing gifts from Austria or Bavaria, usually the toy soldiers, dolls, or clocks for which both regions were famous. He always had stories about his experiences in Europe, and would indulge in his favorite foods—turkey club sandwiches and coffee ice cream. Since Flynn's return trips to Massachusetts were nearly always in the summer, he would often spend many afternoons at Fenway Park watching his beloved Boston Red Sox, in an era where playoff success eluded the team, despite the consistently superb play of Ted Williams, his favorite baseball player. Often, when Flynn's older cousins, all of whom referred to him as "Uncle Phil," came to Europe, he would take them on guided tours of Salzburg, Vienna, Munich, and occasionally, Rome. Maintaining his connections to his "old life" in Boston was one of the things that helped Flynn through the rough periods of work for CRS in Austria.[33]

---

32. Ibid. Ultimately, there was a lack of understanding between Flynn and other members of his order, not regarding the value of Flynn's work for CRS, but whether a Passionist should be engaged in such work.

33. Patricia Chisholm, Interview with the author, June 8, 2015. One thing Flynn was always reluctant to speak about was his time during the Second World War, preferring to change the subject when the matter was brought up.

By mid-October 1952 Flynn seemed to have thrown himself back into his familiar work. He informed Keough that Caritas was engaged in a seemingly endless process of reorganizing itself to operate more efficiently, trying to model itself on the West German *Caritasverband*, widely viewed as one of the most effective charitable agencies in Europe. A more "formal and businesslike" environment was needed, but the easygoing Austrians had difficulty adapting to it. Reading reports, scanning building plans for new refugee facilities, and meeting officials from the Catholic Church, the city of government of Salzburg, and state functionaries from Vienna dictated Flynn's days. The State Department was busy setting up the United States Escape Program (USEP), which had a budget of $3 million for Austria alone. Since 77 percent of the refugee population in Austria was Roman Catholic, CRS would receive much of that money—or at least whatever was left (in a statement characteristic of Flynn's cynical view of government bureaucracies) "following all of the tremendous governmental overhead."[34]

No evidence has emerged that Flynn worked for the Central Intelligence Agency, as he was accused of during the trial of Mindszenty in Budapest in 1949, but he is mentioned in one declassified CIA document. Dated October 13, 1952, the report is not from the CIA itself, but from the Intelligence Directorate of the Office of the Chief of Staff, Headquarters of the United States Army in Austria. Marcel van Cutsem, a Dutch priest and contact for U.S. Army intelligence and for the CIA, who worked extensively with Russian émigrés in Austria, is credited as its author. He oversaw the publication of a Russian-language newspaper, *Lutah* (The Beam), which translated major news articles and editorials from English- and German-language newspapers into Russian for the émigré community. It was one of the press organs for the National Solidarity Union (NTS—*Narodno Trudovoj Soyuz*) one of the largest anticommunist Russian émigré organizations, which operated in North America, Europe, and, clandestinely, in the Soviet Union. In his report, Cutsem mentioned that *Lutah*, lacking dependable subscribers, was desperately short on funds to continue operations; he mentioned having borrowed 3,000 Schillings from Flynn and anoth-

---

34. Letter from Flynn to Keough, October 16, 1952. PHA Record Group 322—3/8.

er 2,000 from Archbishop Rohracher to keep the journal in operation. Flynn informed Cutsem he could not provide him with any more
funds, but encouraged him to contact officials in the USEP offices in
Wels and Vienna to see if they had any funds to spare. The unnamed
Army supervisors' comments concede that the USEP could provide
funds for the publication of *Lutah* in Salzburg. The report is a fascinating microcosm of the Cold War, with a confluence of Austrian, Dutch,
and American clergymen, American government officials, and Russian
émigré organizations working toward a common goal.[35]

Relations eventually improved between Welch and Flynn, as they
exchanged letters in the spring of 1953 concerning the twenty-second
anniversary of their ordination as Passionist priests. Flynn still humorously referred to Saint Michael's Monastery as "the Kremlin." A few
months later, Flynn notified Welch that both Cardinal Innitzer and
Archbishop Rohracher wanted to honor both himself and Swanstrom
in some manner, perhaps a ceremonial title or university degree. Flynn
assured Welch he had told both Innitzer and Rohracher he did not
want any titles, and he certainly did not want to run afoul of the Passionist order again. He informed Welch that, if he did win any honors,
it would not be something he had engineered.[36]

The two men consulted each other on certain issues relevant to
the Passionists. Welch wrote to Flynn in late July asking for advice on
urging Passionists to serve as U.S. Army chaplains, to meet pressing va-
cancies, especially in Army units serving in occupation duty in Germany and Austria. Flynn responded that Welch should select only those
of the most sterling moral and intellectual character, as Army life in
peacetime was "enervating, demoralizing, and beset with numerous
moral pitfalls, dangers to the Faith, and inducements to lead a lazy,
comfortable life that can easily lead to neglect, to spiritual tepidity,
and forgetfulness of the great vocation of the Priesthood." He mentioned how the Army did a good job covering up scandals on the part

35. The report at http://www.foia.cia.gov/sites/default/files/document_conver
sions/1705143/CUTTSEM,%20MARCEL%20VAN_0037.pdf reveals that Flynn was not
averse to using some of the CRS budget to engage in direct aid to anticommunist
publications, if he found it a prudent investment.

36. Letter from Flynn to Welch, June 1, 1953. PHA Record Group 322—3/8.

of chaplains, whether they were Catholic, Protestant, or Jewish. These were quietly removed from their positions for public drunkenness and/ or alcoholism, fighting, homosexuality, or—as was the habit among many U.S. Army personnel in Germany and Austria, including married men—keeping local mistresses. Left without much supervision and with considerable free time, many could not handle this kind of liberty, Flynn wrote, and Welch should take this into consideration.[37]

In the meantime, in August 1953 Swanstrom again appealed to the House Judiciary Committee, this time concerning the number of laws intended for the United States Escape Program (USEP), pleading again for Congress to make special considerations for the two groups that composed the clear majority of the refugee population in Germany and Austria: ethnic Germans and refugees from communism. He couched his appeal in terms of the refugee aid, applied realistically and practically, being a valuable weapon in the Cold War:

> It is true that we are fighting communism and the threat of communism on many fronts. We cannot hope to bring relief to every area of the world through immigration to the United States. However, if the above-mentioned groups can be assisted in some small measure through immigration, and we can help alleviate this threat we will have made an invaluable contribution toward effectively putting the lie to Soviet propaganda that the United States is only interested in its own monopolistic practice and is particularly disinterested in the fate of individual defectors of communism and other victims of misfortune.

Swanstrom concluded his remarks, in words that could have easily come out of Flynn's pen, that CRS and the other relief agencies operating in Europe were still dealing with the consequences of the decisions made at Potsdam—that ethnic Germans would be transferred out of Poland and Czechoslovakia in an "orderly and humane" manner; the reality had been anything but. Many were transferred on cattle cars and they had died by their tens of thousands at the end of the Second World War.[38]

37. Letter from Flynn to Welch, July 24, 1953. PHA Record Group 322—3/8. Flynn's concern about moral failings of Army chaplains in occupation duty was shared by many throughout the military hierarchy.

38. "Statement of Edward Swanstrom, National Catholic Welfare Conference, June 8, 1953," CLA, Record Group 287, Eighty-Third Congress, Hearings Before

The Shadow of the Cold War, August 1953
to December 1955

It was clear that Flynn's work was nowhere near its conclusion. Karl Alter, the newly appointed archbishop of Cincinnati and the chairman of the board of trustees of the NCWC, wrote to Welch that Flynn had done a magnificent good over the previous year, much as he had from 1946 to 1951. But considering the recent establishment of the United States Escape Program (USEP) and still-desperate refugee situation in Austria, CRS would need Flynn for at least three more years, the intended length of the USEP.[39] This lead to what became a yearly ritual for the next decade: Welch and the Passionist superior general, now the American Passionist Malcolm La Velle, would grant their approval for Flynn to remain at CRS, but not without first sharply criticizing Flynn for some kind of failing of his Passionist vows; the criticism would be met by Flynn's indignant denial of the charges. This time, the criticism was that Flynn, although he visited the Passionist monastery of Saints John and Paul during his visits to Rome, he did not stay there. In a November 1953 letter to Welch, Flynn angrily and unsuccessfully attempted to refuse this charge, somewhat disingenuously claiming that reporting to the Passionist monastery upon arrival in Rome was a suitable substitute for actually staying there. He stated he had been to Rome 25 times since 1946 and had checked into the SS John and Paul every time but one: "Any talk to the effect that I didn't or don't visit there when I am in Rome is simply a lie. I may not have stayed there, but I always reported there." Flynn informed Welch he had just completed the thoroughly unpleasant duty of showing a number of congressmen around the refugee camps; Flynn had to pretend to be civil to them and the "phonies from Washington" had to pretend to be interested in visiting the camps rather than the Vienna nightlife.[40]

Subcommittee Number 1, House of Representatives Judiciary Committee First Session on Bills to Provide for an Emergency Immigration Program.

39. Letter from Alter to Welch, August 15, 1953. PHA Record Group 322—3/8. McNicholas, who had died of a heart attack in April 1950, was replaced by Alter, both as archbishop of Cincinnati and as chairman of the NCWC.

40. Letter from Flynn to Welch, November 10, 1953. PHA Record Group 322—3/8. Following Flynn's return to Austria from *The Sign* in September 1952, there was little

Such hosting was a necessary task, because of the amount of aid from the United States government for CRS programs. During 1953 and 1954, CRS received $2,523,649.52 from outside sources, all but $130,000 of which came directly from the United States government in the form of grants, supplies, and reimbursements of ocean freights. The overall budget for all of CRS activities for the fiscal year 1953–54 was slightly over $3,000,000, of which $25,000 was designated for the CRS office in Austria. During this time, CRS distributed 80,103,273 pounds of relief supplies, including 9,917,000 pounds of clothes, which were valued at $22,943,796.81, of which slightly over 8,000,000 pounds were distributed in Austria.[41]

Flynn returned to the United States again for another publicity tour with Swanstrom and Norris in January 1954, as well as for surgery consultation on his left eye. Vision in his right eye had never recovered from the shrapnel injury during the Sicilian campaign, and by the end of the war Flynn had lost sight in it entirely. Now, his left eye was "acting up" and this threatened to make him entirely blind. After considering his options in a clinic in either Vienna or Zurich, Flynn decided to combine a fundraising tour with other CRS officials with a doctor's visit in Boston. Throughout the 1950s, Flynn had constant problems with his left eye, his kidneys, and his stomach. None of them ever incapacitated him, but he was left in constant pain throughout much of his time with CRS. Problems with his eyesight caused him concern, as he feared that a failure of an experimental eye operation to restore some sight to his right eye and to fix the problems with his left one could make him a "blind old man at the age of fifty." Ultimately he decided it was simply not worth "playing around with his eyesight," given that he still had considerable work ahead of him, and so he passed on the surgery.[42]

---

suspense whether the Passionist order would continue to allow Flynn to serve CRS, given all the pressure they received from the NCWC officials. That did not mean, however, that they would not make Flynn pay for it.

41. War Relief Services—NCWC Summary of Operations October 1, 1953 to March 31, 1954. CUA, NCWC—International Affairs—Relief—CRS, 1950–1966, Box 49, File Folder 5. Much of the rest of the external aid came from the UNHCR and, to a lesser extent, from the Ford Foundation.

42. Letter from Flynn to Welch, January 30, 1954. PHA Record Group 322—3/8. Flynn was also careful to inform Welch that, while he was back in Boston, he stayed at Saint Gabriel's Monastery in Brighton.

Flynn continually reported to his superiors in the Passionist order, especially Welch, on what he was doing in Austria and why it was important. In May 1954 he sent Welch a memorandum from his office concerning a seventy-year-old Croatian priest, Father Michael Juric, who had recently arrived in the American zone of Austria following his escape from Yugoslavia. Juric had heart disease, walked with a limp, and his poor command of German made it difficult for him to function in day-to-day life. All he wanted was new clothes, or, more specifically, warm underwear, to replace the shabby ones he had worn for the past five years. Under the memorandum Flynn wrote a postscript to Welch: "This is the kind of priest we give help to at CRS, using generous donations from the Passionist order and from other loyal Catholics. I just thought you might like to see this. All the best."[43]

Ten years after the liberation of Austria from Nazi rule, Chancellor Julius Raab's famous agreement with Soviet Foreign Minister Vyacheslav Molotov secured permanent Austrian neutrality in return for the end of the four-power occupation. The American, French, and British governments reluctantly accepted the deal, known as the State Treaty. Flynn described the joy felt by nearly every citizen of "this little Alpine country," although he was not sure what the future entailed for Austria once the occupation ended. Regardless, he felt the event was perhaps the most significant development in European politics since the end of the Second World War and had the potential to "change of the face of Europe." Not necessarily in a positive way, Flynn continued, writing he feared the Soviet government would offer a similar deal to West German chancellor Konrad Adenauer, with the "sweetener" they would offer not only the GDR but also territories lost to Poland in 1945. This in turn would create a "neutral space" of Germany, Austria, and Switzerland between the NATO and communist countries, and would "tip the balance of power in the hands of Moscow." Following a series of meetings in Vienna, he was assured the future of CRS was not in doubt, as thousands of *Volksdeutsche* and political refugees remained in the DP camps.[44]

43. Office Memorandum from Windsor to Flynn, May 7, 1954. PHA Record Group 322—3/8. In almost every letter, Flynn requested, from both Saint Michael's and Saint Gabriel's, Mass intentions for refugee priests.

44. Letter from Flynn to Welch, May 13, 1955. PHA Record Group 322—3/8.

According to the records of the UNHCR, more than 300,000 refugees remained in Western Europe in the summer of 1955; 225,000 of them were located in private homes, churches, or monasteries, and more than 75,000 were spread out over 200 refugee camps, the bulk of them in West Germany, Austria, Italy, and France. Austria had 109,000 refugees, the highest number of any country in Europe, with West Germany close behind with 99,000; France had 40,000; and Italy, 22,000. The camp population had been reduced by 35,000 in the previous two years; some of the inhabitants, though, had been there since the end of the Second World War. There were three preferred methods of dealing with the refugee population: emigration abroad; integration into the economy of the country where they had found refuge; and—a distant third—voluntary repatriation to their home country.[45]

Providing more detail on CRS operations, James Norris testified on June 16, 1955, to a session of the Senate Judiciary Committee during a hearing on Amendments to the Refugee Relief Act of 1953. CRS had brought more than 409,000 refugees to the United States from all over the world since 1945, with Austria and West Germany contributing the greatest number of these. He mentioned to Senator William Langer of North Dakota that the CRS offices in Europe had 25,000 more refugees they were ready to send to the United States, and they were processing background material for 25,000 more. Furthermore, Norris noted, CRS would try to send similar numbers to the United States for at least the next three years. In a supplemental letter Swanstrom offered to the committee, he urged the Senate to pass the amendment to streamline the process by which refugees were placed with American sponsors. Sponsorship of refugees by American families or religious or civic institutions was a requirement of the Refugee Relief Act, and one both Norris and Swanstrom said they agreed with.[46]

45. Letter from Stanley Wright, deputy director of the UNHCR, to Robert Allen of the *New York Post*, June 17, 1955. UNHCR Fond 17—Records of the Office in Vienna, Series 1 Central File 1951–1970, Section 8/27—Repatriations, Box 4. It was also during this month that CRS adopted its new name, abandoning the title War Relief Services, which had been in use since 1943.

46. "Statement of James Norris, European Director of the National Catholic Welfare Conference June 16 1955." CLA, Record Group 287, Eighty-Fourth Congress, Subcommittee of the Senate Judiciary Committee on the Amendments to the Refugee

Flynn was also an active member of the Joint Food Programming Committee, a branch of the United States of America Operations Mission to Austria, which had been created as part of Austria's participation in the Marshall Plan. Run by State Department officials who worked out of the American embassy in Vienna, the Operations Mission to Austria supervised the transfer of surplus medicine and food from the United States to Austria, where the embassy workers then transferred it to various aid agencies operating in the country, including CRS, as well as giving some directly to the Austrian government. The Joint Food Programming Committee consisted of State Department officials, representatives from the Austrian Ministry of the Interior, and CRS, Caritas, the main Protestant Austrian charity, Evangelische Hilfswerk, and the American Friends Service Committee. For most of Flynn's time in Austria, much of the aid distributed by his agency came directly from this program. Even before the flood of Hungarian refugees in 1956, the amount distributed throughout the country was enormous; in 1955 alone the U.S. Joint Operations Mission to Austria sent 8,377 tons of foodstuffs. The amount sent the previous five years was even higher, for at times it totaled more than 10,000 tons.[47]

Visits by representatives of the Soviet government posed one of the thorniest problems at the Austrian refugee camps. Incidents in 1953 and 1954 were marked by some refugees screaming insults at Soviet representatives, with the Soviets occasionally responding in kind. By 1955, these visits occurred only two or three times a year. Before the signing of the Austrian State Treaty in the summer of 1955, the Soviet authorities were making a final push to persuade former Soviet citizens

---

Relief Act. Within eighteen months, such an approach would not be possible, because of the flood of Hungarian refugees pouring into Austria.

47. Minutes of the Joint Food Committee for the United States of America Operations Mission to Austria, April 18, 1955. Österreiches Staats Archive (OSA—Austrian State Archive—Vienna) Archiv der Republik Bestand BMI (Bundesministerium für Inneres) 1945–2002: U.S. Hilfe. At times, the costs related to the transportation of the food surpluses from ports in northwestern France, Belgium, or Italy to Austria could not initially be met by the relief agencies, and this led to occasional delays in food distribution, both to the refugee camps and to the homes for the impoverished. Flynn temporarily had to turn down 1,000 tons in food aid because of the budget crunch in his office in November 1954, although he was able to get the situation resolved.

to repatriate themselves; delegates arrived at the camps in Klagenfurt, Sankt Martin, Spittal, Weidmannsdorf, and Graz Nord in the month of June 1955. These Soviet delegations occurred only after advance notification to the American, British, and French authorities, and Soviet officials were accompanied in the camps by representatives from the Allied authorities, the UNHCR, and occasionally from CRS, including Flynn himself. Usually the Soviets persuaded only a small number of refugees to return to the USSR or its satellite states. The Soviet officials had to follow a number of precise guidelines: they could ascertain whether Russians, Lithuanians, and Ukrainians lived at the camps, and they could ask to meet with them, but the inhabitants would not be required to meet with the Soviet delegation. The Soviets could walk through the camps in the company of other officials, but they could not enter the barracks for the refugees unless they were explicitly invited in.[48]

Flynn and the head of the UNHCR mission in Austria, Dr. Victor Albert Beermann, agreed that the occasional visits to the camps by Soviet delegates were necessary, given the special position of the Soviet Union as one of the occupying powers in Austria, but UNHCR and CRS officials had to accompany them to ensure that the refugee population did not suffer "undue pressure" during these meetings. Despite these precautions, a minor international scandal broke out over the visits by Soviet delegates when Countess Alexandra Tolstoy, the youngest daughter of Leo Tolstoy and head of the Tolstoy Foundation—which worked to help inhabitants of the former Russian Empire emigrate to the West—reported to the *New York Post* that the UNHCR was deliberately helping the Soviets "seize" as many inhabitants of the camps as possible to be sent back to prison terms in the USSR. Therefore, neither CRS nor any other aid agency should work with them, and the U.S. Congress should cut off all financial assistance to the UNHCR.

48. Internal Memorandum for UNCHR officials by Deputy Director of UNHCR—Austria, Nikolai Wyrouboff, June 10, 1955. UNHCR Fond 17—Records of the Office in Vienna, Series 1 Central File 1951–1970, Section 8/27—Repatriations, Box 4. Many of the precautions were due to the dark legacy of British acquiescence to Stalin in 1945, when they turned over thousands of Soviet citizens who had ended up in British-occupied Austria, especially from General Andrei Vlasov's Russian Liberation Army; many of these were executed or sent to the Gulag.

Neither Flynn nor anyone else in CRS or the other relief agencies followed the lead of Alexandra Tolstoy, whose foundation's relationship with the UNHCR ended abruptly.[49]

Shortly after Norris's June testimony to the Senate, the Vatican Migration Commission requested that he and Flynn visit four countries in South America to discuss with clerical and government leaders about whether they would receive refugees from Europe—specifically, ethnic Germans and some Croatian and Slovenian refugees from Yugoslavia. The tour, which lasted from late June to early August 1955, took Flynn to Bolivia, Chile, Ecuador, Peru, and Colombia. The reason for the urgency of the trip was the CRS officials' fear that, once the Austrian State Treaty was completed, the Slovenians and Croatians, 98 percent of whom were Roman Catholic, would simply be repatriated to Yugoslavia.[50]

The first destination was Bolivia. Following a bumpy flight across the Atlantic, the CRS officials spent a week touring the country, much of which was spent in the capital of La Paz. Flynn, as he remarked to Welch, found the thin air and cold temperatures difficult to adjust to, while the condition of the Church reminded him of the poor situation of religious institutions in parts of Europe, with too few priests spread out over a large country, and few young men taking up the vocation. There were numerous Protestant missionaries coming into the country, which Flynn described as a "grave threat." The Bolivian government offered to take in about one hundred refugees, but only 10 to 12 at a time, and only "professional men."[51]

The trip to Chile proved more successful, as the government offered to take in any Yugoslav citizen who had experience as a fisherman—which many of the Croatians refugees did. Flynn also found

49. Letter from Dr. V. A. Beermann to Fabian Flynn, July 9, 1955. UNHCR Fond 17—Records of the Office in Vienna, Series 1 Central File 1951–1970, Section 8/27-Repatriations, Box 4.

50. Letter from Flynn to Welch, June 13, 1955. PHA Record Group 322—3/8.

51. Ibid. One thing Flynn disliked in particular was the lack of central heating in the Andean countries, as they used "silly little heated stoves on wheels." Flynn did ask Welch to send any American Passionists he could spare to Bolivia, as the country had a dire shortage of priests, and the local "Spanish Passionists" desperately needed some assistance.

the Catholic Church to be stronger there than in Bolivia, and the political situation more stable. This was not true of Ecuador, which Flynn described as a "primitive country, with an unstable economy and an insecure government." The Church was caught between "rightist forces" and anticlerical politicians, and it faced the same problems of priest shortages and an influx of Protestant missionaries that existed in Bolivia. While little was accomplished in Colombia, the Peruvian government offered a similar arrangement to Chile's, offering to take in refugees who had at least some fishing experience, whether they were Germans or Croatians. Not returning to Austria until mid-August of 1955, Flynn missed that country's lengthy celebrations of the State Treaty.[52]

A sense of solitude was constantly on Flynn's mind throughout the fall of 1955; the American military personnel were leaving the country, and he had gotten used to seeing many of his old friends in the U.S. Army. For all Flynn's criticisms of Army life in occupation duty, his lingering affection for his time in uniform continued. Welch was not able to accede to his request to send some American Passionists to Bolivia, as he informed Flynn in October he had none to spare. Flynn told him he understood, although he felt a deep sympathy for those who served the Catholic Church in South America: "I would rather be the Pastor of the poorest Parish in the United States than the Nuncio to Bolivia."[53]

Despite a largely cordial relationship with Austrian government, there remained several issues of contention between it and the CRS authorities. Both Norris and Flynn complained to the international press that Austrian border police were intercepting Yugoslav refugees, classifying them as "economic migrants," and then promptly deporting them without allowing UNHCR or CRS officials to speak with them. A by-product of this policy was thousands of Yugoslavs who, to avoid the border police, went immediately to West Germany, where they were interned by the Bavarian government. Norris further claimed this only

52. Letter from Flynn to Welch, August 2, 1955. PHA Record Group 322—3/8. The numerous close calls his plane experienced traveling throughout South America probably did not improve his mood.

53. Letter from Flynn to Welch, October 13, 1955. PHA Record Group 322—3/8.

served to further the interests of the Soviets and their satellites, who wished to discredit the refugees and make the Western nations lose interest in their plight.[54]

A month after his return from South America, Flynn had a chance to visit the former Soviet zone of Austria in November 1955. In a fascinating and prescient observation to Welch, Flynn vividly described what he saw at the Austrian-Hungarian and Austrian-Czech borders:

> To behold the barbed wire, and the mine fields stretching for miles and miles, as far as the eye could distinguish, along the border was a frightening and tragic spectacle. Standing there 50 yards or so from a watch tower with a mounted machine gun on the Hungarian or Czech side one realizes that the expression "The Iron Curtain" is not just an oratorical phrase. How anyone ever escapes is nearly a miracle. Those who erected the Iron Curtain and who murdered their brothers as they attempted to cross it, are supposed to be Christians, at least they were at one time in their lives. It is indeed a sorry world in many respects today.[55]

The World in 1956

In 1956, as Flynn's seventh year as director of CRS in Austria began, the stage was set for another year of revolutionary upheaval throughout Europe and the broader world, one of the most significant of the post-1945 era. In the West, the 1956 presidential election in the United States was shaping up to be a repetition of the 1952 contest between Eisenhower and his Democratic opponent, Adlai Stevenson. Despite running on "rollback" of communism in 1952, Eisenhower had, maintained, for the most part, the containment policies of the Truman administration, refusing to intervene in the 1953 East German uprising, for example. An increasingly economically prosperous and politically stable West Germany had been integrated finally into NATO with the

54. UNHCR—Austrian branch report on James Norris's letter of November 14, 1955. UNHCR Fond 17—Records of the Office in Vienna, Series 1 Central File 1951–1970, Section 8/16-Expulsions, Box 2. Norris, like Flynn, saw no distinction between Yugoslavia and the other European communist regimes, despite Belgrade's disputes with Moscow.

55. Letter from Flynn to Welch, November 25, 1955. PHA Record Group 322—3/8.

creation of a West German Army, the Bundeswehr. The CIA continued to broadcast messages of rebellion to the captive nations through Radio Free Europe, inspiring hope among many—especially Hungarians—that the West would intervene in the event of a revolution against communist rule.

The Austrian Second Republic had won its independence, and an end to the four-power occupation had come the previous summer with the State Treaty; true "neutrality" in the Cold War, though, proved to be frustratingly difficult to achieve. Throughout the communist world east of the Austrian border, pressures that had been building since the death of Stalin in 1953 were reaching the boiling point. The death of the Soviet dictator had led to the supposed return of "collective leadership" in Moscow. It also contributed to a series of diplomatic breakthroughs on a handful of issues frozen by the Cold War, such as the end of the Korean War, the first Four-Power summit in ten years in Geneva, and the end of the occupation of Austria. Following the withdrawal of Soviet forces from Austria, the Soviet Union formally created its answer to NATO, the Warsaw Pact alliance, tying Warsaw, Sofia, Prague, Bucharest, and Budapest militarily to Moscow.[56] Relations also improved between Moscow and Belgrade, although Tito resisted entreaties for Yugoslavia to join the Warsaw Pact. Instead, he preferred to be one of the principal leaders of the "non-aligned" movement along with India and Egypt.

In the USSR, Stalin's successor had emerged. That man was the volatile, bombastic, and both intellectually and emotionally insecure Nikita Khrushchev—Stalin's "fool." He had distinguished himself through repressions in Ukraine and as the boss of the Communist Party organization in Moscow, and later as the leading political commissar during the Battle of Stalingrad. Like all members of Stalin's inner circle, Khrushchev was complicit in millions of deaths, but, unlike some of them, he was convinced that communism would become a worldwide phenomenon. While he would prove himself willing to use mass violence to uphold communist authority, Khrushchev also believed the Soviet Union had to reform itself; more specifically, its authority had to

---

56. East Germany would join the Warsaw Pact in 1961, after the Berlin Wall went up.

rely on offering its citizens a better life—equal to and eventually superior to what existed in the capitalist world—in contrast with merciless application of state terror. Khrushchev also believed these reforms had to be implemented immediately, or else the Soviet population would force them on the Communist Party leadership.

The opening salvo of what became known as the "thaw" (*ottepel* in Russian) in the Soviet Union and "de-Stalinization" in the West was a speech Khrushchev gave to the assembled leaders of dozens of communist parties as well thousands of Soviet communists on February 25, 1956, at the 20th Party Congress of the CPSU. Known as the "Secret Speech," it was one of the most significant of the twentieth century. In this speech stretching over three hours, Khrushchev criticized Stalin by name for ruining relations with Yugoslavia; for persecuting innocent communists in the late 1930s and again in the late 1940s and early 1950s; for perpetuating a ridiculous "*kulti lichnosti*" (cult of personality); and—perhaps most significantly—for making dozens of tactical and strategic errors during the Second World War, wasting the lives of millions of Soviet citizens and soldiers.

On the one hand, Khrushchev gave a limited critique of Stalinism—limited because of his own complicity in its crimes and his lack of a specific agenda of political reforms. Khrushchev did not acknowledge the horrors of collectivization, especially the Holodomor in Ukraine. Nor did he call for any specific rehabilitations of those such as Lev Kamenev, Gregori Zinoviev, Karl Radek, or Nikolai Bukharin, who were tried and executed as German, Polish, and Japanese spies during the infamous Purge Trials in Moscow in the late 1930s. His critique of Stalin's personality cult was disingenuous, given that he was rapidly developing one of his own. Nevertheless, the speech had an enormous impact on both sides of the Iron Curtain. Khrushchev had been specifically warned by Molotov—the Soviet Foreign Minister and Stalin's oldest and closest associate—not to criticize Stalin by name. Molotov prophetically argued it would have a destabilizing effect on the People's democracies in the Soviet bloc, as Stalin had imposed communism on Eastern Europe after the Second World War, and those communist governments had precious little domestic legitimacy.

Molotov was correct, especially about Hungary, where the leadership of the MDP had been caught up in a bitter struggle between reformists and Stalinists since 1953. Khrushchev had forced Rákosi, after a brutal eight years in power, to step down from his position as head of the MDP in the summer of 1956 and go into exile in the Soviet Union. His replacement, Ernö Gerö, another doctrinaire Stalinist, seemed to the seething Hungarian population to offer little improvement. Many aspired to see a return to power of Imre Nagy, the prime minister from 1953 to 1955, who was widely viewed as a reformer and a moderate. Many more desired the end of communist rule entirely. The success of Hungary's former imperial partner, Austria, in freeing itself from Soviet occupation and winning a neutral position in the Cold War (although tacitly aligned with the West) the year before presented a tantalizing opportunity. In Budapest, the leadership fight between reformers and Stalinists, egged on by Moscow's seeming renunciation of Stalinism, threatened revolutionary upheaval against communist rule. By the fall of 1956 this would be precisely what happened, and it changed Flynn's life and career with CRS in Austria forever.

∽6

THE HUNGARIAN REVOLUTION AND
ITS AFTERMATH, 1956–1962

The nationalist movement in Hungary was triggered, as that in Poland had been, into national revolt by the intervention of Soviet troops. The Hungarian government called them in during the first hours of the uprising. The people's subsequent demands on the government went far beyond those originally sought and became anticommunist as well as anti-Soviet. Under Imre Nagy, the Hungarians moved from a program of modest reform to one in which the Nagy government (a) announced the withdrawal of Hungary from the Warsaw Pact and (b) appealed to the UN for aid in obtaining the cessation of Soviet intervention, the withdrawal of Soviet troops, and the recognition of Hungarian neutrality. On November 4, the Soviet government renewed its efforts to suppress the Hungarian revolt by installing a puppet regime headed by János Kádár, and by deploying greatly increased Soviet forces. The direct intervention of Soviet troops in fighting the Hungarian population, and the threat of intervention of Soviet forces in Poland, illustrated that—at least in those countries where Soviet troops were stationed—the Soviet Union was willing to use force to prevent the coming to power of a non-communist government, or to prevent a communist government altering its policy of close political and military alliance with the U.S.S.R.[1]

1. Document No. 99, National Security Council Report NSC 5616/2, "Interim U.S. Policy on Developments in Poland and Hungary, November 19, 1956," In *The 1956*

So argued a dispassionate analysis from the National Security Council two weeks after Nikita Khrushchev ordered the Red Army to enter Hungary and crush its move toward independence. Neither U.S. President Dwight Eisenhower nor Secretary of State John Foster Dulles, the recipients of the report, would have disputed the description of the events or its conclusions about Soviet objections. A watershed of the Cold War and one of the monumental events of European history in the twentieth century, the Hungarian Revolution demonstrated the inability of the United States to "roll back" communism in the era of Mutually Assured Destruction. It showed also the ruthlessness of the Soviets in maintaining their hold on their conquests of the Second World War.

The second half of Flynn's twelve years in Austria had much in common with the first half. He continued to have issues with his Passionist superiors back in the United States, both over his finances and over his continued employment with Catholic Relief Services. He helped find homes and employment for the slowly declining numbers of *Volksdeutsche* in the refugee camps in Austria, while occasionally traveling to Rome or Geneva to confer with other CRS officials, especially Swanstrom and Norris. There were the occasional fundraising trips back to the United States, which in turn offered opportunities to visit his relatives in Boston. He also indulged in his first love, journalism, writing occasional articles for both *The Sign* and *The Brooklyn Tablet*.

The upheavals of 1956 ensured one issue dominated all the others during the last six years of Flynn's tenure as the director of CRS in Austria. The Hungarian Revolution, or, to be more accurate, the 200,000 refugees it created, most of whom fled across the Austro-Hungarian border, was one of the greatest challenges in the history of Catholic Relief Services. Despite daunting circumstances in the aftermath of the Soviet invasion of Hungary, CRS—with the assistance of the Austrian government, the Catholic Church, the United Nations High Commissioner for Refugees (UNHCR), several other aid agencies, as well as the Eisenhower and Kennedy administrations—would help nearly all of the Hungarian refugees start a new life in the West.

Hungarian Revolution: A History in Documents, ed. Csaba Bekes, Malcolm Byrne, and János Rainer (Budapest: Central European University Press, 2002), 437–42, at 438.

For his services during the Hungarian refugee crisis, Flynn, for an almost unprecedented second time, received the Golden Cross in 1963, the highest honor the Second Republic could give to a non-Austrian citizen. These achievements in assisting Hungarian refugees proved to be the crowning moments of his career as relief official in Europe, and, as Flynn saw it, his lifelong work as a priest who fought against tyranny in its many forms.

At the Front Lines Again: Catholic Relief Services and the Hungarian Revolution, 1956–1957

After spending last two months of 1955 in Austria, Flynn returned to the United States in January 1956, to accomplish business for Catholic Relief Services and to fulfill obligations to the Passionists. He divided much of the month of January between Boston and Union City. In Boston, Flynn returned to what had been his original duty when he first became a Passionist: leading a series of spiritual retreats in Boston for the laity of Saint Gabriel's Monastery in Brighton. He also had time to visit Saint Michael's Monastery to celebrate his Silver Jubliee, the twenty-fifth anniversary of his ordination to the priesthood, and also that of his provincial, Ernest Welch. Flynn then traveled to San Francisco to meet with Swanstrom, Norris, and most of the other CRS officials to discuss activities for the upcoming year. One of the items on the agenda was scaling back the operations of the CRS offices in Austria and transferring them to Caritas.[2]

The annual report of CRS activities from October 1955 to September 1956, submitted by the CRS administrative board to its board of trustees, reported these statistics for the period: 12,054,091 pounds of surplus food sent to Austria, with 30 percent of it going to poor families and the remainder going to the various refugee camps. Out of this aid, only 14.2 percent came from the Catholic Church in America, and the remainder came either from reimbursements for Ocean Freights from various European governments (although not Austria) or (the vast ma-

2. Letter from Flynn to Welch, January 17, 1956. PHA Record Group 322—3/8. Flynn also promised he would submit the yearly amount of money due to the order, which totaled $750. He sent the funds to Welch the next month.

jority) from the U.S. government, which contributed 71.8 percent of all donated aid. The report also detailed how the CRS officials in Austria actively in worked with Caritas under the leadership of Leopold Ungar, as well as with the other aid agencies and the Austrian government to assist in integrating the remnant of the ethnic German refugees into Austrian society, including helping them move out of the camps and into homes of their own. The report provided information about the larger numbers of Yugoslav refugees who had been entering Austria since the summer of 1956, as well as hundreds of Hungarians.[3] In comparison, most of the ethnic Germans were being granted citizenship in either Austria or West Germany, or they were granted visas to the United States, Canada, the United Kingdom, or Australia. By the beginning of 1959, there were only about 490 *Volksdeutsche* left in Austria without visas, and 652 who had been approved to leave the country; at the beginning of 1956, they had numbered 3,000.[4]

Austrian Chancellor Julius Raab—based on a recommendation by the Federal Ministry of Social Administration—decided to bestow on Flynn the highest honor any non-Austrian citizen could receive, the Golden Cross. It honored both Flynn and CRS for their enormous contribution to the country's recovery. Perhaps, also, the award served to signal that their work was nearing completion. Per the government report, the work CRS had done for the Austrian government was twofold. The first element was the establishment of a welfare aid program for impoverished Austrians suffering from the effects of the Second World War and eight years of Nazi rule. The second was in refugee relief, not only in helping construct shelters and camps for the largely German ethnic refuges who came into the country from Poland and

---

3. National Catholic Welfare Conference, Report to the Board of Trustees—Catholic Relief Services, October 1, 1955–September 30, 1956. CMS Collection 026—War Relief Services, National Catholic Welfare Conference, Box 2 (Hereafter 026—2). The report also mentioned that CRS and the UNHCR were working to ensure refugees could resist the extradition demands of neighboring communist governments, which had been "increasing in frequency."

4. Letter from Edward Cummings, Executive Assistant of CRS, to Flynn, February 5, 1959. UND James Norris Papers, Box 23 Folder 09. Even during the height of the Hungarian and Yugoslav refugee crisis, CRS continued its older work of resettling the *Volksdeutsche*.

Czechoslovakia, but also in assisting those who arrived to find a new home abroad if the Austrian government was unable to accommodate them. The report concluded Flynn had performed an "incredible service" to the Austrian republic, and he was deserving of their highest honor. After receiving permission from both Swanstrom and Welch, Flynn received the Cross at the American embassy during a visit to Vienna on April 5, 1956.[5]

Although it would not be until 1962 when he would actually refer to it as "my second home," it was clear Salzburg had become this for him. He had come to love the city, especially its medieval quarter, often going on walks there when he had finished his work. He lived at a small house on the banks of the Salznach River and employed a *Volksdeutsche* war widow and her daughter as a housekeeper and a cook. Despite the difficulties of work in one of the CRS "hot spots" and the occasional conflicts with his superiors in the Passionist order, he genuinely enjoyed working for Catholic Relief Services, and, in all honesty, was in little hurry to return to either Brighton or Union City. When his various nieces and nephews came to visit him in Salzburg, he would always take them to the Mirabell Palace Gardens and the Salzburg fortress, and, if they desired it, would serve as a tour guide to Geneva, Munich, Vienna, and Rome. These familial visits proved invaluable in helping Flynn escape, if only temporarily, from his often isolated routine while working in Salzburg.[6]

He continued to have mixed views about the country, especially the position of the Catholic Church in Austria. Under his pseudonym Fay Behan, Flynn discussed his feelings about the state of Austrian Catholicism in an article entitled "How Catholic Is Austria?" in the September 1955 issue of *The Sign*. Flynn wrote that, on the surface, it

5. Report for Austrian Chancellor Julius Raab compiled by the Ministry of the Interior, February 13, 1956 OSA—Archiv der Republik Bestand BMI (Bundesministerium für Inneres) 1945–2002: Präsidentschaftskanzlei. Flynn would later tell both men that receiving the Golden Cross was a great honor not just for himself but also for CRS.

6. Laura Wilson, Interview with the author, December 13, 2015, Scranton, Pennsylvania. Three years after Flynn left Austria, the Mirabell Palace Gardens would become world famous when they were featured in the "Do-Re-Mi" number in the gargantuan 1965 hit, *The Sound of Music*.

was a "Catholic country," with over 90 percent of its population being members of the Church. This, Flynn argued, was deceptive, as only about a third of those—somewhere between 25 and 35 percent—were religiously observant. Even the name "Catholic country," Flynn argued, was problematic, as it can be used in a positive or a derogatory manner, or could be used to cover up deep-rooted problems or uncomfortable issues.[7]

The article contained both a history of the Austrian Church and an observation of Catholic clerical and lay life. For centuries, Catholicism was the official state religion in the ancient Habsburg Empire, and Flynn argued this had led to many "grievous errors and abuses"—such as priests, and especially bishops, acting like government rather than religious leaders, and the accumulation of massive amounts of wealth by the Church that was not "used productively." The Church, like many other elements of Austrian society, was struck with a deep identity crisis in the interwar era following the end of Habsburg rule. This identity crisis, when combined with the unremitting hostility of the Austrian Socialist Party, led numerous Catholic clergy foolishly to attempt to accommodate themselves to Nazi rule following the *Anschluss*. The result of their accommodation was a "tornado of Nazi oppression" over the next seven years, as well as the disaster of the Second World War, with the destruction of hundreds of Church buildings. Moreover, the bombings during the war, and to a lesser extent, combat between the Wehrmacht and the Red Army in the spring of 1945, led to the death of hundreds of Catholic clergy throughout the country.[8]

The ten years of the occupation were the story of how the Austrian Catholic Church again tried to recover, from another war and in a vastly different political environment. The hostility of the SPO to the Church was still prevalent, while the OVP, despite its sympathy for Catholic teachings, was no more an exclusively "Catholic" party than

7. Fabian Flynn, "How Catholic Is Austria?" *The Sign*, September 1955, 15–18, at 15. One wonders why Flynn used such an obvious pseudonym in his writings for *The Sign* and *The Brooklyn Tablet*, given the fact his writing style did not change at all.

8. Flynn, "How Catholic Is Austria?" 16. Although Flynn did not mention him by name, Vienna's Cardinal Innitzer was a quite obvious example of clergy whose "opportunistic foolishness" had accommodated to Nazi rule.

its West German equivalent, the CDU. The Church had also, during the twentieth century, lost support from both the Austrian working class and much of the urban population, which in turn led to an increasingly secular atmosphere in most of the cities. Most of the schools had been secularized, and religious education in them was often inadequate. Not all was lost, for, as Flynn wrote, the country still had a vibrant Catholic intellectual tradition; in the countryside, Catholic social life was flourishing; a "renewed commitment" to charitable endeavors had improved the Church's moral reputation among much of the country, including some Socialists; and, since the country had avoided Soviet rule, there had not been an aggressive push to destroy the institutional Church as had happened in so many of Austria's neighbors. Thus, Flynn concluded, the conditions were there for a revival of Catholic life; the country was not destined to sink into merely nominal Catholicism, but that could be avoided only if the Church hierarchy took advantage of these favorable social and political conditions.[9]

When Flynn returned from the United States to Austria in mid-February 1956, Khrushchev was about to unleash an earthquake on the communist world. Once Khrushchev had overthrown Lavrentiy Beria and Georgy Malenkov, his rivals for power, he had exerted intense pressure on the various capitals behind the Iron Curtain for political and economic reforms, especially following the June 17, 1953 uprising in East Germany. In Hungary, the situation was particularly bad: a wave of AVH terror under Rákosi's orders had profoundly embittered the population toward the regime, a condition worsened by the deteriorating economy.[10]

Rákosi and his trusted deputy Ernö Gerö were extremely reluctant to make substantial reforms, especially regarding a scaling back of state terror. The Hungarian prime minister, Imre Nagy, who had replaced Rákosi in this office in July 1953 (Rákosi remained general secretary of the MDP), was far more receptive to an agenda of moderate reforms. His attempts were ultimately thwarted by his removal as prime minister at Rákosi's instigation in April 1955. Following Khrushchev's "Secret

9. Ibid., 17–18.
10. Borhi, *Hungary in the Cold War*, 230.

Speech," the MDP in Hungary openly split into reformist and Stalinist wings. As was typical of relations between the Soviet Union and its "socialist brothers" in Eastern Europe, the Kremlin temporarily "solved" the leadership struggle in Hungary with Khrushchev's insistence Rákosi step down as MDP party secretary in June 1956. Since Rákosi's deputy Ernö Gerö took his place, the leadership situation remained completely unacceptable to most Hungarians, who demanded that reformers such as Nagy or János Kádár take over the state and party leadership. Khrushchev's decision to demand an ardent Stalinist like Rákosi step down as the general secretary of the Party but then replace him with his equally Stalinist deputy Gerö was emblematic of the Soviet leader's contradictory style of decision-making in both foreign and domestic policy. It made an already tense situation in Hungary worse for the communist regime.[11]

Unlike in the Soviet Union, where the "Secret Speech" could conceivably lead to the reform of a communist system that had been in power for decades, in Eastern Europe, the effects of de-Stalinization challenged the entire existence of the communist order. Nowhere was this more evident than in Poland and Hungary, where economic conditions were miserable, the Russians were despised, and the communist leadership was viewed as completely subservient to Moscow. By the summer of 1956, political conditions in both countries were increasingly unstable.[12]

In Poland, this took the forms of workers' and students' demonstrations, beginning with riots in Poznań in June 1956, demonstrations that continued in size and intensity to October. The protestors demanded the "nationalist" Polish Communist Władysław Gomułka replace the Stalinist Edvard Ochab in the party and state leadership, as well as a more independent relationship with the Soviet Union. The "Polish October" was successful in its first objective, and at least temporarily in the second, symbolized by the removal of the Red Army Field Marshal Konstantin Rokossovsky as Polish defense minister. Poland's success encouraged many Hungarian students and workers to take more daring

11. Ibid, 238.

12. Johanna Granville, "1956 Reconsidered: Why Hungary and Not Poland?" *Slavonic and East European Review* 80, no. 4 (October 2002): 656–87, at 664.

actions, in the belief that, since Khrushchev had "let Poland go," Hungarian freedom was soon to follow.[13] The catalyst for the Hungarian Revolution were events on Tuesday, October 23, as thousands of Hungarian students surrounded the main radio station in Bem Square to demand that a document called the "Sixteen Points" be aired throughout the country. When MDP and AVH personnel first stalled and then responded to the crowds by shooting into them, the surviving students, with the aid of hundreds of Hungarian soldiers, raided several military armories. The next day, in Hero's Square, the massive statue of Stalin was torn down, and it seemed Hungary had escaped from Stalinism.[14]

Shortly thereafter, János Kádár replaced Gerő as MDP leader and Imre Nagy returned as prime minister. In Moscow, the Kremlin leadership hoped these actions would prevent a counterrevolution and that the new government would maintain Hungary's ties to the Warsaw Pact and the MDP's political monopoly of power. After fighting against revolutionaries for few days, most of the Soviet soldiers were withdrawn from the streets of Budapest and other Hungarian cities. Many of the Hungarian cities and towns outside Budapest, where the Soviet military presence was scarce, had already gone over to the side of the Revolution.[15]

By the fourth week of October, the hold of the MDP, and more specifically the AVH, over the population had effectively collapsed. Dozens of agents of AVH had been lynched on the streets of Budapest by angry mobs and many more had gone into hiding. Thousands of Hungarian soldiers freed numerous political prisoners. Imre Nagy, partially to preserve some of the MDP's standing in the country, promised the return

13. Ibid., 665–66. The situation worsened in Hungary as Gerő and much of the rest of the MDP were not even in the country when major street demonstrations broke out in Budapest, having spent the prior two weeks at a summit in Yugoslavia.

14. Victor Sebestyen, *Twelve Days: The Story of the 1956 Hungarian Revolution* (New York: Vintage Books, 2006), 107–18. The "Sixteen Points" demanded, among other things, the withdrawal of Soviet soldiers from the country, Nagy's appointment as prime minister, and the legalization of other parties besides the MDP.

15. Borhi, *Hungary in the Cold War*, 249. Notably, one Soviet leader who did not share Moscow's hopefulness was the Soviet ambassador to Hungary, future KGB chairman Yuri Andropov, who argued that a massive military intervention by the Red Army was necessary to stabilize the situation.

of multi-party elections for the Hungarian Parliament and a thorough reexamination of Hungary's role in the Warsaw Pact.

Officials in CRS in neighboring Austria and in the United States viewed these events with great interest and hope. Back in December 1955, Norris had mentioned in a letter to Swanstrom that the political conflict in Hungary might eventually allow CRS to resume its activities in that country. Swanstrom wrote back to him in agreement and urged him to monitor the situation closely. As the situation became even more chaotic by the fall of 1956, Flynn wrote to Norris that a return to Hungary by CRS was now a possibility and expressed hope that a settlement similar to the one granted to Austria the year before would come to its next door neighbor.[16]

CRS conducted some work on Hungary's borders in late October and early November 1956. Under the orders of both Swanstrom and Norris, Flynn supervised three different missions in which he and other CRS staff brought substantial amounts of food, clothing, and medical supplies to the Hungarian people, including to thousands who had taken to the streets to fight the communist rule in Hungary. The first two missions went off successfully, as Flynn encountered his old friend, Cardinal Mindszenty.[17]

In Budapest, it was clear that the Stalinist atmosphere which had characterized Hungary since the late 1940s had (at least temporarily) faded. Mindszenty was released from his imprisonment at the medieval castle of Felsopeteny, located 65 kilometers north of Budapest, by his AVH captors on October 30. Mindszenty refused to be moved away from the castle that morning, preferring to await his fate, whatever it was, at his current place of imprisonment. By mid-afternoon, thousands of local farmers and laborers surrounded the castle and demanded the release of all the prisoners. The AVH authorities, heavily outnumbered and fearing for their lives, abandoned the castle and slipped away. Consequently, when a Hungarian military unit arrived

16. Letter from Flynn to Norris, October 2, 1956. CUA National Catholic Welfare Conference International Affairs Collection File 9 Box 49.

17. Letter from Swanstrom to Norris, October 24, 1956. Center for Migration Studies Archives Collection 023, National Catholic Welfare Conference, Department of Immigration Records Box 1.

an hour later to liberate the cardinal, they found him released from his cell and among his flock.[18] With Mindszenty were numerous other Catholic, Lutheran, and Calvinist clergy who had been imprisoned on the orders of the AVH, including, most notably, the number two cleric in the Hungarian Catholic Church, Archbishop József Grösz of Kalocsa, who had been tried and imprisoned in 1951 in circumstances like those of Mindszenty. Both men returned to Budapest on October 31, 1956.[19]

By this point Flynn had been given formal permission by Nagy's government to return to Hungary to resume charitable work for Catholic Relief Services. On November 2 he sent a report to the *New York Times* concerning his meeting with Cardinal Mindszenty, describing how dozens of Hungarian soldiers who had joined the revolutionary forces currently guarded the cardinal in a run-down section of Budapest. He wrote: "The Cardinal looks fine, although his face is shrunken. He has the same piercing eyes and his voice is full and vigorous. He remained most gracious and seemed to be in complete control of the situation." Flynn repeated Mindszenty's request to Catholics in the United States to provide charitable relief for the Hungarian people. During the next week, Flynn traveled from Budapest to Vienna and back again to provide supplies for the soldiers and students who had gone over to the side of the Revolution.[20]

The freedom of József Mindszenty proved vexing for Nagy. As a U.S. Army intelligence report from January 1956 had correctly observed, the arrest and persecution of Mindszenty in 1948–49, which symbolized the attack on religious faith in Hungary by the communists, was "perhaps productive of more dissidence and resistance potential than any other single action of the regime."[21] Nagy and his ministers feared the cardinal's potential for rallying the Hungarian people, not merely

18. Sebestyen, *Twelve Days*, 204–5. Mindszenty's combination of incredible courage and an unbending, stubborn will, was mirrored in Flynn; the two men were, in many ways, kindred spirits.

19. Ibid., 207–9.

20. *New York Times*, November 2, 1956, 12.

21. Document #8 Study Prepared for U.S. Army Intelligence, "Hungary: Resistance Activities and Potentials," *The 1956 Hungarian Revolution: A History in Documents*, 86–105, at 92.

against Stalinism, but against Nagy's brand of reformist communism as well. On October 23, Nagy and the journalist Miklós Gimes engaged in a heated debate regarding Mindszenty's role in Hungary's future. Gimes insisted on free elections and the possible reestablishment of a multi-party democracy in Hungary, stating: "The wishes of the Hungarian people must and shall prevail." Nagy then asked Gimes whether he would accept a scenario in which the Hungarian people elected Mindszenty as leader of Hungary in an open election. Gimes replied that he deeply desired this would not come to pass, but even if it did, the Hungarian people would soon come to realize the error of their judgment, for "Mindszenty is not suitable for the resolution of their problems."[22]

On November 1, 1956, Nagy delivered a radio address to the Hungarian people, repeating the same message he had just given to various diplomatic missions in Budapest. Hungary was officially withdrawing from the Warsaw Pact, and it aspired to achieve the same neutral status as Austria. He appealed to Hungary's neighbors, especially the Soviet Union, to respect the country's new status, as it wished to live in peace with all its neighbors. Nagy proclaimed: "The revolutionary struggle fought by the Hungarian heroes of the past and present has at last carried the cause of freedom and independence to victory. The heroic struggle has made it possible to implement, in the international relations of our people, its fundamental national interest—neutrality."[23]

Despite Nagy's fears, when Mindszenty made his own radio address two days later, his tone was generally reserved and conciliatory. The Hungarian government was not taking any chances, as Nagy's deputy

22. Janós Rainer, *Imre Nagy: A Biography*, trans. Lyman Legters (New York: I. B. Tauris Press, 2009), 93. The left-wing British historian A. J. P. Taylor was less willing to accept this outcome than Grimes, snidely noting after the Soviet invasion in early November that the new leader, János Kádár, was still preferable to the "reactionary" Mindszenty.

23. Document #68 Imre Nagy's Declaration of Hungarian Neutrality, November 1, 1956. *The 1956 Hungarian Revolution: A History in Documents*, 334. Ultimately, the decision of Nagy's new government to break away from the Soviet empire, as well as the increasingly violent attacks on the hated AVH officials, broke the inertia in Moscow regarding the question of military intervention. Khrushchev began making plans to launch a full-scale invasion of Hungary to install a new puppet Communist government that would be led by Nagy's former ally, János Kádár.

Zoltán Tildy sat next to the cardinal during the radio address, and had already requested of Mindszenty that he not address the issue of communist land reforms or the presence of Soviet soldiers in the country.[24] Mindszenty did not call on the Hungarian people to take up arms against their government, or against the Red Army. He emphasized Hungarians should leave the streets and return to work, to begin reestablishing "normality" throughout the country. Mindszenty demanded early, open, and genuinely democratic elections to form a Hungarian government that would represent all of those who lived under it. Although not criticizing the land reforms that had occurred after the end of the war, he called on government authorities to respect private property. Unsurprisingly, Mindszenty also demanded the government should honor Catholic Church's special position as spiritual leader of the majority of the population, and persecution of all religious institutions cease immediately. He concluded his speech by arguing this task was in the hands of "heirs to a fallen regime," regarded by many as an oblique criticism of Nagy and his ministers.[25]

Neither Nagy's nor Mindszenty's intended future for Hungary came to pass. As had happened in East Germany three years earlier, and as happened to Czechoslovakia twelve years later, Hungary remained a pawn in the hands of the Soviet government, its destiny ultimately to be decided by the leaders in the Kremlin. The decisive steps were taken on October 30 and October 31, 1956. Politburo members Anastas Mikoyan and Mikhail Suslov reported to Khrushchev on October 30 that the decision by many soldiers and officers of the Hungarian army, to go over to the side of the Revolution, meant that a massive Red Army intervention was almost certainly a necessity. The next day, KGB chief Ivan Serov—who, like Suslov and Mikoyan, was present in Budapest—reported back to Moscow: "The political situation in the country is not getting better, it is getting worse. In the leading organs of the party there is a feeling of helplessness. In the party organizations there is a process of collapse. Hooligan elements are seizing regional party committees and killing communists." Following the reception of this report, the Politbu-

24. Mindszenty, 210.
25. Rainer, *Imre Nagy*, 132.

ro decided to invade Hungary, remove Nagy's government, and replace it with one led by the more compliant János Kádár, who had already signaled his receptiveness to Moscow for such a solution.[26]

An interview with Fabian Flynn by one of his hometown newspapers, *The Boston Herald*, provides some details on his activities during the revolutionary weeks in Hungary. "Boston Priest Lauds Mindszenty Spirit" appeared at the top of the front page of the November 3, 1956 issue of *The Boston Herald*. Flynn wrote how he brought two massive shipments of food, clothing, and medical supplies to the beleaguered Hungarian population, and, once the Soviets had invaded, returned across the border with thousands of Hungarian political prisoners who had been freed by revolutionary soldiers and workers during October. Flynn answered in the affirmative to the *Herald* reporter's inquiry whether his assisting political prisoners to flee to Austria could be considered similar to the nineteenth-century Underground Railroad in the United States. Without hesitation, Flynn responded "It is just like that."[27]

Flynn described the situation of the Hungarians with a typical mix of admiration and hard-headed realism: "It is part of the Russian strategy to seal off the border, starve the population, put down the uprising and force the population into submission and back to the work. The Hungarians have vowed they will maintain a general strike and keep the country at a standstill until the last Russian soldier departs. To which the Reds will always respond, 'very well, we will seal off the borders and you will starve.'" The Hungarians told Flynn they were fighting for "freedom and for their Western Allies, especially the United States of America, against Communist tyranny," although there was considerable bitterness toward the British and French for their actions during the Suez Crisis, which enabled the Soviets to take a free hand in Hungary. Flynn praised Eisenhower for promising $20 million in aid for the Hungarians but argued that far more was needed.[28]

26. Granville, "1956 Reconsidered," 685–688.

27. Stanley Eames, "Boston Priest Lauds Mindszenty Spirit," *Boston Herald*, November 3, 1956. The article's prominence also indicates Flynn had become a minor celebrity in his hometown.

28. Ibid. Years of tension between Egypt's leader Colonel Gamal Nasser and the British and French governments over the control over the Suez Canal came to a head in the summer of 1956, with Nasser's decision to nationalize the canal. His action led to

On all three of the aid missions into Hungary, Flynn and the other CRS members dodged convoys of Soviet tanks. He described Mindszenty as being in excellent spirits, encouraged by the revolutionary spirit of his fellow Hungarians, and guarded by the same soldiers who had liberated him from the hands of the AVH a week before: "Our youth, our workers and farmers, and many soldiers from the army who revolted against the regime. Our country is full of heroes and there are many wounded in our hospitals. We all need the support of the West, now more than ever." Mindszenty told Flynn he had received a supportive telegram from Pope Pius XII and he hoped this would be the first step in the free world helping Hungary to join its ranks. Flynn also wrote that the Revolution had led to a revival of religious freedom throughout the country; during the eve of the Feast of All Saints, "every window" in Budapest held a lit candle, most for the first time since the communists had come to power nine years before.[29]

The third attempt by Flynn and a CRS convoy—accompanied by some members of Caritas and even a handful of French representatives from Catholic charities in that country—to bring medicine to the Hungarian revolutionaries was less successful in avoiding the Soviet military. A tank convoy stopped the CRS trucks after they had gotten eighty miles into Hungary, and ordered Flynn to return to Austria, escorting them to the border. Once again, the Reds forced Flynn and CRS out of the country. Flynn described the Russian soldiers as possessing a cold, vacant look on their faces as they went about their "horrible duty"; and the whole experience reminded him (he wrote), more than anything else in his CRS career, of his time with the 26th Infantry Regiment during the Second World War. As for the fate of Hungary, Flynn admitted to Eames, "Only God knows" if the Hungarians could hold out against the renewed Soviet invasion.[30]

---

an Anglo-French-Israeli attack on Egypt simultaneous with the Hungarian Revolution. Political, diplomatic, and economic pressure from the Eisenhower administration, as well as fear of the propaganda effect on the third world that invasion might produce, forced the British, French, and Israelis to back down, leaving Nasser in power.

29. Ibid. Mindszenty had also informed him he would never again allow himself to be a prisoner of the regime.

30. Ibid.

Khrushchev—who, for all of his denunciations of Stalin, ultimately resorted to the same methods of his former boss when faced with popular resistance—followed the recommendations of Yuri Andropov and Mikhail Suslov: to crush the Revolution, to dispose of Nagy, and to replace him with his more compliant colleague János Kádár.[31] The day after Flynn's interview with *The Boston Herald*, the Red Army returned to Budapest in force. After a few days of brutal street fighting on a scale not seen in Europe since 1945, fighting that cost the lives of thousands of Hungarians and hundreds of Russians, the tanks and soldiers of the Red Army crushed the Hungarian Revolution, and Mindszenty sought refuge to avoid imprisonment or execution. After a brief visit to the Hungarian parliament building on the morning of November 4, where Nagy's ministers informed the cardinal that the Red Army had attacked Budapest, Mindszenty enquired from his staff as to the nearest embassy. Mindszenty, together with a handful of fellow priests, hid their cassocks under their coats and walked past a line of Soviet tanks to the American embassy. Welcomed by Ambassador Edward Thompson Wailes as a "symbol of liberty," Mindszenty was granted, by executive order of U.S. President Dwight Eisenhower, an indefinite refugee status, which would last until 1971.[32]

The Salzburg diocesan weekly newspaper, *Rupertibote*, published a series of articles concerning the tragic situation in Hungary. The first was published on November 4, 1956, the same day the Red Army returned in force to the country, and was entitled *"Gebet und Hilfe für Ungarn!"* (Prayers and Help for Hungary!) The front-page article informed the readers of Pope Pius XII's appeal to all the Catholics to pray for the Hungarian people and to do whatever they could to assist the country in its darkest hour. The article also asked its readers in

31. Sebestyen, *Twelve Days*, 152–53. Khrushchev's other emissary, the Armenian Anastas Mikoyan, had urged a more peaceful solution, but Khrushchev ignored him, much as he would six years later when he ordered the massacre of Russian workers in the city of Novocherkassk.

32. Mindszenty, *Memoirs*, 212. The exact circumstances of Mindszenty's escape to the American embassy remain shrouded in controversy, especially regarding who initially called for it. Mindszenty asserted in his memoirs that Imre Nagy asked the Americans on November 3 to take him in, something for which he expressed deep gratitude.

Salzburg to follow the example of all the political parties in Austria, by supporting their neighbor's bid for freedom, specifically by donating funds for Caritas, which was preparing efforts with other aid agencies to assist the Hungarian people.[33]

The following issue, entitled "*Tragische Wendung in Ungarn*" (Tragic Turning Point in Hungary), discussed the bloody denouement of the Hungarian Revolution. The front-page article discussed how "a horrible tragedy had engulfed the Hungarian nation" as the massive influx of Russian soldiers and tanks had overwhelmed the Hungarians; the reformist government of Nagy had fallen; and the capital and most of the country were effectively occupied by the Red Army. Mindszenty had fled to the American embassy, and thousands of Hungarians had crossed over the Austrian border, with tens of thousands more to come. The article conceded that the government in Vienna could not have prevented these awful events; the Austrian people, though, should provide all the physical and financial aid they could to "those who have lost their home."[34] The next issue, on November 18, 1956, was also dedicated to the Hungarian tragedy. It included appeals from Andreas Rohracher and a reprint of a radio address from Pius XII, who claimed the "blood of the Hungarian People cries out to God." Both men denounced the "Russian and Hungarian criminals" who had responded to demands of freedom and peace with tyranny and war. Rohracher also reminded the Austrians to assist both Caritas and its "foreign allies" in helping the Hungarian refugees who continued to come into the country.[35]

During the immediate chaos that surrounded the Soviet invasion, and for a number of months after the Revolution, Flynn continued his work for Catholic Relief Services along the Austrian/Hungarian border, especially in assisting Hungarians to escape into neutral Austria. Back in New York, the American Council for Voluntary Agencies for Foreign Services—which consisted of, among others, CRS, the LWF, the YMCA,

---

33. "Gebet und Hilfe für Ungarn!" *Rupertibote*, November 4, 1956.

34. "Tragische Wendung in Ungarn," *Rupertibote*, November 11, 1956

35. "Das Blut Ungarns schreit zum Herrn," *Rupertibote*, November 18, 1956, 1–2. Later issues of the newsletter contained shorter articles and pictures about the activities of both Caritas and CRS distributing food and medicine, as well as conducting religious services, at the various Hungarian refugee camps across the country.

the American Friends Service Committee, and the American Jewish Defense Council—met on December 3, 1956. On that occasion, they agreed to work with the Austrian, Italian, and Yugoslavian governments, as well as the UNHCR, to aid the Hungarian refugees for as long as necessary. The CRS mission in Austria received 150 tons of milk, 350 tons of cheese, 25 tons of clothing and blankets, 1750 pounds of medicine supplies, 100,000 pounds of baby clothes, and $20,000 in cash from CRS headquarters in Geneva, and $5,000 worth of medical equipment from France. Flynn distributed this aid in cooperation with Leopold Ungar of Caritas.[36]

Flynn also helped bring about a reversal of the initial policy of the Department of Immigration and Naturalization Services (INS) to those Hungarian refugees in Austria who were scheduled to be brought to the United States. The visas these Hungarians initially received from the U.S. embassy were marked "parole" rather than having permanent residence status. This would have meant the Hungarians who came to America would have to spend weeks in a relocation facility until their backgrounds were examined, as part of the McCarren Immigration Act. Hearing of this, Flynn refused to help process any more Hungarian refugees for emigration to the United States unless they received permanent residence status. Since CRS, in cooperation with the UNHCR, had processed nearly all of the Hungarians bound for America, this led to a holdup of the initial plane flights intended to take hundreds of Hungarians to America. Ultimately, State Department pressure over the delay led the INS to drop the "parole" status, and, by early December, participants in the Hungarian Revolution began to arrive in the United States.[37]

Flynn also wrote several articles for various Catholic and secular newspapers regarding the tragic fate of the Hungarian people following the Soviet invasion. One example comes from *The Brooklyn Tablet*

36. Meeting of the American Council of Voluntary Agencies for Foreign Services, December 3, 1956. CMS Collection 026—1. Flynn worked with Ungar on a daily basis from mid-November 1956 until mid-January of 1957.

37. "U.S. Drops Parole Status for Hungarians," NCWC News Service, November 23, 1956. This was a considerable victory for Flynn, but most Hungarian refugees ended up at Camp Kilmer, New Jersey, anyway, since they did not have a home, employment, or relatives waiting for them in the United States.

in late November 1956. In this article, Flynn appealed for massive assistance from American Catholics for the beleaguered Hungarian population, especially those crowded in refugee camps on the Austrian/Hungarian border. He told of how supplies for Hungarian refugees had been practically exhausted, and they desperately needed food and medicine. Flynn concluded that the courageous example of Hungary should be more than enough for Americans to provide whatever was necessary for the victims of communism.[38]

Three months later, Flynn's tone regarding the status of Hungarian refugees was, if anything, more dire. Speaking to dozens of directors from Catholic dioceses along the U.S. eastern seaboard who were taking part in the Catholic Bishops' Relief Fund Appeal, he stated that "immoral and obscene conditions" prevailed in the overcrowded Hungarian refugee camps. He bitterly attacked the United Nations for its dual failure: first, to come to the aid of Hungary during the Soviet invasion, and then, to address the refugee crisis afterward. Flynn argued that unless their situation was alleviated, the refugees might be forced to return to Hungary, where they would face certain imprisonment by Kádár's government. He avowed that CRS were instructing young Hungarians who had grown up under communism in "Christian living," so they could be resettled in other countries.[39] By January 1957, Kádár and his Soviet allies succeeded in suppressing armed opposition, more than 2,500 Hungarians had been killed, and more than 200,000 had fled, most to neighboring Austria. While Kádár's government was not nearly as repressive as Rákosi's, Hungary remained tightly in the Soviet embrace until the late 1980s.[40]

The border between Austria and Hungary remained largely open until February 1957. Consequently, tens of thousands of Hungarians fled during the four months from mid-October to mid-February. The Austrian government, despite official neutrality, announced it would open its borders to 20,000 refugees fleeing the Soviet military. The desperate situation in Hungary, especially the acts of vengeance com-

38. *The Brooklyn Tablet*, November 17, 1956, 4.
39. "Refugee Centers Scoured by Priest," *New York Times*, February 27, 1957, 17.
40. Borhi, *Hungary in the Cold War*, 311.

mitted by Hungarian and Soviet communists against the defeated rebels, drove far more to flee to the country—by December 1956, more than 158,000 Hungarians had already fled to Austria, a further 25,000 would follow during the next two months.[41]

Perhaps anticipating such a situation, when the Red Army invaded Hungary on November 4, 1956, the Austrian government sent an urgent appeal to the Eisenhower administration, asking the United States to admit a number of Hungarian immigrants. Eisenhower initially agreed to admit 5,000 refugees as part of an extension of the Refugee Relief Act of 1953. By early December 1956, President Dwight Eisenhower agreed to admit another 21,500 Hungarian refugees to the United States and to establish, as part of the State Department's United States Escape Program, a special emergency program for Hungarians. The program lasted until December 1957, and during this time 38,000 Hungarians relocated to America.[42] Eisenhower launched the program with an open letter sent to Hungarian refugees that read, in part: "The circumstances that have separated you from your homeland and your loved ones fill American hearts with deep emotion and compassion for what you are enduring, We feel a solemn and responsible pride that in your time of need you have come to our shores."[43]

Aftermath of the Soviet Invasion: CRS and the Hungarian Refugees, 1957–1962

Approximately 155,000 refugees have crossed the border between Hungary and Austria from October 23 1956 and January 1 1957. An average

41. Internal NCWC Memorandum. CMS 026—1. A considerably smaller number of Hungarians made their way initially to Yugoslavia and Italy as compared with the number who crossed into Austria, especially after February 1957, when Hungary's border was closed.

42. "The Refugee Status in Europe," CRS Report, January 1958. UND Joseph Hartnett Papers Box 2, Folder 32. One wonders if this policy was the product of guilt over the failure of United States to support the Hungarian people more actively against the Soviet invasion following constant encouragement by Radio Free Europe to the "captive peoples" behind the Iron Curtain to rebel in the late 1940s and early 1950s.

43. Official Statement by President Dwight David Eisenhower, December 9, 1956. CMS 026—1.

of 800 people a day are coming across the border at this time. The quality of the people who fled Hungary is of the highest order. For the most part they were in the fight for freedom and fled only when the choice was death or deportation at the hands of foreign invaders or temporary flight to a foreign land to await the inevitable freedom of Hungary. The large majority are young people, students, technicians, craftsmen, and professional people. There are many family units, including a large number of children. 88,000 of the 155,000 refugees have already been settled in other countries besides Austria; of this 88,000, 15,000 have been relocated to the United States and 73,000 have been relocated to other countries. This leaves 67,000 in Austria, of which 37,000 remain to be settled in other countries.[44]

So wrote Vice President of the United States Richard Nixon to President Dwight D. Eisenhower three months after the Soviet invasion of Hungary. As János Kádár restored the authority of the Hungarian Workers Party (MDP) over the country, tens of thousands of Hungarians lived in harsh conditions in refugee camps hastily set up in eastern Austria and in other parts of the world, including the United States.

The most important American charitable agency that attempted to fill President Eisenhower's promise, both in Austrian refugee camps and in the United States, was Catholic Relief Services. The task ahead of them was daunting. Initially the Austrian army simply transported Hungarian refugees around the country in "ghost trains" until temporary shelters were constructed for them. The two largest refugee camps, Camp Kaiser-Ebersdorf and Camp Traiskirchen, were both located near Vienna. Later, the United States Army transported the majority of the 38,000 Hungarians who were relocated to the United States to Camp Kilmer in New Brunswick, New Jersey. The fate of Hungarians at these camps, whether in Austria or the United States, was largely in the hands of the UNHCR, CRS, and a handful of other organizations that also worked in the camps, such as Lutheran World Federation, the World Council of Churches, the American Jewish Defense Committee, and the YMCA.[45] In all, in excess of $71,075,000

44. "The Text of Nixon Report to President on Problems of Hungarian Refugee Relief," *The New York Times*, January 2, 1957.

45. World Refugee Year Report 1959. UND James Norris Papers Box 51 Folder 04.

came from the United States to assist Hungarian refugees, more than $20,000,000 of which came from various private sources, including the NCWC. The remainder of the funds came from the American government. CRS used these funds to provide food, clothing, and medical care for the refugees. Austria, during the fiscal years of 1956 to 1960, was among the main recipients of resources from CRS.[46]

The amount of aid distributed by CRS to the Hungarians was massive, on a scale that had not been seen since the end of the Second World War. In 1956 alone, CRS distributed 12,534,004 pounds of food, clothing, and medical supplies, most of it surplus food that had been donated by the U.S. Department of Agriculture; only 750,000 pounds were clothing and medicine. In order to meet the increased administrative workload, Swanstrom and Norris allowed Flynn to expand his staff in Austria from its regular size of 165 workers to 225. Many of the extra sixty staff members were recruited from the Hungarian refugee population; those who had language abilities in German and English were given special priority.[47]

Following initial interviews of the Hungarian refugees by officials from the UNHCR, CRS processed more than 60 percent of all remaining Hungarians who were admitted to the United States as part of the USEP. More than half of the 40,000 refugees processed by CRS throughout the world in 1957 were Hungarians living in Austrian refugee camps. The CRS offices in Austria also engaged in several smaller tasks, such as printing and distributing 25,000 prayer books and Bibles for the refugees. A Catholic youth center was also set up for hundreds of young Hungarian Catholics who had arrived without their parents.[48]

46. Final Report on the Hungarian Escape Program, Standing Conference of Aid Agencies Working with Refugees, December 8, 1961. CMS 023—NCWC Immigration Records, Box 3 (hereafter CMS 023—3). Camp Kilmer housed the Hungarian refugees until late May 1957, when those who by this point had still not been placed in a home were transferred to the Saint George Hotel in Brooklyn; the final Hungarian refugees left in February 1958.

47. National Catholic Welfare Conference, Report to the Board of Trustees—Catholic Relief Services, NCWC October 1, 1956 to September 30, 1957. CMS 023—10.

48. 1957 Appeal Handbook for the Catholic Bishop's Relief Fund. CUA NCWC International Affairs: Relief CRS 1950–1966 Box 49 Folder 8.

During the first few weeks after the Soviet invasion of Hungary, as over 150,000 refugees began to enter Austria, Salzburg city and provincial officials—including the *Landeshauptmann* of the province, Josef Klaus—were on a tour of the United States, visiting Washington, D.C., Baltimore, New York, Boston, and New Orleans. When they returned home in early November, Klaus wrote to Flynn that he had met with Archbishop Francis Keough, chairman of the CRS administrative board, as well as Swanstrom at the Empire State Building in New York, and both men had praised Flynn's work over the past seven years. As Klaus wrote, "we informed them, they had found the best possible representative for the NCWC in Austria we could have wished for in the personage of Father Fabian Flynn."[49]

Many Hungarian refugees were housed in camps outside the cities, where they joined the remaining *Volksdeutsche* and some political refugees from Yugoslavia. The Salzburg city authorities had little control over the camps, for jurisdiction was divided between the UNHCR and the Austrian government. Since, for a while, the tasks of assisting the Hungarian refugees simply overwhelmed all other demands on CRS, Flynn was out of contact with Klaus and the other Salzburg authorities for the first two months after the Hungarian Revolution. He apologized for this in his letter to Klaus on January 3 1957, admitting that "this enormous Hungarian problem, which suddenly fell on top of us, has occupied nearly all of my attention since the end of the year." He did promise that CRS would send a belated Christmas gift of 100,000 Schillings to benefit kindergartens in both the city and the province, and expressed hope that by March he would be able to turn his attention back to the concerns the two of them had traditionally shared. Flynn thanked Klaus for giving an excellent speech in English on the radio in which Klaus had thanked Vice-President Richard Nixon for his recent visits to the Hungarian refugee camps and for the efforts made by America in behalf of Austria since the end of the Second World War.[50]

49. Letter from Klaus to Flynn, November 12, 1956. SLA Präsidalakten 1956 Karton 187 PRÄ (Personalangelegenheiten) 1956.

50. Letter from Flynn to Klaus, January 3, 1957. SLA Präsidalakten 1956 Karton 187 PRÄ1957. Most of Flynn's correspondence with Klaus, like his correspondence with

The relationship between Klaus and Flynn followed a similar pattern over the next five years. Flynn consistently sent Klaus materials concerning the activities of CRS in Austria, fundraising appeals for the CRS missions, and articles he had written for either *The Sign* or *The Brooklyn Tablet*. Klaus would usually respond to these materials positively. A letter he sent to Flynn on January 2, 1957, was typical, as Klaus thanked Flynn for reminding the world, or at least his American readers, that Austria had dealt with the "terrible situation in Hungary" by responding to the refugees from the Soviet invasions with "an open door and a friendly heart." Klaus mentioned Flynn's stories were an inspiration for people on both sides of the Atlantic, and Flynn would always have Salzburg's gratitude for what he had done.[51] CRS also provided a financial gift every year to the orphan kindergartens administered by the Salzburg provincial government. Usually this came to between 85,000 and 100,000 Schillings. Many of the students at these schools were from the various refugee groups that had made it into the country without parents.[52]

Despite the efforts by CRS and other agencies that were aided by the USEP, conditions in Hungarian refugee camps in Austria were miserable. By early 1957, about 30,000 refugees remained in the Austrian camps. Since quotas for many of the Western countries had filled up, these people were trapped in a legal and political purgatory, one that continued for four years.[53] Flynn had no illusions about the enormity of the task ahead of CRS. On February 25, 1957, he made this statement to the Associated Press: "There are still 70,000 Hungarians stranded outside of Vienna. This is what we are left with when all the do-gooders

---

most other Austrian officials, both clerical and secular, was written in fluent German: his education at the Boston Latin School was continuing to pay dividends.

51. Letter from Klaus to Flynn, February 1, 1957. SLA Präsidalakten 1956 Karton 187 PRÄ 1957.

52. Letter from Klaus to Flynn, November 2, 1959. SLA Präsidalakten 1956 Karton 187 PRÄ 1959.

53. Report of the Zellenbach Commission on the European Refugee Situation, December 1959. UND James Norris Papers, Box 51, Folder 04. Besides the usual suspects of Austria, Switzerland, the United States, Canada, Australia, and New Zealand, other countries as diverse as the Dominican Republic, Italy and Panama took in a number of Hungarian refugees.

have finished handing out chocolate bars at the border, when all the shouting about Hungary's glory is over. We are left with the dirty work, 70,000 people whom nobody has any room for right now."[54]

In a speech given to twenty-five diocesan directors in a fundraiser for the annual Catholic Bishops' Relief Fund Appeal the next day, Flynn wrote "One thing that cries to heaven in Austria these days is the condition of the refugees. The utter overcrowding in the camps was morally indecent and without privacy." Flynn laid the blame for this squarely at the feet of the UNHCR, which he believed had placed far too many obstacles to allowing the remaining Hungarians to emigrate abroad. In an oblique criticism of the Austrian government, Flynn pointed out that neither Vienna nor the UNHCR had allowed CRS or other relief agencies to screen and register the remaining refugees in preparation for their eventual emigration. At the end of the speech Flynn sharply rejected claims by the Pennsylvania Democrat, Representative Francis E. Walter, that many of the Hungarian refugees were secret communists whose goal was to spread subversion throughout the West.[55]

Flynn spent from late February to mid-April of 1957 traveling throughout the United States, meeting with numerous clerical and lay officials in charge of the Catholic Bishops' Relief Fund to impress on them the need to raise funds specifically for relief work among the Hungarians Refugees. One of the largest meetings took place in New Orleans, where Flynn met bishops from Louisiana, Texas, and Arkansas to inform them of the situation in Hungary and Austria, and how they could portray the situation to their parishioners.[56]

At a meeting of the heads of various relief agencies in Geneva, Switzerland on April 16, 1957, to address the Hungarian problem, Dr. Auguste Lindt, the head of the UNHCR in Europe, echoed some of Flynn's criticisms of the situation in the Austrian refugee camps. Lindt stated that while CRS and other relief agencies did a commendable job in meeting the material needs of the refugees, the moral atmosphere in the camps was abysmal. Comparing the mood to that in

---

54. "Hungarian Refugees in Vienna," *Associated Press*, February 25, 1957.

55. "Refugee Centers Scoured by Priest," *New York Times*, February 27, 1957.

56. "Arkansan at Southern Appeal Confab," *Arkansas Catholic*, March 29, 1957, 3.

the aftermath of the Second World War, Lindt reported that many of the Hungarians who had failed to obtain refuge in other countries simply sleepwalked through each day, and a feeling of general despair set upon the camps.[57]

What to do with the remaining 30,000 Hungarians in Austria was a difficult question for CRS and UNHCR officials in Europe over the next four years. At the same time CRS was providing housing and employment for the 30,000 Hungarians at Camp Kilmer in New Jersey and later at the Saint George Hotel in Brooklyn. At a meeting of the President's Committee on Migration and Refugee Problems on May 16, 1957, Edward Swanstrom admitted the inability of the U.S. Congress to address the immigration status of Hungarian refugees remaining in Austria, Italy, and Yugoslavia. It would be better for the various relief agencies to continue to work toward providing a basic standard of living for the refugees in the camps, accepting that they could be there indefinitely. Swanstrom noted that many of those in the camps were either young men or women, or the very old.[58]

One of the more painful duties for Flynn and other CRS officials in Austria, in coordination with Caritas members, was helping to reunite Hungarian children with their parents, as in many cases they had been separated from them during the Soviet invasion of Hungary or during the journey to the Austrian border. This initiative involved distributing lists of missing children to adults throughout the camp, advertising in refugee and local newspapers, and frequent announcements on the radio. The task was not new to Flynn, as he had performed this service since his arrival in Freiburg in 1946. Although the attempt to reunite parents and children was often frustrating, he at least had the advantage of having a natural rapport with children, something that a number of CRS officials on both sides of the Atlantic noted in their correspondence.[59]

---

57. Meeting of the Standing Committee of Voluntary Aid Agencies Assisting Refugees, April 17, 1957. CMS Collection 026—1.

58. Ibid. Also complicating the matter was that, whereas more than 3,000 Hungarians had fled to Yugoslavia, thousands of Yugoslavs, mostly Croats and Slovenians, had fled to Austria.

59. Eileen Egan, *Catholic Relief Services*, 248–50.

Besides the regular work in his Salzburg office, Flynn frequently traveled to Vienna to meet with representatives with the Austrian government and to Munich with the directors of the CRS mission in West Germany, as the work between the two often overlapped. There were also occasional trips to Geneva to meet with Norris and there were conferences with the other directors of CRS missions in Europe. These trips were combined with weekly visits to the various refugee camps and centers all over Austria, but especially in the eastern part of the country. By the summer of 1958, the extensive work schedule was having its effects on his shaky health, and he underwent another round of hospitalization and surgery, as he started bleeding from an adhesion from an appendectomy performed in 1948. This time, Flynn did not return to the United States for treatment but instead had surgery at the University of Munich's medical school. During his recovery, which stretched through most of the month of July 1958, Flynn received a letter from Cardinal Francis Spellman, wishing him speedy recovery and asking God to bless him in his work. Spellman also promised he would strongly consider Flynn's recommendation that CRS missions in Africa bring African-American Catholics to talk to the native populations in sub-Saharan Africa about the civil rights struggle in the United States. By mid-August 1958, Flynn had returned to Salzburg and had resumed his regular work schedule.[60]

Flynn also served as consultant for the treatment of Hungarian refugees in the United States. Conditions for Hungarians at Camp Kilmer were considerably better than conditions in the refugee camps in Austria. Refugees' presence in the United States naturally allowed them to take advantage of certain opportunities that were not available to those in the Austrian camps. CRS, working with the NCWC's Education Department, provided hundreds of scholarships and tuition waivers for young Hungarian men and women at Camp Kilmer to attend Catholic universities and colleges in the northeastern and midwestern United States. William McManus, the official in charge of running the program, admitted to Swanstrom on June 17, 1957 that financial aid

60. Letter from Spellman to Flynn, July 22, 1958. ANY—Francis Cardinal Spellman Collection, Collection 007. Box S/C 34, Folder 1. CRS missions did eventually follow through on Flynn's suggestion, although not for a few years.

from many relief agencies for the program had been disappointingly inadequate.[61] CRS not only provided for much of the material needs of the camps' inhabitants, which at its height in early 1957 numbered more than 30,000 people, but also worked to provide housing, language and civics instruction, and employment to those Hungarians who lacked a sponsoring family in the United States, which was more than 85 percent of them.[62]

Fact-finding committees from various relief agencies, including CRS, arrived at Camp Kilmer during 1956 and 1957; they usually judged that the military base—which had been set up as a refugee center for Hungarians in the emergency situation of the winter of 1956–57—was not up to the task of housing them. The committees frequently complained about the large size of the camp, the ease with which the refugees could simply slip outside for unapproved excursions into New Jersey, and the inability of American civilian and military authorities to determine which people were living in which part of the camp. Despite this, none of the agencies found an alternative to the use of Camp Kilmer. Eventually, by 1961, most the refugees at Camp Kilmer had been made permanent residents of the United States. A handful relocated to Canada just as Kádár's government offered a general amnesty for participants in the Hungarian Revolution.[63]

Few Hungarians took Kádár up on his offer, and nearly all of those who did lived in the refugee camps in Austria. From January of 1957 to March 1958, only 290 Hungarians out of the 30,000 in the camps accepted repatriation back to their homeland, although the total number of those repatriated increased slightly over the next few years. The United States ultimately accepted seven times the number Eisenhower had originally proposed: 35,026 were resettled in the United States, which included nearly all the inhabitants of Camp Kilmer as well as another 5,000 who had been living in Austria. The UNHCR and CRS provid-

---

61. Letter from McManus to Swanstrom June 19, 1957. CMS C26—1. The President's Committee for Hungarian Refugees, formed by President Eisenhower on December 12, 1956, consisted of representatives from 15 different relief agencies.

62. Ibid.

63. Final Report on the Hungarian Escape Program, Standing Conference of Aid Agencies Working with Refugees, December 8, 1961. CMS 23—1.

ed application forms to nearly every Hungarian who was interested in applying for asylum in America from 1957 to 1962. By 1957, 24,525 had been relocated to Canada, 20,590 in the United Kingdom, 14,720 in West Germany, 11,962 in Switzerland, 10,232 in France and 9,423 in Australia, which included many of the players and coaches on the Hungarian Olympic delegation who had come to Sydney for the summer Olympic games shortly before the events of October and November 1956.[64]

On December 28, 1957, Eisenhower released a statement announcing the United States was terminating the Hungarian Emergency Refugee Program. The president credited the work of the UNHCR, the Austrian and Italian governments, and the various aid agencies that had enabled the American government to bring almost 38,000 Hungarian refugees to the United States. Camp Kilmer would soon be closed as refugee center for Hungarians; those who were still there would be sent to the Saint George Hotel in Brooklyn. Eisenhower congratulated those who had worked to ameliorate the effects of the Hungarian tragedy, including CRS: "The success of the United States' emergency program of assistance to Hungarian refugees stems basically from three factors: America's traditional humanitarianism, the dedicated work of the religious and other agencies which transformed that spirit into action, and finally, the quality of the refugees themselves."[65]

The situation in the Austrian camps was considerably more complex. While the country's economy had considerably improved by the late 1950s, much of the aid for the Hungarian refugees was coming from abroad, especially from the United States' surplus food program, distributed through various aid agencies in the country. A report from the Austrian Ministry of the Interior from April 1959 noted that since the Hungarian refugee crisis began in November 1956, the United States alone had sent 700,000 tons of surplus goods, to aid them in

64. Summary of the Hungarian Escape Program by the CRS Resettlement Division of CRS March 12, 1958. CUA NCWC International Affairs: Relief CRS 1950–1966, Box 49 Folder 9.

65. Dwight D. Eisenhower, "White House Statement on the Termination of the Emergency Program for Hungarian Refugees December 28, 1957," in The American Presidency Project, ed. Gerhard Peters and John Wooley, http://www.presidency.ucsb.edu.

providing for the Hungarian refugees as well as the increasing number of Yugoslavs who were also starting to come into the country. By
this point, there were 15,987 Hungarian refuges remaining in Austria:
5,888 were in refugee camps, 2,016 in homes set up by charitable organizations, and 8,083 in private homes throughout the country. Most
were located in major cities such as Vienna, Salzburg, Innsbruck, and
Graz. The report concluded many of those remaining, inspired by their
meetings with American aid workers, desired to go to America, especially those who were separated from family members who had already
gone there.[66] The remaining 15,000 in Austria made great demands
on the resources of the CRS mission: of the $215,230 spent in aid in
the year 1958, for example—which comprised cash grants, clothing,
food, and medical supplies—more than half, $116,960, was dedicated
to assisting the Hungarian refugees.[67]

Official termination of the Hungarian Emergency Resettlement
Program, itself a branch of the USEP, meant CRS faced a sharp reduction in funds. Two weeks before Eisenhower announced his decision,
the CRS mission in Austria was informed its budget would be cut by
thirty percent, as it would receive a total of $170,000 from the State
Department for the upcoming year. This forced CRS to lay off staff
at their offices in Graz, Linz, and Innsbruck, and to consolidate their
efforts largely around Salzburg and Vienna.[68] This caused a minor
panic on the part of the Austrian Catholic Church, especially since
the leader of Caritas, Leopold Ungar, felt they could not handle the
refugee situation on their own. Consequently, Flynn spent much of
the winter of 1958–59 conducting damage control with the Austrians
to assure them that, while CRS was reducing its operations because of

66. "Finanzierung der Betreunng der Neuflüchtlinge in Österreich durch
Lieferung US-Überschußgüttern," April 9, 1959. OSA—Archiv der Republik Bestand
BMI (Bundesministerium für Inneres) 1945–2002: U.S. Hilfe.

67. Report from Norris to Monsignor Paul Tanner concerning CRS Aid to Nationality Groups, March 25, 1959. CUA NCWC International Affairs: Relief CRS 1950–1966
Box 49 Folder 11. The Yugoslavs, most of them Croats, were the next largest recipients
of aid, followed by ethnic Germans and smaller numbers of Poles, Romanians, and
Russians.

68. Letter from Norris to Flynn, December 10, 1958. UND James Norris Papers,
Box 23 Folder 09.

budget constraints, it would not pull out of the country entirely. In his correspondence with Norris, Flynn admitted looking forward to the day when Caritas could take over from CRS, especially regarding the refugee question.[69]

Flynn was even angry with Norris for, in his mind, not having done enough to pressure the head of the USEP at the State Department, Dick Brown, to provide funds for the CRS missions in Austria to assist the Hungarian and Yugoslav refugee programs. He wrote to Norris on March 3, 1959, stating he was "angry and disappointed at him" for his failure to procure funds, given Flynn's efforts to assure the Austrian government and the Catholic Church that the CRS mission was still capable of performing its tasks. Norris was nonplussed, to put it mildly, and informed Swanstrom of Flynn's complaints. Swanstrom responded in a letter on March 10 assuring Norris he felt both men had done everything they could to get more money—not only for Flynn, but also for Monsignor Landi of the CRS mission in Italy, who operated under similar pressures. Swanstrom also admitted this type of behavior was typical of Flynn, who had not attended several crucial meetings in Geneva, nor sent representatives. Flynn's lashing out at authority figures for not doing their duty, Swanstrom acknowledged, was something they had dealt with from the beginning of his employment.[70]

Some of Flynn's frustration came from the complicated dealings with both the State Department and UNHCR officials. In a letter to Norris from June 5, 1959, Flynn complained how the officials in charge of the USEP in Vienna had informed the CRS offices in Salzburg they had to send all funding requests for all of their refugee projects in three days. Flynn had his staff drop everything they were doing to draw up all of their funding requests, rush to Vienna to present them, work until late into the night, then take an overnight plane to Munich followed by a dawn train ride to Salzburg to make a morning meeting

69. Letter from Norris to Flynn, February 26, 1959. UND James Norris Papers, Box 23 Folder 09.

70. Letter from Swanstrom to Norris, March 10, 1959. UND James Norris Papers, Box 23 Folder 09. Norris and Flynn eventually patched up their differences, as can be seen in their correspondence over the following months, which became considerably friendlier.

at the CRS headquarters. There they presented their project-funding requests at a morning meeting with George Warren, the head of USEP in Europe. After having taken an overnight flight from Frankfurt am Main, Warren had only two hours to meet with them before heading to Greece. With his usual exasperation at bureaucracy that complicated aid distribution during a major humanitarian crisis, Flynn concluded with: "All of this is ridiculous, and to me seems so unnecessary. With all the great brains who are running this, WHY, why can we not have calm and order and common sense instead of hysteria?"[71]

A year later, in the fall of 1960, the relationship between Dick Brown, the overall head of the USEP, and Flynn had not improved. Flynn sent a letter informing Brown that if the USEP wanted to continue to "contract" with CRS for work involving the refugees from Hungary or Yugoslavia—jobs the State Department representatives in Austria felt they could not do—then the USEP needed to provide greater financial support for the CRS staff engaged in these projects. Furthermore, the USEP should stop requesting that CRS write endless reports justifying their expenditures simply so the USEP could submit them to Washington, D.C. Since the USEP was responsible for its own budget, it should write the financial reports regarding the projects for which it contracted with CRS, rather than forcing CRS to waste time and resources to perform this work. Flynn informed Brown that both of these conditions would have to change if the collaboration between the USEP and CRS was to continue.[72]

In response, a furious Brown wrote to Norris, informing him that Flynn's recent letter was the "snottiest" he had ever received. Norris eventually asked Flynn to send him a copy of the letter he had sent to Brown. Flynn obliged, writing to Norris he could not see what the fuss was about, as he was merely answering the USEP to discuss the subject of concern between the two. He was not interested in pursuing the matter further, writing: "I intend to do nothing about this contemptible

71. Letter from Flynn to Norris, June 3, 1959. UND James Norris Papers, Box 23 Folder 09. The unsaid assumption was, if Flynn was to jump through all these hoops to obtain funding, the funding should be increased, as CRS genuinely needed it.

72. Letter from Flynn to Brown, July 9, 1960. UND James Norris Papers, Box 23 Folder 09.

action of his [Brown] because, I am weary of struggling with the USEP, USEP mentality, USEP bureaucracy, and USEP abuse. CRS/NCWC has accomplished more for USEP and given USEP less trouble in Austria than any other Agency. Notwithstanding, CRS/NCWC is the one Agency the USEP seems bent on constantly needling and aggravating."[73]

In his response nine days later, Norris agreed that Flynn's letter was slightly "snotty"; he reminded Flynn that Brown and other USEP staff were "very sensitive" about critical letters, and Brown had always been an "admirer of yours, especially how you handled the Hungarian crisis." Norris suggested that, since Brown was arriving in Europe soon, Flynn should meet with him and have a face-to-face conversation to reconcile their differences. This occurred a few weeks later. The meeting served to patch things up enough that CRS and the USEP continued their work together until the end of CRS activities in the country in the spring of 1962.[74]

CRS officials working in the camps also found themselves under pressure from the Austrian and, ironically, Hungarian governments. Austrian Chancellor Julius Raab—seeking to reassert his country's neutrality, which the housing of thousands of Hungarian revolutionaries endangered—made clear to CRS his intention to move most of the Hungarians out, one way or another. At the same time, Kádár's regime in Budapest attempted to draw thousands of Hungarian youths back into the country by offering the possibility of "family reunions" without any punishment from the communist regime.[75]

Conflicts between CRS and the UNHCR were also commonplace. In November 1959, the UNHCR sent a list of 878 Hungarian refugees in Austria who desired to emigrate to the United States. The list was rife with errors and, in the view of both Norris and Flynn, demonstrated the lackadaisical nature of the UNHCR's record keeping. Flynn sent Norris a breakdown of the various errors in the report; many of the names on the list had no business being on it. Of the first 93 names on the

73. Letter from Flynn to Norris, September 19, 1960. UND, James Norris Papers, Box 23 Folder 09.

74. Letter from Norris to Flynn, September 28, 1960. UND James Norris Papers, Box 23 Folder 09.

75. World Refugee Year Report 1959, January 1960. UND NOR, Box 52 Folder 1.

list, Flynn's office revealed 12 had already come to the United States, 11 had been rejected for any emigration on medical or security grounds, 4 were young men and women who wanted to finish their studies before leaving for another country, 25 had clearly stated they wanted to stay in Austria, 10 had registered to emigrate to countries besides the United States, and CRS lacked all records for 12 other people. On December 14, Norris sent the entire report to Dick Brown, warning him not to take the word of UNHCR director Auguste Lindt as gospel. In his response, Brown promised to take CRS's concerns into consideration when deciding how to admit more Hungarians into the United States.[76]

Flynn, Norris, and Norris's deputy director of the CRS mission in Europe, Jean Chenard, spent much of 1960 in an ugly financial dispute with the UNHCR officials from both Vienna and Geneva. By this point, Norris had relocated his own office to New York City, leaving Chenard in charge of day-to-day activities in Europe. His letter informing Auguste Lindt, the director of the UNHCR of this on January 14, 1959, was cordial, saying, "I want to thank you for your extremely helpful cooperation and understanding support of the activities which are of our common concerns." Norris thanked Lindt's staff as well, both in Geneva and in all of the branch offices throughout Europe. There was little hint of the problems about to emerge.[77]

The conflict started in January 1960, as the UNHCR had launched in April 1959 a major project to process refugees out of the camps and into private residences, the final step before either integrating the refugees into Austrian society or allowing them to emigrate abroad. The nickname of the project was the "Out-of-Camp Cases." There had been similar attempts by the Austrian government to reduce the number of refugee camps and eventually to close them all within a three to four-year period. The UNHCR asked all the charitable organizations in the countries that had large refugee populations, especially Italy, West Germany, and Austria, to work on this project. What irritated Flynn was that members of his staff had to be used for this project,

76. Report from James Norris to USEP Director Dick Brown December 14, 1959. UND, James Norris Papers, Box 23 Folder 09.

77. Letter from Norris to Lindt, January 14, 1959. UNHCR, Fond 11, Series 1, Box 4 Folder 39.

which took them away from other CRS tasks. Since these were paid staff, Flynn requested financial compensation from the UNHCR offices in Vienna, especially when he heard that such an arrangement had already been worked out between the UNHCR offices in West Germany and Italy with the CRS missions in those countries. UNHCR offices in Vienna were unable to come to a financial agreement with CRS, and Flynn informed Norris that he had received only minimal instructions from the UNHCR as to how this project was to be completed. Finally, he was angry at the "glacial pace" of the UNHCR's review of the case files Flynn's office had put together; out of the 570 dossiers the CRS mission in Austria had sent to the UNHCR offices in Vienna in 1959, only fifteen had been reviewed by the end of the year.[78]

A series of requests passed back and forth between the CRS offices in Geneva and Salzburg, and the UNHCR offices in Vienna and Geneva over this issue, but there was no resolution. In essence, UNHCR offices in Vienna approved Flynn's funding requests, agreeing to pay the salaries of the CRS staff who were working on the "Out-of-Camp" project, but they repeatedly informed him the final approval would rest with UNHCR headquarters in Geneva. The latter would then inform Flynn they were still waiting on "definitive recommendations" from their office in Vienna. By September, Flynn's patience ran out. He sent a blistering letter to Jean Chenard accusing the UNHCR officials in both Austria and Switzerland of rank incompetence and ingratitude: "This latest incident just about strains my patience to the breaking point, and renders intolerable the deceitful buck passing of the UNHCR, as if all of us in the CRS/NCWC were administered by a group of nincompoops, persons who can be pushed around at will, and kidded up to the ears with empty promises."

Flynn expressed even greater anger over the fact some Arab charitable agencies had demanded and received 100 percent financial compensation for dealing with Palestinian refugees, but CRS could not receive a salary for a few clerical workers engaged in a vital refugee project at the request of the UNHCR. As a man who rarely raised his voice, he concluded the letter by stating: "What in God's Holy Name

78. Letter from Flynn to Chenard, January 25, 1960. UND, James Norris Papers, Box 23 Folder 09.

is the UNHCR actually doing with all the millions given to it by the governments of the world to aid refugees?" The real answer, Flynn claimed, rested on an overabundance of clerical and administrative staff; Flynn estimated that, out of the 70 people who worked in the UNHCR offices in Vienna, "I will wager that 65 of them never got nearer to a refugee than the registration cards and dossiers that they are fiddling with from morning to night."[79]

Following appeals from Norris, Chenard, and Swanstrom, in December 1960 the UNHCR and CRS negotiated an agreement for the CRS staff members engaged in the "Out-of-Camps" project in Austria. On January 12, 1961, Warren Pinegar, the deputy director for the UNHCR operations in Europe, along with William Grant of the Vienna office, traveled to Salzburg to meet with Flynn and his staff regarding the previous year's difficulties. The meeting went cordially, and Pinegar reported back to Chenard on February 13, 1961: "The exchange of views with Father Flynn provided the basis for a re-affirmation of the friendly relations and division of functions that exist between our branch office and the NCWC in Austria."[80]

Relations deteriorated again in the fall of 1961. Both Norris and Flynn engaged in a similar tug of war over funding with the UNHCR officials, since the UNHCR suspended reimbursement projects for the "Out-of-Camps" project until CRS made a 20 percent "matching contribution" to the UNHCR operations in Austria. Norris objected to this demand, since CRS, like the UNHCR, operated all over the world and could not increase funds for the CRS mission in Austria's budget without cutting services elsewhere. This galled both men, for CRS already contributed in excess of 30 percent of the total costs of the project. Each month of 1960 CRS spent about 81,500 Schillings on the project: they processed more than 173 cases in Austria from the refugee populations in Vienna, Salzburg, Liz, Graz, Klagenfurt, and Innsbruck, and the average cost per case was 4,100 Schillings.[81]

79. Letter from Flynn to Chenard, September 29, 1960. UND James Norris Papers, Box 23 Folder 09. As stated before, Flynn could be difficult to deal with at times, which may have contributed to this standoff, but he was not going to blame himself.

80. Letter from Pinegar to Chenard, February 13, 1961. UNHCR 11—Records of the Central Registry, Series 4/39 NCWC/CRS, Box 102.

81. Internal CRS memorandum on the "Out-Of-Camps" Project, April 12, 1961.

The impasse lasted for as long as CRS conducted activities in Austria. CRS could not count on financial reimbursements from the UNHCR toward completion of this project, and Norris, Flynn, Chenard, and Swanstrom all agreed the amount CRS had already spent on the project was more than enough for its "supporting contribution" to the overall refugee work in Austria. After thanking Norris for his efforts to resolve the problem with the UNHCR officials, Flynn disgustedly wrote: "The whole long story of our negotiations over this project is a mass of deliberate and disgusting UNHCR deceit. The Geneva crowd are not only cheap, they are treacherous." Flynn mentioned how the UNHCR had offered refugee cases intended for CRS to Quaker relief agencies as a way of "punishing our agency." He concluded it was not worth fighting over any more: "I am weary of writing, of complaining, of arguing, of discussing, and of thinking of the UNHCR 'Out-of-Camps' project. The case of the administrative grants can be considered finalized." He notified the UNHCR officials: "CRS helped refugees before the UNHCR was even formed, and would continue to do so, even if we never receive another penny from Geneva." One can hear in Flynn's letter two decades of aggravation at entrenched bureaucracies, whether military, religious, or governmental in nature; they were led by people who rarely saw those who were affected by the decisions they made. Further, the bureaucratic leaders did little to help those who had to deal with unfortunate consequences of their policies. It is also possible to hear reflected, to some extent, Flynn's traits of impatience and self-righteousness.[82]

The CRS mission in Austria appeared to have little problem working with either the hierarchy of the Austrian Catholic Church or Caritas. Flynn's correspondence with Archbishop Andreas Rohracher and with Leopold Ungar was almost always warm and friendly, and there are few instances of Flynn informing Chenard, Norris, or Swanstrom of problems. The letter from Flynn to Rohracher on February 10, 1960 provides an illustration. Flynn thanked Rohracher for arranging the transfer of the large shipment of medical supplies from Salzburg to the

UND James Norris Papers, Box 23 Folder 09. Expenses included personnel costs for the CRS staff, travel, telephone, postage, and office supplies.

82. Letter from Flynn to Norris, September 15, 1961. UND James Norris Papers, Box 23 Folder 09.

Thurnfeld Cloister located in the province of Tyrol, which was also being used a refugee shelter for elderly Hungarian and Croatian women. Flynn mentioned to Rohracher that three weeks earlier he had personally delivered the medical supplies, and they caused a "great joy with their reception" (*großer Freude in Empfang*). He thanked Rohracher for his help, adding that both the speed of its delivery and the quantity of the shipment were typical of aid provided by the Salzburg archdiocese to CRS since their arrival in the country.[83]

In July 1960, Flynn informed Rohracher that CRS had recently been notified of the decision by the Austrian bishops at their recent conference in Feldkirch to send religious books to priests and theologians in countries behind the Iron Curtain. Flynn told Rohracher that CRS fully supported this endeavor and would do whatever it could to assist the Austria Church, such as procuring books in a variety of languages from Catholic sources in the United States. He praised Rohracher and the other Austrian bishops for this "superb proposal," since those who had "stayed behind" in Hungary and other communist countries needed all the help they could get in an "aggressively atheist" environment. Flynn, his Cold Warrior persona as strong as ever, suggested that, if they could keep religious faith alive, it would outlast the ideology of the communists. The project would last until the late 1980s, far past the end of CRS's activities in the country.[84]

The transfer of banned religious books by Caritas to Catholics in communist countries was clandestine. CRS and Caritas could, however, openly resume their aid work, albeit limited, to the population of Hungary, but this was largely restricted to packages sent to Catholic priests. Even then, they had to pay high mailing taxes imposed by the Hungarian government.[85] Also, once Soviet forces withdrew from Budapest in

83. Letter from Flynn to Rohracher, February 10, 1960. AES Bestand 2.1 Rohracher 20/94 NCWC.

84. Letter from Flynn to Rohracher, July 8, 1960. AES Bestand 2.1 Rohracher 20/94 NCWC. The process of smuggling "banned books" to communist countries was undertaken not only by the Catholic Church in Austria. It was also a major CIA project, often done in coordination with officials from Radio Free Europe and Radio Liberty. Alfred Reisch's 2013 book *Hot Books in the Cold War* details this project in excellent detail.

85. Letter from Norris to Swanstrom, May 5, 1957. UND James Norris Papers, Box 23 Folder 09.

early February 1957, Kádár's government allowed the International Red Cross to enter the country until May 1957. CRS agents traveled with the Red Cross to Hungary and helped distribute more than $1,000,000 in clothes, food, and medical supplies to Actio Catholica. Hungarian families still in Hungary also were allowed to make requests for medicine from CRS offices in Geneva. Flynn did not take part in the visits to Hungary, although he had his staff prepare many of the packages. He had been declared *persona non grata* by Kádár's regime.[86]

By the fall of 1957, Kádár decided the International Red Cross had served its purpose, and he closed off much of the country to further assistance from CRS and other charitable agencies. The government continued the policy of allowing Hungarians to request medicine from CRS. Also, it allowed CRS to ship clothing duty free from Austria to Hungary to be distributed to needy families, but halfway through the year, Kádár removed this provision; thenceafter, high duties were charged for their distribution in Hungary. Although CRS authorities considered ending the program because of the duties, appeals from Actio Catholica convinced them to continue the program, which used Vienna as a transit point.[87]

That was the status quo in 1961 and 1962. In Hungary, with Church/state relations frozen in place between Kádár's government and Mindszenty in his exile in the American embassy (his exile in turn having created a leadership crisis in the Hungarian Catholic Church), the regime also ratcheted up restrictions on religious activities. Used clothing sent through Vienna and medicine sent through Geneva to Budapest continued, but in decreasing quantity.[88]

CRS officials had to deal also with the religious differences among the refugees who were living in the Austrian camps. Hungary's population at the time was about 70 percent Catholic and 25 percent Prot-

---

86. National Catholic Welfare Conference, Report to the Board of Trustees—Catholic Relief Services, NCWC October 1, 1957 to September 30, 1958. CMS 023—5.

87. National Catholic Welfare Conference, Report to the Board of Trustees—Catholic Relief Services, NCWC October 1, 1959 to September 30, 1960. CMS 023—5. By this point, Kádár had allowed Actio Catholica to resume operations.

88. National Catholic Welfare Conference, Report to the Board of Trustees—Catholic Relief Services, NCWC October 1, 1961 to September 30, 1962. CMS 023—5.

estant (largely Calvinist); the refugees were about 85 percent Catholic and 10 percent Protestant. CRS and the other relief agencies all strove to find Hungarian clergy of their respective faiths to provide religious services for the refugees during their time in the camps, and were largely successful in doing so.[89]

The non-official ties between CRS and the Hungarian—and, by extension, Soviet—governments came at a price. Both governments asked to send representatives to visit refugee centers and camps in order to inquire formally of the inhabitants whether they wished to return home. Kádár's government requested this as early as January 1957, shortly after the Soviet and Hungarian forces had regained control of the country and much of the Hungarian-Austrian border. During a meeting held by the Austrian Ministry of the Interior on January 10—attended by representatives of the UNHCR, CRS, and numerous other charitable agencies—the arrangements for these visits were set in place. There would be only one Hungarian mission to Austria to visit the refugee population; only the large "federal camps"—such as Traiskirchen—would receive representatives from Kádár's regime; and the representatives of the Hungarian government would be accompanied by a member of the Austrian Interior Ministry, the UNHCR, at least one charitable agency, and a member of the local police force. The camp inhabitants would be informed of the visit two days in advance, and only those who agreed to receive a visit would meet with the Hungarian representatives.[90]

The extensive security arrangements were undertaken to assure refugees they would not be taken against their will—a reasonable concern, as kidnappings of refugees and dissidents by communist secret police agencies were common in Europe during the 1950s. Correspondence between Flynn and Arnold Rorholt, the head of the Austrian Mission for the UNHCR, reveals that both men viewed the visits by Hungarian or Soviet officials to the refugee camps as a necessary evil at best, a price of keeping some connections open on the other side of

89. World Refugee Year Report 1959, January 1960. UND James Norris Papers, Box 52 Folder 1.

90. Internal Memorandum, "Hungarian Repatriation Missions," UNHCR 47—Records of the Vienna Office, Series 8/27 Repatriations, Box 3.

the Iron Curtain. In a letter written to Flynn on June 26, 1958, Rorholt reminded him to inform the refugees they never had to meet communist officials if they did not wish to, and, if necessary, he could also call out extra Austrian police and gendarmes to handle security concerns. Flynn later responded he had already done so and would continue whenever these "unpleasant meetings" occurred.[91]

With the substantial cuts to the CRS budget, other financial difficulties emerged in the dealings they and Caritas had with the U.S. State Department regarding the costs involved in distributing surplus food. Flynn attended a meeting of the Joint Food Programming Committee at the American embassy in Vienna on September 29, 1959. During the discussions at that meeting, the participants reviewed the amounts donated by the surplus food program to the CRS mission in Austria alone was 6,023,322 pounds, out of 12,113,477 pounds donated to all U.S. charitable agencies in Austria for the year of 1959. During the meeting, Flynn thanked the State Department and Agriculture Department officials for their assistance, but he pointed out there were number of problems CRS had to deal with that were damaging their financial resources. The first was that dried milk, cheese, and flour, the most common food items, often came in enormous packages—dried milk came in 200 pound barrels; cheese arrived in 7 pound cans; flour usually came in sacks weighing more than 20 pounds. CRS officials had to repackage them. They contracted with businesses in Austria to do so, as they lacked the staff to accomplish the repackaging. Pastor Joseph Ries, the main representative of the Lutheran World Federation, agreed that smaller packaging would be useful. The American government representatives, led by the Joint Food Program Committee Chairman Donald Baron, promised to do what they could to alleviate the problem but were confident they could send the surplus food in smaller packages.[92]

Flynn was slightly less successful in his second appeal at the meeting. He stated that the United States government paid for only half of

91. Letter from Rorholt to Flynn, June 26, 1958. UNHCR 47—Records of the Vienna Office, Series 8/27 Repatriations, Box 3.

92. Minutes of the Meeting of the Joint Food Committee, September 29, 1959. OSA—Archiv der Republik Bestand BMI (Bundesministerium für Inneres) 1945–2002: U.S. Hilfe. There were a few Austrian representatives at the meeting as well.

the transportation costs of all surplus food to Austria, leaving Caritas —in other words, the Catholic Church in Austria—to pay for the other half; in 1959 alone the cost for 50 percent of surplus food transportation came to slightly more than $35,000. Flynn thought this was especially galling, as Caritas had to pay a considerable amount of money for an American "gift," which in turn limited their charitable activities throughout the country. Ries again agreed with Flynn's point but argued the United States was due some kind of compensation for sending food across the Atlantic and into Central Europe. Austria was a middle case between food aid sent to Germany, where Bonn paid for all transportation costs, and Yugoslavia, where Washington paid for everything. Flynn responded by saying, if a communist dictatorship under Tito could get all expenses paid for surplus food, then a democracy like Austria should have this as well. He pointedly noted that transportation costs for Austria's surplus food had been paid by Washington until 1956, when the Agriculture Department decided Austria should pay half the costs. (This decision was made right before the Hungarian situation exploded.) In Flynn's view, the Austrian economic situation had not improved to such an extent that it should carry the surplus food transportation costs, regardless of "what the newspapers say." Until Austria was ready to handle the refugee situation entirely on its own, the United States should shoulder the financial burden of the refugees. He concluded: "There either is a need for help or there is no need." It was classic Flynn: a mix of stubbornness, occasional insensitivity to other points of view, fierce protection of CRS and his local allies from Austria, and painful awareness of the reality about a terrible situation for which the American government bore some responsibility. All Baron could promise to do was to "look into the matter."[93]

The CRS authorities in Austria turned over to Caritas many of their duties in caring for the remaining Hungarian refugees in 1960 and 1961. Funds from the United States Escape Program, on which CRS heavily depended, began to dry up, especially when Kennedy's presidency began. CRS helped reduce the refugee population, in some part through

93. Ibid. Ultimately the United States government agreed to remove more, but not all, of the financial burden from Caritas—Caritas still had to pay between 25 and 35 percent of the cost.

repatriation back to Hungary, but mostly through refugees gaining permanent residence in Austria, Switzerland, the United States, the United Kingdom, Australia, and other countries. There was also a new crisis appearing in the Austria—the Yugoslav refugees—and in most cases refugee camps vacated by Hungarians were filled again by Croats and Slovenians. By the end of 1961, CRS's role in providing for Hungarian refugees in Austria was concluded. Within a year, CRS ceased activities in Austria entirely, and Caritas took over completely in late 1962.[94]

In retrospect, the accomplishments of CRS in assisting the victims of the Soviet invasion of Hungary from 1956 until the early 1960s were amazing. Ultimately, the clear majority of Hungarian refugees who fled to Austria found new homes, some in Austria itself, and others in the United States, Canada and Australia, among many other countries. Few returned to Hungary despite all the difficulties in the refugee camps. The efforts of CRS and many other American service agencies, with considerable financial support from the Eisenhower administration, provided a basic standard of living for the refugees in the camps and helped them start a new life in the West—a necessary task, since communist rule persisted in Hungary for another thirty-three years.

Caring for the Hungarian refugees proved to be a Herculean endeavor, fraught with bureaucratic conflicts, financial hardships, and political controversies. CRS officials such as Edward Swanstrom, James Norris, Jean Chenard, and Fabian Flynn occasionally clashed with both the U.S. and Austrian governments, which often seemed motivated to wrap up the unexpected "Hungarian problem" as soon as possible. The attempt to deal with the most visible legacy of the Hungarian Revolution—the presence of almost 200,000 Hungarians in Austrian and American refugee camps—was often a frustrating and difficult task. As Flynn wrote to his family in 1957, CRS performed the Church's sacred mission against communism by assisting the Hungarian freedom fighters in exile, but it was by no means an easy or rewarding duty.

94. Ibid. Another irritating issue for Flynn and Norris was the return of some "professional refugees" to Austria from their original exile countries, especially from the Dominican Republic. Flynn wrote a number of times that he was no longer interested in providing aid to those who, in his estimation, had abused the assistance of CRS and other relief agencies.

Figure 6. Flynn meets with Hungary's Cardinal József Mindszenty, on the far right, in 1948

Figure 7. Flynn in Salzburg in December 1955 with a number of his frequent collaborators in Austria: from left to right, Father Flynn; Monsignor Josef Stefan of Catholic Spiritual Relief for Refugees; Salzburg Provincial Governor Josef Klaus; and Andreas Rohracher, the archbishop of Salzburg

Figure 8. Flynn bids farewell to his colleagues Father Alfred Schneider, Bishop Edward Swanstrom, and Father Aloysius Wycislo in Boston before heading back to Austria in the summer of 1956, shortly before the largest challenge of his career in Catholic Relief Services, the Hungarian uprising

Figure 9. Flynn receives Austria's Golden Cross for the second time from President Johannes Wilfort on May 5, 1963, at the Austrian consulate in New York City

Figure 10. At the International Catholic Migration Conference in Ottawa, Canada, on August 20, 1960: from left to right, Bishop Edward Swanstrom, executive director of Catholic Relief Services; Monsignor Leopold Ungar, director of Caritas in Austria; Bishop Joseph Gilmore of Helena, Montana; Father Flynn; and James Norris, director of the European branch of Catholic Relief Services

$\mathscr{\infty}7$

YUGOSLAV REFUGEES, 1956–1962

*Yugoslavia: The Independent Communist Dictatorship
in Eastern Europe, 1941–1955*

Tito's regime in Yugoslavia had been on Flynn's radar since the early 1950s. Flynn wrote numerous articles about religious and political freedom in Yugoslavia, as well as Yugoslav-American relations, under his pseudonym "Fay Behan" for the Catholic diocesan newspaper, the *Brooklyn Tablet*. During the Second World War, Josip Broz Tito cleverly kept many of his own best soldiers in reserve while letting the royalist Chetniks—the other large guerrilla army besides Tito's communists— do the bulk of the fighting against the German and Italian occupation forces. The Chetniks were the "official" resistance movement in Yugoslavia and were supported by its monarchy in exile. Their slogan was "For king and fatherland, freedom or death." The leader, Draža Mikhailović, had, like Tito, occasionally made temporary deals with the Axis authorities from 1941 to 1945, but his long-term goal was to remove the Italian and German occupiers, and then destroy his rivals, Tito's communists. Tito, however, expertly used his contacts with the British military in nearby Greece to convince London that he was the more effective fighter against the Axis powers and was the future of an independent Yugoslavia. Following the withdrawal of the Axis powers, the communists and Chetniks fought a brief civil war from which Tito emerged victorious, and the independent Croatian state was crushed and reincorporated into Yugoslavia. The Serbian monarchy was dissolved. Yugoslavia became a one-party dictatorship, much like the other states of Eastern Europe, with the important difference that, unlike Walter Ulbricht, Mátyás Rákosi, and Bolesław Bierut, Tito had not been placed in power by the force of the Red Army.[1]

Tito, much like these other men, started out as a fervent Stalinist. Yugoslavia under his rule initially followed the Soviet model of development, with the nationalization of all major industries, the abolition of private property, and, as we will see, the persecution of religious institutions. There was one notable exception. Tito believed his country, having lost almost a fourth of its population in the Second World War, was not yet ready to collectivize agriculture, especially having seen the costs of the same process in the Soviet Union in the early 1930s. Stalin, who was not used to other communist leaders disagreeing with him, was not pleased. A further rift opened up over the Greek civil war; Stalin warned the Greek communists not to rise up against the non-communist government in 1945, but to wait for a full withdrawal of British soldiers in a few years' time. When the Greek communists rose up anyway, Stalin was decidedly unenthusiastic about supporting them. Tito, eager to ensure that the Greek communists should succeed in establishing a Marxist regime in Athens, publicly criticized Stalin for his lack of support.[2]

By 1947, an open split emerged between Belgrade and Moscow. The Communist Information Bureau (Cominform), the post–World War II successor to the Communist International, formally expelled Yugoslavia. Tens of thousands of members of communist parties throughout the Soviet bloc were purged as "Titoists"; many of them had been advocates in 1945 and 1946 of "national roads to communism." Tito was the primary symbol of ideological heresy in the late Stalinist period of the late 1940s and early 1950s—rather as Leon Trotsky had been in the mid- to late-1930s, during the purge trials. In 1940, Stalin had finally succeeded in getting Trotsky assassinated; none of the attempts on Tito's life (ordered by Stalin over many years) ever succeeded. Yugoslavia

1. John Lampe, *Yugoslavia as History: Twice There Was a Country* (New York: Cambridge University Press, 1996), 225.

2. Lampe, *Yugoslavia as History*, 241–45.

was denounced as a traitorous regime in league with the Western imperialist powers. This last charge had some truth to it, as Tito's regime secretly received economic and military aid from the British and American governments, with the expectation that Tito's example would encourage other "nationalist communist" movements in other Eastern European states. In the words of the secretary of state in 1949, Dean Acheson, "Tito was a son-of-a-bitch, but he was our son-of-a-bitch."[3]

One person who thought this U.S. policy was composed by sons-of-bitches was Fabian Flynn. On December 9, 1950, the *Brooklyn Tablet* published a Flynn article entitled "Tito's Guests are Whitewashing Him." In it, Flynn reported that Tito allowed few American and West European journalists to interview the imprisoned Croatian Archbishop Alojzije Stepinac, who—as the archbishop of Zagreb since 1937—was the effective leader of the Catholic Church in Croatia. Stepinac always gave the same canned responses to the reporters' questions, stating he was in good health, had plenty of time for prayer, was working on his memoirs, etc. Flynn argued that none of the reporters, nor the American and West European governments, contested the legitimacy of Stepinac's imprisonment (he had been sentenced by a "rigged court," as a political prisoner of a dictatorship). He concluded by noting that, in his capacity as the director of CRS in Austria, he had recently welcomed hundreds of children who had been expelled from Yugoslavia by Tito's regime, to join their parents who had already fled across the border. Although never in numbers comparable to the *Volksdeutsche* or the Hungarians from 1956 and 1957, thousands of refugees from Yugoslavia arrived in Austria each year from the late 1940s to the early 1960s, with a considerable uptick from 1955 to 1962.[4]

3. Robert Beisner, *Dean Acheson: A Life in the Cold War* (New York: Oxford University Press, 2006), 158. The Truman administration's response to Kim Il-Sung's invasion of South Korea in 1950 may have prevented a Soviet invasion of Yugoslavia from occurring in 1951 or 1952.

4. Fabian Flynn, "Tito's Guests Are Whitewashing Him," *The Brooklyn Tablet*, December 9, 1950, 6. Even more than Vienna's Cardinal Innitzer, the role Stepinac played during the Second World War—especially his relations with the extraordinarily brutal Ustaše regime under Marshal Ante Pavelic—was very controversial. Some on both sides of the Iron Curtain viewed him as scarcely a victim. Recent scholarship, such as Robin Harris's recent biography, *Stepinac: His Life and Times* (Gracewing, 2016), has attempted

A few months later, Flynn wrote another piece for the same newspaper in which he detailed his experiences with other Yugoslav refugees in Austria, most of whom were originally from either Slovenia or Croatia. "Refugees Tell of Terror in Yugoslav 'Paradise'" began with a discussion of a visit by Flynn and his secretary, Minerva Mores, to a refugee facility near the Austrian/Yugoslav border, which had formerly been a Habsburg military academy. Flynn admitted the Austrian authorities had unearthed a few spies working for Tito's intelligence services, some passing themselves off as laborers, others as peasant women. Yet most were "genuine refugees" fleeing political or religious persecution, often with only the clothes on their backs and whatever they could fit into one suitcase. Hundreds continued to arrive in Austria every month, testifying to the cruel nature of a regime that the Truman administration continued to support. Flynn also commented favorably on a proposal by Massachusetts Republican Senator Henry Cabot Lodge Jr. to create a "Volunteer Freedom Corps" of young male refugees from communist countries, part of which would be providing them with military training.[5]

In the fall of 1951, Flynn wrote a series of articles for the *Brooklyn Tablet* further developing this theme. The longest, "Tito Fetes Harriman, Gets $50,000,000 Gift," appeared in the September 15, 1951 issue. Harriman, a former U.S. ambassador to the United Kingdom and to the Soviet Union, had been placed in charge of the Marshall Plan by President Truman in 1948. Flynn explicitly compared the meeting between Harriman, U.S. ambassador to Yugoslavia William Allen, Tito, Eduard Kardell, the Yugoslav foreign minister, and Alex Rahkovic, the head of the Yugoslav secret police, to the 1938 Munich summit between Chamberlain, Daladier, Mussolini, and Hitler. Using hyperbolic language, he denounced as a "moral obscenity" the decision to give Tito's dictatorship $50 million in Marshall Plan aid. Flynn gave three specific reasons. First, little of the money would help the poor in Yugoslavia. Instead, it

---

to rehabilitate Stepinac's reputation, especially the charge of open collaboration with Pavelic.

5. Flynn, "Refugees Tell of Terror in Yugoslav 'Paradise,'" *The Brooklyn Tablet*, March 10, 1951, 7. Flynn was also highly critical of NATO Supreme Allied Commander Dwight Eisenhower, who had recently expressed some reservations about Lodge's proposal.

would assist the upper echelons of the Communist Party, including Tito himself, who lived in "incredible luxury." Second, the aid was a lifeline to a regime on the verge of collapse, and this was the third time the American and British governments had supported it. Last, and most important, the United States could not call upon its own citizens and those of other countries for a grand battle against Soviet communism while simultaneously propping up its Yugoslav variant.[6]

Flynn's views on Tito's regime were shared by Norris. A memorandum Norris sent out to all CRS missions in Europe in 1951, entitled "Religious Oppression in Yugoslavia," outlined testimony from Catholic priests who had fled the country. The communist regime banned religious youth and women's organizations, censored homilies, arrested those clergy who criticized not just the regime or Tito personally but even those who said something that reflected negatively on communism. Religious instruction was banned in the schools, and there was mandatory adherence to atheism for government and military officials. Norris conceded: "Persecution today in Yugoslavia is neither violent nor brutal, but it is an oppression and harassment which is intended to prevent the Church from carrying out her traditional spiritual role, to keep people away from the Church, and eventually to have Marxism as the religion of the state."[7]

The September 27, 1957, issue of the *New York Times* published "Yugoslavs in Austria." It reported that more than 8,000 Yugoslavs had entered Austria during the past three months, 4,000 having arrived in the month of August alone. The Austrian government complained its

---

6. Flynn, "Tito Fetes Harriman, Gets $50,000,000 Gift," *The Brooklyn Tablet*, September 15, 1951, 4. Flynn discounted how the Truman administration's Yugoslav strategy fit into its doctrine of containment, although he was certainly not wrong about how Tito lived, as he had many of the trappings of a king, despite his poor upbringing. Flynn also demonstrated considerable foresight in criticizing Truman's policy, as it would later lead to Western support for the even more repressive communist regime in Romania under the monstrous dictator Nicolae Ceaușescu. Tito had also supported Khrushchev's decision to invade Hungary in 1956 in the name of crushing the "counter-revolution."

7. James Norris, "Religious Oppression in Yugoslavia," CRS Europe Memorandum, October 5, 1951. CMS 026—2. The unsaid assumption was that all CRS missions in Europe were to keep these facts in mind when dealing with Yugoslav refugees, and in struggling on their behalf with Western governments.

refugee camps for Yugoslav refugees were filled to bursting, and this placed a tremendous burden on a country that was already sheltering more than 26,000 Hungarians. It appealed to the United Nations for immediate assistance with this additional refugee burden. The article concluded: "Most of the Yugoslavs appear to be seeking better economic conditions, but they also plead political conditions."[8] This final sentence proved to be the crux of the issue regarding the fraught status of Yugoslav refugees in Austria. From the mid-1950s to the early 1960s, in excess of 18,000 Yugoslav refugees came to the country, with the hope of starting a new life in Austria or another country in the West.

These refugees occupied a unique position in Austria. Despite the neutrality it had won through the State Treaty in 1955, the country continued to be affected by the Cold War and the division of Europe. Yugoslav refugees lacked the status of martyrs to communism in the manner of the Hungarians in the aftermath of their failed revolution against communism in 1956. Although Yugoslavia under Tito was undoubtedly a communist dictatorship, it was not a satellite of the Soviet Union, and so refugees from the country proved an awkward issue both for the Austrian government and for the country that paid for much of Vienna's refugee aid, the United States. A popular line in both capitals was that Tito's government was a different kind of communist regime, one not nearly as repressive as those in the Warsaw Pact, and that most of those who fled were "economic," not political, refugees, looking for higher wages and better living conditions rather than political and/or religious freedom.

Whether Yugoslav refugees were "genuine refugees from communism"; whether one's status as an economic refugee did or did not mean you were entitled to the same status as a political refugee; whether one could be both—these were thorny questions for the four-way relationship between the United Nations High Commissioner for Refugees, the Austrian government, the relief agencies, and the American government, which provided much of the financial support for refugee relief efforts. Nor were these questions ever satisfactorily resolved. Most

8. "Yugoslavs in Austria," *New York Times*, September 2, 1957, 24. One ironic fact was that 15,000 Hungarians had fled to Yugoslavia rather than to Austria in the aftermath of the Soviet invasion, and most of them were living in refugee camps supervised by the UNHCR.

Yugoslav refugees were not immediately repatriated to Belgrade by the Austrian government, although there were spurts of forced deportations. Even more than those from Hungary, Yugoslav refugees found many obstacles placed in their way before they could receive a permanent home far removed from Tito's regime.

Because of its long border with Yugoslavia, specifically with the republic of Slovenia, Austria was a popular destination for refugees, especially the Chetniks as well as Slovenian and Croatian Catholics, who were visible opponents of Tito's regime. During the years immediately after the Second World War, both groups were subject to state repression, which was symbolized by the show trials of the Chetnik leader, Draža Mihailović, and the Catholic primate of Croatia, Archbishop Alojzije Stepinac, in 1946. From 1947 to 1952, more than 4,000 Yugoslavs escaped to Austria; 1,742 were afterward repatriated.[9]

The Yugoslav Refugees and Austrian Neutrality, 1955–1960

During the Moscow negotiations between Austrian Chancellor Julius Raab and the Soviet government in July 1955, Raab raised with the Soviets the matter of the "dumping" of refugees into the country by the Yugoslav government. Most of those refugees were "comintern" refugees from Hungary, Bulgaria, and Romania who had come to Yugoslavia following that country's open split with the Soviet Union. Both the U.S. State Department and high-ranking officials of the CRS believed the Austrian government had reached a secret quid pro quo with the Soviets to return nearly all refugees back to their own countries—including Yugoslavia, with whom the Soviet government was attempting a rapprochement. The Americans also leaked this information to the press, in the hope of preventing the "repatriation" of the refugees.

Ultimately, the U.S. State Department publicly retracted the earlier leaks that suggested the Austrians were forcibly returning Yugoslav refugees. On August 21, 1956, Austrian State Secretary Franz Grubhofer clarified Vienna's refugee policy: Austria would set up a few "central transit

9. Letter from Flynn to Swanstrom, "Report on U.S. and Austrian government treatment of Refugees," February 1959. UND James Norris Papers, Box 24 Folder 5.

camps" from which refugees, who by this point were largely coming from Yugoslavia, could stay until they immigrated to another country. The Austrian government, the United Nations High Commissioner for Refugees, and international relief agencies would administer the camps. Grubhofer also announced the government was strongly considering banning the settlement of refugees in the border territories of Carinthia and Styria and would refuse asylum to any refugee under eighteen years old or with a criminal record. He also emphasized the Austrian government did not have the financial resources to handle the refugee problem on their own; he appealed directly to the UNHCR for greater financial support and more speed in expediting the emigration of refugees.[10]

The events of November 1956 meant that Hungarians replaced Yugoslavs as the primary concern of refugee efforts in Austria and throughout Western Europe. Still, throughout the 1950s and early 1960s Croatians and Slovenians continued to take advantage of the relatively porous border between Yugoslavia and Austria. Not only was Yugoslav border security lax in certain areas, but border guards often accepted bribes to allow through those who wished to escape into Austria. And while the Yugoslav government kept its distance from Moscow and was a recipient of considerable American aid, its economy remained a top-down, centrally planned economic system on the Soviet model. The economic reforms that would make Yugoslavia the most economically free communist country in the world did not begin until 1963. Poor economic conditions, when combined with the repressive political and religious environment in the country, drove thousands of economic and political refugees into Austria, some of whom lived in the same refugee camps as the Hungarians.[11]

Just as Hungarians had filled up the refugee camps in Austria when most of the *Volksdeutsche* were leaving in 1956–1957, so the Yugoslav refugees were now, from 1957 to 1958, replacing the Hungarians, albeit in slightly smaller numbers. The 1958 annual report compiled by Swans-

10. Press Release by Franz Grubhofer, August 21, 1956. OSA—Archiv der Republik Bestand BMJ (Bundesministerium für Justiz) 1920–2013, ZR Konv Jugoslawien 1954–1960.

11. National Catholic Welfare Conference, Report to the Board of Trustees—Catholic Relief Services, NCWC. October 1, 1957 to September 30, 1958. CMS 026—5.

trom and his staff and sent to the CRS board of trustees in the early autumn of 1958, made this case: "While the number of Hungarian refuges remaining in Austria continues to decrease substantially each month
as many immigrate to various western countries, the problem of the Yugoslavs becomes more and more acute. There are more than 20,000 of
the refugees now, arriving at the rate of 1,000 per month. They arrived
in Austria in rags, with practically no personal possessions. Even in the
dead of winter the refugees continued to come over the snow-covered
mountains, many of them enduring severe hardships."[12]

The 1959 report revealed Austria remained one of the primary recipients for CRS aid programs, receiving 6,183,794 pounds of surplus
food, distributed to 360,000 families, 70,000 schools, and 30,000 institutions throughout the country, distributed in a partnership between
Caritas and Catholic Relief Services. The CRS also worked with both
the Austrian government and the UNHCR to construct housing for
Yugoslav refugees. At the same time, the government in Vienna told
CRS officials to reduce the level of aid they sent to the country, setting
a distribution maximum of 6,500,000 pounds of surplus food. The report also mentioned, with some pride, the CRS mission in Austria was
increasingly turning over to Caritas responsibility for cooperating with
the UNHCR to deal with refugee issues. The report pointed ahead to
a time when it could end its mission and CRS resources could be dedicated to other trouble spots in the world.[13]

By this point, the patience of the Austrian government with Yugoslav refugees was running out. As a former part of the Third Reich and
the neighbor of a number of communist counties, for fourteen years
Austria had been a magnet for political, economic, and ethnic refugees. Over 1,500,000 refugees had passed through the country since
1945. Nearly all of them came from four distinct groups: forced laborers from all over Europe sent to work in the Third Reich by the Nazis;
ethnic Germans expelled from Poland, Czechoslovakia, Hungary, and
the Soviet Union; Hungarians fleeing the Red Army; and, finally, the

12. Ibid.

13. National Catholic Welfare Conference, Report to the Board of Trustees—
Catholic Relief Services, NCWC, October 1, 1958, to September 30, 1959. CMS 026—5.
The report also noted resources directly from the United States government came to
only slightly more than 51 percent of the CRS aid distributed worldwide.

Yugoslavs who abandoned Tito's regime. The Austrian government claimed its economy was not yet strong enough to integrate many of the refugees into their country, which meant it was willing to send the refugees to any country that would take them in, including, for the Yugoslav refugees, back to Tito's regime.[14]

Here lay the central conflict between the CRS officials and the UNHCR, especially its new lead official in Austria, Robert McCullum. The UNHCR would classify most refugees from Yugoslavia as economic refugees, and the Austrian government would simply repatriate many of them across the border, in many cases before they had even met with representatives of the CRS. Political refugees, by contrast, were given sanctuary in refugee camps in Austria until most of them could emigrate to different countries in the West. Like the other charitable agencies, the CRS was unable to alter this situation, although this did not mean they did not try to persuade officials at the UNHCR headquarters in Geneva and in the Austrian government to allow more of the economic refugees to stay.

On June 1, 1959, Flynn wrote to Norris regarding this dispute between the CRS and the UNHCR. Flynn claimed that there were now fewer Yugoslav refugees entering into Austria, not because political repression exercised by Tito's regime had lessened, but because the Austrian border was now "almost hermetically sealed." Also, the UNHCR exhibited an almost complete indifference to the plight of the Yugoslavs through its classifying almost 80 percent of them as economic refugees; from this group, in excess of 95 percent were repatriated. A side effect of this process was that it drove more Yugoslav refugees to Italy, where the UNHCR authorities were more likely to classify them as political refugees. Norris admitted that McCollum refused to recognize the Yugoslavs as legitimate refugees, and that this was a sentiment shared by many, both at the United Nations and in the State Department in Washington.[15]

14. World Refugee Year Report by the ICMC 1959, January 1960. UND James Norris Papers, Box 52 Folder 1. There were also much smaller groups of Poles, Russians, Czechs, and Ukrainians living the camps, whose number totaled about 5,000.

15. Letter from Flynn to Norris, June 1, 1959. UND James Norris Papers, Box 23 Folder 9.

Norris, Chenard, and Flynn, as well as Swanstrom, agreed that the best solution was to voice their concerns to sympathizers in the secular and Catholic press, and to use their connections with the Catholic Church in Austria to exercise leverage over the Austrian government. Chenard, in a public address to aid organizations in Geneva on June 20, noted that in 1957 only 15 percent of Yugoslav refugees were deported by the Austrian government; this figure rose to 60 percent in 1958 and to 80 percent in 1959. He argued that Austria was fulfilling its obligation to the political refugees, but needed greater financial support from the rest of the world to provide for the economic refugees. Chenard also suggested that many Yugoslavs were wrongly classified as economic refugees because of their confused responses to UNHCR interviewers. In a letter to Flynn dated July 20 1959, Norris admitted that the attitudes in Washington and Vienna, which continued to view the question of Yugoslav refugees as an "economic problem only," exacerbated the problem.[16]

Five days later, Flynn sent to Norris a report of a meeting of the Arbeitsgemeinschaft der freiwilligen Hilfsorganisation (Working Society of Voluntary Charitable Organizations) in Vienna. The meeting consisted of representatives from the CRS and other charitable organizations, the UNHCR, and various agencies of the Austrian government, in particular the Ministry of the Interior. Flynn told Norris the only real reason the meeting even happened was the public complaints of the CRS about how the UNHCR was "derelict in its duty" toward the Yugoslavs, and the tendency of officials of that agency, including McCollum, to "hide behind the Austrian government." Flynn claimed he had been as conciliatory to the representatives of the Austrian government as possible, acknowledging their right to admit or refuse as many refugees as they wished. He expressed gratitude toward Austria's policy of allowing Yugoslav refugees to stay up to March 1958, and he said the CRS "did not want to create a refugee crisis in Austria, it wanted to help solve an existing one."[17]

16. Letter from Chenard to American Council of Voluntary Agencies Abroad, June 20, 1959. CUA—National Catholic Welfare Conference, International Affairs Collection, File 9 Box 49.

17. Letter from Flynn to Norris, June 6, 1959. UND James Norris Papers, Box 23 Folder 9.

The Austrian representatives at the meeting demanded the UNHCR's legal affairs section do a better job of classifying refugees who had come to Austria; otherwise, the government would allow the CRS and other agencies to issue appeals for refugee status directly to the Ministry of the Interior. The representatives also insisted CRS representatives be allowed into the transit camps to meet with Yugoslav refugees and assist them with their interviews with UNHCR representatives. The representatives from Vienna admitted they might be willing to go back to a more liberal policy of allowing economic refugees from Yugoslavia to remain, if the "international community" were to assist Austria with this problem financially. Some of Flynn's colleagues in the CRS, such as Norris and Chenard. tended to blame officials in the Austrian government as much as the UNHCR for the situation; they argued the Austrians repatriated the Yugoslavs because most American funds were directed toward the Hungarian refuges.[18]

On July 26, in full view of a group of American, British, Dutch, and Belgian tourists, Austrian border police forcibly repatriated twenty-two Yugoslav refugees—including two Croatian men who were trying to enter a seminary in Austria. Flynn described the "ugly scene" to Norris: the Yugoslavs, who had been classified as "economic refugees," were placed on a bus, driven fifty yards over the border into Yugoslavia, and then dragged onto another bus run by Yugoslav police. Flynn could not say what role the UNHCR authorities played in this process, but events like this were obviously damaging their reputation.[19]

Three weeks later, Chenard informed Norris that the ugly incidents involving Yugoslav refugees (and CRS's calling attention to them) were starting to influence UNHCR policies. Besides the large repatriation on July 26, two weeks later, two Yugoslav refugees committed suicide while awaiting repatriation from Austria. One of them had, the day before, written a letter to UNHCR headquarters in Geneva begging for her case to be reevaluated. Chenard noted he met with an official of the UNHCR, Thomas Jamieson, who argued he could not change the methods or the questions used by the UNHCR to process Yugoslav

18. Ibid.
19. Letter from Flynn to Norris, July 30, 1959. UND James Norris Papers, Box 23 Folder 09.

refugees; he said, though, that he would ask request the Austrian government to avoid repatriating the refugees for at least two weeks until
they had an opportunity to meet with a representative from a voluntary agency. Chenard's letter concluded: "UNHCR-Geneva is getting
very nervous about this problem of Involuntary Repatriation and they
would like to get off the hook somehow."[20] By the end of August 1959,
the situation had begun to improve for Yugoslav refugees.

The American Council of Voluntary Agencies for Foreign Services
declared the year of 1959–1960 as the "World Refugee Year" in order to
draw the world's attention to the problem of refugees. The CRS leadership wanted to use this opportunity to assist as many refugees in Austria
as possible to immigrate to the United States. On March 24, 1960,
Swanstrom testified to the House of Representatives, this time to a Subcommittee of the Judiciary Committee, urging them to ease the requirements to allow refugees to enter the United States. Swanstrom informed
the committee that the CRS mission in Austria and the UNHCR officials calculated there were still 27,780 refugees living either in camps,
public housing, or private residences in Austria, of whom about 10,180
still desired to come to the United States; of this group, the CRS could
expedite 1,400, mostly Croatians. He urged the committee members not
to allow the World Refugee Year to pass without some American legislative initiative to assist those feeling political or ethnic persecution from
communist regimes. He explicitly called for waiving a deadline for visa
applications to the United States, given that those who "fled over the
barbed wire and machine gun emplacements" had to do so regardless
of deadlines established by the State Department, and would continue
to do so as long as half of Europe lived under dictatorial rule.[21]

20. Letter from Chenard to Norris, August 18, 1959. UND James Norris Papers,
Box 23 Folder 09.

21. "Statement of Reverend Edward Swanstrom, National Catholic Welfare Conference, March 24 1960." Center for Legislative Archives, National Archives, Washington, D.C. (CLA), Record Group 287—Publications of the Federal Government.
Eighty-Sixth Congress, Hearings Before Subcommittee Number 1, House of Representatives Judiciary Committee Second Session on HR 397. In a humorous exchange,
Congressman Walter Frank hand-waved Swanstrom's statement that Australia had
already doubled the number of refugees it had promised to take in, quipping "Australia will take anyone it can get."

The Conclusion of the Yugoslav
Refugee Affair, 1960–1962

By April of 1960, the repatriations of Yugoslav refugees from Austria dropped significantly, partially in response to the negative publicity surrounding deportations, and also because of frequent contacts between the CRS and Yugoslav refugees, which enabled more of them to qualify as political rather than economic refugees during their initial interviews with UNHCR officials. Nevertheless, officials from the Austrian foreign ministry made it clear in a meeting with Chenard and other CRS officials that they would continue the policy of treating only about 20 percent of the Yugoslavs as political refugees (who would be entitled to look for housing and employment outside the refugee camps). The remaining 80 percent, designated as economic refugees, would be treated as, in Chenard's words, "unwanted refugees," basically confined to the camps until they could emigrate to any country that would take them in. The suggestion, offered by the Austrians, that the CRS and other agencies work out an arrangement with Tito's government to bring economic refugees out of the country, was rejected by Belgrade since, as Chenard argued, communist governments could not publicly admit the existence of unemployment and dissatisfaction with the regime.[22]

In late June 1960, the Austrian government informed the CRS it wished to close the last of the refugee camps in the country, as part of a step forward to moving the refugees into their own homes, and symbolically, to demonstrate that Austria's status as Europe's primary destination for refugees was over. The Austrian ambassador to the United States, Wilfred Platzer, met with Swanstrom and informed him Vienna wanted to begin a two-year project to close all of the refugee camps. Swanstrom told Platzer the CRS would certainly support this project, given its own interest in gradually ending its operations in the country, but it had no funds to donate to this project. Platzer replied that Vienna had already received assurances from Norway and Switzerland of $200,000 each for the project, and had appealed to the West

22. Meeting between Austrian Foreign Ministry and CRS officials in Europe, April 14, 1960. OSA—Archiv der Republik Bestand BMI (Bundesministerium für Inneres) 1945–2002: U.S. Hilfe.

German government for $3,500,000. Flynn admitted to Norris the plan was an excellent one, as living in private residences, even small apartments, was far better than living under the conditions of the camps.[23] A *New York Times* article from March 14, 1961, "Austria Hopes to Close Last Camps for Refugees," detailed how the Austrians had been successful in closing most of the "emergency camps," which had been in continual operation since 1945. They still needed to raise additional funds from private and public sources, the goal being the closing of all the camps by late 1961 or early 1962. The vastly improved economic situation in West Germany allowed that country economically to absorb many of the refugees who were ethnic Germans or those from Yugoslavia or Hungary who had a good command of the German language.[24]

Another factor that eased the emptying out of camps was the greater willingness of foreign governments to take in the remainder of the refugee population. By the spring of 1961, Flynn had successfully persuaded the Swedish government to take in a few hundred of the 12,000 Yugoslav refugees who remained in Austrian refugee camps. He later informed Norris and Chenard that, despite its public statements that, given more financial assistance from the international community, it would take in more refugees, Vienna was mainly interested in wrapping up the refugee problem. Flynn noted that the refugee issue complicated the Austrian government's attempts to reestablish diplomatic and economic ties with the communist regimes in Eastern Europe. By November 1961, the number of Yugoslav repatriations from Austria rose to 51 percent—that is, of those Yugoslavs who attempted to escape to Austria, half were being returned to Tito's realm by their intended host. At the same time, Belgrade opened up ties with Bonn, Vienna, and Bern to allow a limited number of Yugoslavs to emigrate legally each year to West Germany, Austria, and Switzerland. It was hoped that this arrangement would cut down on the number of economic refugees who slipped over the Yugoslav-Austrian border.[25] This remained the status quo throughout the 1960s.

23. Letter from Flynn to Norris, January 28, 1960. UND James Norris Papers, Box 23 Folder 09.

24. Frederick Scheu, "Austria Hopes to Close Last Camps for Refugees," *New York Times*, March 14, 1961, 8.

25. Letter from Flynn to Chenard December 14, 1961. CUA—National Catholic Welfare Conference, International Affairs Collection, File 9 Box 49.

On November 20, 1961, the NCWC News Service formally announced the official transfer of Fabian Flynn from his position as director of the CRS mission in Austria to a new position as director of the office of information for Catholic Relief Services. He would take over from William Maloney, who had occupied the position over the previous six years. He would be based at the CRS offices in the Empire State Building. This was Flynn's penultimate role in what would be twenty-six years of work for the charitable agency.[26]

Flynn stayed in Salzburg until the CRS formally ended its activities there in the summer of 1962 and turned its operations over to Caritas. The U.S. State Department continued to fund the refugee programs until 1967; in 1962 alone, Austria received $4,000,000 from the United States to maintain its refugee camps. The UNHCR continued its operations in Austria until 1974, largely following its established pattern of action with the dwindling numbers of refugees from Yugoslavia, classifying 80 percent as economic in character. The repatriation rate during this time hovered between 50 and 80 percent. As Chenard had pointed out, Yugoslavs simply did not have the same "political value" as those from other communist countries.[27]

The CRS activities with the Yugoslav refugees in Austria cannot be considered the same unqualified success as their activities on behalf of refugees from Hungary, even though the total number of refugees from Yugoslavia who came to Austria from the mid-1950s to the early 1960s was only one fifth the number of those who came from Hungary. Paradoxically, there were only slightly fewer Yugoslavs than Hungarians in Austrian refugee camps, since it was much more difficult for the Yugoslavs to emigrate out of Europe. Austrian authorities were much more likely to repatriate Yugoslavs back to their homeland, and those Yugoslavs who did not get repatriated tended to spend much more time in transit camps before leaving Austria than did their Hungarian counterparts. The CRS officials were able to ameliorate this situation, but not prevent it. Yugoslavs lacked a national tragedy that captured the world's attention in the manner of the Soviet invasion of Hungary in

26. NCWC News Service Press Release, "Priest Who Aided Freedom Fighters Named CRS-NCWC Director of Information," November 20 1961. CMS 023—10.

27. Letter from Chenard to Swanstrom, April 3, 1967. CMS 023, Box 10.

November 1956. Tito's regime was widely considered to be more politically lenient and pro-Western than any other communist regime in
Europe, by both the American and Austrian governments.

These same divisions eventually emerged in the ranks of the CRS
as well. Norris steadfastly insisted that most Yugoslav refugees left Tito's
regime because of political persecution; pursuing economic opportunity had clearly been secondary. In Norris's eyes, CRS had to pressure the Catholic hierarchy of the Catholic Church in Austria and the
government in Vienna to admit as many Yugoslavs as possible. Flynn,
who was closer to the ground in Salzburg, broadly sympathized with
the Austrian state's dilemma regarding the Yugoslav problem. Flynn
believed the Austrian government had a legitimate fear that the presence of too many Slovenians and Croats would further complicate the
issue of the Slavic minorities in the Austrian provinces of Styria and
Carinthia. Flynn concluded that Norris "frequently seemed to be missing" these points. He argued with Norris that many, if not most, of the
Yugoslav refugees were "economic," and while this should not mean
an automatic deportation back to Belgrade, the Austrian government
could not be expected to take on too many Yugoslavs if the American
government refused to take in the majority of refugees. Refugees feeling political, ethnic, or religious persecution should be prioritized over
the "economic refugees," but Flynn believed both the American and
Austrian governments allowed more of them in as well. As the world's
largest economy and its brightest beacon for freedom and democracy,
America had to lead by example in admitting refugees of the Cold War.

Despite all these problems, some of the Yugoslavs who made their
way into Austria during this time eventually sought out both economic
opportunity and political freedom in the West. The CRS played a pivotal part in this process, during a tense period in the histories of two
countries, Austria and Yugoslavia, that despite their different political
structures, occupied a similarly ambiguous position in Cold War geo-
politics.

On June 18, 1962, Flynn wrote a formal "farewell letter" to one of
his most important partners over the years, Archbishop Rohracher.
Flynn informed Rohracher that CRS was formally ending its activities
after seventeen years in the country. He noted that the Austrian am-

bassador in Washington had by this point informed the Kennedy administration that the standard of living in Austria was "higher than it had ever been in its history"; he noted that much of this had to do with aid that had been given by the United States, through the State Department and by various private charities. This, when combined with the fact there was no longer a "serious Refugee problem" in the country—most of the *Volksdeutsche*, Hungarians, and Yugoslavs having been moved out of the country—CRS's services were needed elsewhere, especially in the countries of Asia and South America.[28]

Flynn went on to thank Rohracher for all the assistance provided to him personally by the Archdiocese of Salzburg, particularly from 1949 to 1952 and then from 1956 to 1957, when the CRS mission, which employed both Americans and Austrians in its efforts, was engaged in "fruitful work in difficult times." He conceded it was emotionally painful to give up his work in his "second home" of Austria, but he realized "all the years I have dedicated myself with idealism towards welfare and refugee relief" had reached their goal of helping create an independent, prosperous, and democratic Austria and had helped thousands escape the horrors of communism and ethnic persecution. As he (Flynn) returned to New York to take up his position as director of information for CRS, he wished Rohracher all the best in the future.[29]

The next year, Flynn received a nearly unprecedented honor: he received the Golden Cross for a second time. The report compiled on October 19, 1962, for Austrian Chancellor Alfons Gorbach discussed Flynn's activities since he had received the honor the first time, in April 1956. Whereas Flynn's first award of the Golden Cross was for his services to the Austrian people, as well as to the *Volksdeutsche* who had come into the country following the Second World War, the second was for his work among the Hungarian and Yugoslav refugees. The report noted that he had shown tremendous courage in returning to Hungary with CRS convoys during its revolution, in order to coordinate

28. Letter from Flynn to Rohracher, June 18, 1962. AES Bestand 2.1 Rohracher 20/9: NCWC Korrespondenz.

29. Ibid. This was part of broader transfer of personnel in the CRS. Jean Chenard was promoted to director of the CRS in Europe; James Norris was appointed deputy director of the CRS, serving immediately under Swanstrom.

efforts with Hungarian aid organizations, and also that he had helped to bring "high-level" Hungarian political prisoners to Austria. The report stated the Austrian authorities simply would not have been able to handle the 180,000 Hungarians who came to the country without the help of the foreign aid agencies, the most important of which was CRS. Particularly impressive, concluded the report, was Flynn's collaboration with Caritas leader Leopold Ungar on behalf of refugee children, especially in providing them with clothes, toys, and games. Since Flynn had returned to the United States, he officially received the award at the Austrian consulate in New York City on May 5, 1963; his old editor at *The Sign*, Ralph Gorman, was with Flynn when Austrian President Johannes Wilfort gave him the medal.[30]

Among the many tributes to Flynn's work in Austria, a unique and most revealing one comes from the weekly newspaper *Sudetenpost*, which was published for the Sudeten German exile community who lived in Austria. In the May 10, 1963 issue, the newspaper related that Flynn had been "justly honored" for his services to thousands of Germans who were expelled from the Sudetenland after 1945 and ended up in Austria. It praised Flynn for performing great service for their refugee community for almost twenty years, service that would not be forgotten.[31] Ultimately, whereas Flynn's first reception of the Golden Cross in the spring of 1956 was supposed to be marking the gradual end to his career as director of the CRS mission in Austria (before the unforeseen emergence of the Hungarian and Yugoslav refugee tragedies), this time his work in Europe was truly done.

The World in 1962

As Flynn completed his thirteen-year sojourn in Austria, the Cold War remained as tense as it had been when he arrived in 1949. The building of the Berlin Wall in August 1961 solidified and enshrined what seemed to be the permanent division of Europe. The construc-

30. Report for Austrian Chancellor Alfons Gorbach compiled by the Ministry of the Interior, October 19, 1962. OSA—Archiv der Republik Bestand BMI (Bundesministerium für Inneres) 1945–2002: Präsidentschaftskanzlei.

31. "Auszeichnung für Father Flynn," *Sudetenpost*, March 10, 1963.

tion of the "antifascist protective barrier" ended the three-year diplomatic standoff instigated by Soviet leader Nikita Khrushchev at the urging of East German party boss Walter Ulbricht. From the perspective of the communist authorities, this had the bonus of reducing the flood of refugees into West Berlin to a trickle, and it demonstrated the ruthless nature of the actions by which the Soviets would hold on to their conquests of the Second World War. The Berlin Wall also revealed that Western powers would acquiesce to these tactics if it meant avoiding a third world war: "A Wall is a hell of a lot better than a War," as the American president put it.

Kennedy's narrow election victory in 1960 over Eisenhower's vice-president, Richard Nixon, had brought the Democrats back to power in the White House after eight years in opposition, and it marked the final ascension of the Irish Catholic community of Boston to the height of power in America. Kennedy and Nixon had competed over who could be a more effective prosecutor of the Cold War. Kennedy's foreign policy demonstrated general continuity with Eisenhower's: he maintained the U-2 spy plane program; he refused to vacate Berlin; he even, in the spring of 1961, staged a (failed) attempt to overthrow the communist dictatorship of Fidel Castro. Regarding Austria, Kennedy's State Department continued to provide financial assistance to both the Austrian government and the remaining charitable agencies to help them with the remaining refugee population.

In Moscow, Nikita Khrushchev's hold on power was as strong as ever. After defeating a coup attempt by the Stalinist Old Guard of Vyacheslav Molotov, Lazar Kaganovich, Georgi Malenkov, and Nikolai Bulganin in 1957, Khrushchev was now both the head of the Communist Party of the Soviet Union and the Soviet premier. The "thaw" (*ottepel*) of political, economic and cultural reforms continued in a haphazard manner, while Khrushchev's foreign policies were characterized by "brinksmanship"—using the threat of nuclear war to get his way on various conflicts with the West, such as Berlin and another Cold War hotspot, Cuba.

Here, Khrushchev embarked on an even more reckless brinksmanship than in Berlin. His romantic view of the Cuban regime under Castro, which reminded him of his own revolutionary youth in Russia, led him in September 1962—over the objections of most of the members of the Presidium—to attempt to safeguard the communist government in Havana by placing nuclear missiles on the Caribbean island. This would place the United States under the same nuclear threat as the Soviets.[32] In mid-October, a U-2 spy plane detected the Soviet missiles in Cuba. During the ensuing two-week Cuban Missile Crisis—a standoff between the United States and Soviet Union—the world teetered on the brink of an all-out war. In the end, both Washington and Moscow conceded something to end the crisis: Khrushchev agreed to withdraw the missiles in return for a secret promise from Kennedy not to invade Cuba and later to dismantle the NATO missiles in Italy and Turkey. Much of the world assumed Khrushchev had blinked first, and this resolution of his reckless gambit humiliated him. What with the failure of the "Virgin Lands" campaign to improve agricultural output and his alienation from the KGB and the military, Khrushchev's rivals in the Presidium began to plot his removal, although two years passed before they made their move.

In Hungary, János Kádár felt confident enough, and far removed enough, from the events of October and November of 1956, to issue a general amnesty to participants in the Hungarian Revolution. Many of those who had been imprisoned in 1956 and 1957 were released, and a small number of Hungarians left refugee camps in Austria to return safely to their homeland.[33] Cardinal Mindszenty continued living in

---

32. Khrushchev had renamed the Politburo, calling it instead the "Presidium," following his defeat of the coup attempt in 1957. The name "Politburo" was revived after Khrushchev fell from power seven years later.

33. Sebestyen, *Twelve Days*, 290–93. Imre Nagy, Pál Maléter, and a number of other senior Hungarian government officials who had supported the country's bid for independence had, on about November 22, 1956, been lured out of their brief exile in the Yugoslav embassy with a false promise that they could retire to private life. Rather than being allowed to retire quietly to their homes, however, they had been detained and, a year and a half later, subjected to a show trial, the outcome of which was, for four of them, execution by hanging, on Kádár's orders, on June 16, 1958. The others had been imprisoned, for terms of three years up to life. For many years, most Hungarians assumed Khrushchev had been the driving force behind Nagy's trial and execution. Recent revelations, though, from Hungarian government records that were declassified following the fall of the communist regime have demonstrated that Kádár was the one pushing for Nagy's death; the deposed leader's mere existence was, in his view, a grave threat to his control over Hungary.

the U.S. embassy in Budapest until 1971, when he was finally released to travel to the Vatican. He would die in exile in Vienna four years later. Kádár, meanwhile, implemented many economic reforms that resembled the New Economic Policy in the Soviet Union in the 1920s. These changes liberalized the economy slightly, and there was a corresponding rise in living standards, which helped to make Hungary the self-proclaimed "happiest barracks in the Socialist camp." Despite Kádár's claims, his regime was no more popular than the others in the satellite states, and it, too, would collapse in 1989, the "year of miracles."

West Germany in 1962 remained under the leadership of Konrad Adenauer, the Christian Democratic leader, who was in his thirteenth year in power. Despite overseeing the *Wirtschaftswunder*, the return of the remaining German POWs from the Soviet Union, the reconciliation with France through a series of summits with Charles de Gaulle, and the stabilization of the democratic system, the Rhinelander's tepid response to the building of the Berlin Wall the year before led to a significant drop in his popularity, even in his own party. The groundwork was laid for a gradual transition wherein Adenauer's economics minister, Ludwig Erhard, whose partnership with Adenauer symbolized how the CDU had bridged the Catholic and Lutheran divide in Germany, would take over as chancellor. The Social Democrats, following a decade of electoral defeats, had formally abandoned the goal of a workers' state at the 1958 party conference at Bad Godesburg, and, with the rising star of Willy Brandt, the charismatic mayor of West Berlin, the party seemed poised for a more successful decade. By its end, Brandt would be the chancellor of West Germany, heading the first SPD government in history.

Austria's economic miracle, although it had started later and did not have the same impact as West Germany's, came into its own, following the signing of the State Treaty in 1955, and it continued into the early 1960s. The foundations had been established during *Anschluss* with Germany—as the Nazi regime had relocated considerable industrial assets to the country—and through Marshall Plan aid from 1949 to 1952. Austria was not a part of NATO, but it was economically tied to Western Europe as an original member of the European Free

Trade Association (EFTA) and also traded extensively with EEC nations.[34] Like West Germany, Austria had been under the leadership of Christian Democrats, the Austrian People's Party (OVP), since the end of the Second World War; OVP leader Alfons Gorbach had been its chancellor since Raab stepped down in 1961. Arguably, it was during his three years as chancellor—1961 to 1964—that the Austrian Second Republic truly stepped out on its own as an economically independent state, and the sharp reduction of American aid to the country, including the conclusion of the work of the CRS, symbolized this. For Flynn and other CRS staff, it was a bittersweet accomplishment.

34. The original members of the EFTA, formed in 1960 as an alternative to the EEC (founded in 1958), were Austria, Portugal, Denmark, Norway, Sweden, Switzerland, and the United Kingdom.

$\backsim 8$

FINAL YEARS, 1962–1973

The U.S. Catholic relief agency will continue its assistance for Haiti as long as possible, because of "desperate human need." This position has been announced by Fabian Flynn, CP, Public Relations director for CRS. The U.S. government has quietly suspended most of its Haitian aid programs, reportedly to indicate disapproval of the oppressive rule of President François Duvalier. Father Flynn said that CRS continues its aid program, despite "almost insurmountable" administrative obstacles and open tension between Church and State, because "almost nowhere in the world is more desperate human need." "Fifty percent of all children in Haiti do not live to the age of five, average income is $50 per year, and death from starvation is not uncommon. The illiteracy rate is near 90 percent." Father Flynn noted that President Duvalier had been excommunicated because of his direct attacks on the Church, including expulsion of the country's leading Catholic officials. Despite this, and other problems such as riots, looting of supplies and the failure of the government to meet its commitment, CRS continues its assistance "in response to appeals from Bishops who pleaded the critical needs of the Haitian people," he declared.[1]

1. "Church Continues to Help Needy Haitian People," *The Anchor*, August 16, 1962, 19. François Duvalier, better known by his nickname "Papa Doc" due to his previous career in medicine, was an almost archetypical "mad tyrant" who was responsible for the deaths of between 30,000 to 60,000 of his own citizens and who kept the severed heads of political opponents in his bedroom closet.

Austria may have been a true success story for Catholic Relief Services, but in Flynn's life of service, once one great task concluded, another emerged. In many third-world countries, controversies persisted regarding how CRS aid was distributed and to whom it was given. A dispute grew among American Catholic clergy and laity about whether CRS was, rather than a Christian relief agency, simply a junior partner in the American government's struggle against communism. These problems dominated Flynn's entire tenure as public relations director from 1962 to 1968. He was finally back home in America, but his staunch anticommunism—combined with his determination to ensure that CRS continue its work free from criticism by those who, in his view, had no right to judge its activities—meant this new period in his life would be a difficult one.

Flynn remained at the center of the major events of history. His time in the military had led him from the invasions of Sicily and Normandy to the Nuremberg Tribunal. During his service with Catholic Relief Services, Flynn had been in Hungary for the earliest days of Rákosi's Stalinist-style dictatorship; he was in Germany during the Berlin blockade, in Austria for the State Treaty, and in Hungary again during its failed revolution. It is not surprising, then, that Flynn was involved in two of the pivotal events of the 1960s. The first one was the Second Vatican Council, where Flynn served as a *peritus* delegate representing both the Passionist order and the Catholic Church in America. The other was the Vietnam War, which divided nearly every American institution, and the Catholic Church was no exception, as the CRS's aid policy to South Vietnam was strongly criticized by a younger generation of radical left-wing activist Catholics, especially the Berrigan brothers. The generational and political divisions between, on the one hand, those two conservative, anticommunist Cold warriors Swanstrom and Flynn, and, on the other, the Berrigans and others who composed the Catholic Peace Fellowship, serves as a microcosm of the divisions in America during this tumultuous period.

After a challenging tenure as public relations director for CRS, Flynn returned to Europe in 1968 at the age of sixty-three to serve as deputy director to Joseph Harnett, the head of the CRS mission for Southern Europe and North Africa. Based out of Rome, Flynn was back doing what he loved, utilizing his many European connections. His health problems, including the emergence of pancreatic cancer, led to his final return to the United States in December 1972, for a retirement at Saint Michael's Monastery in Union City, New Jersey, passing away less than two months later on January 28, 1973.

Back to America: CRS Public Relations Director, 1962–1966

The CRS offices were in the Empire State Building in downtown Manhattan, so Flynn's place of residence would have to be somewhere in the New York Metro area. His new provincial, Gerard Rooney, choose not to send Flynn to the larger Passionist monasteries either in Jamaica, New York (Immaculate Conception) or Union City, New Jersey (Saint Michael's). Instead, Flynn was sent to the smaller Passionist residence in Riverdale, New York, part of the borough of the Bronx.[2]

This would Flynn's home for the next six years, the Vincent Strambi Passionist Residence, which consisted of a 62-year old estate house, two smaller cottages, and a small chapel constructed on 14 acres of land. Rooney and the rest of the Saint Paul of the Cross Province reflected that—after nineteen years removed from monastic life (with the small exception of Flynn's brief return to *The Sign* in 1952), and with a full-time job as the public relations director for CRS—Flynn could not be inserted into a Passionist monastery like a nail into a plank of wood, and so sent him to Strambi House. This residence, with a much smaller community, proved a more appropriate fit. To his fellow Passionists at the Residence, like Columkille Regan, most of whom were ten to fifteen years younger than Flynn, his exploits in the 1940s and 1950s had made him a somewhat legendary, and initially intimidating, figure. This eventually dissipated, as Flynn proved to be a quiet, business-like, introverted fellow, but always ready to share a story of his experiences if requested.[3]

2. Letter from Rooney to Flynn, April 3, 1962. PHA Record Group 379—Personnel Files, Deceased Passionists, Fabian Flynn, Box 23.

3. Columkille Regan, CP, Interview with the author, Yonkers, New York, February 5, 2014.

Flynn also engaged in some traditional Passionist activities. During his six years in Riverdale, the Strambi Residence expanded into the Passionist Spiritual Center/Cardinal Francis Spellman Retreat House. The last of a number of retreat centers established by the Saint Paul of the Cross Province in the 1950s and 1960s, it performed this function until 2011. During his time off from work with CRS, Flynn assisted with the planning and construction of the Retreat Center, and, after its completion in 1966, directed occasional spiritual retreats of Catholic laymen from the New York metropolitan area. He loved directing retreats again, as it reminded him of his earliest days with the Passionist order in the late 1920s and early 1930s.[4]

Some of the more difficult aspects of monastic life returned to Flynn's daily routine. Most of his CRS salary went to his order, ending the relative financial independence he enjoyed for the previous two decades. The beginning of each week, Flynn had literally to get down on his knees to beg Strambi Residence's director for funds to pay for his train fare into Manhattan, and occasionally for food expenses as well. He rose between 5:30 and 6:00 a.m. every weekday to join the other Passionists for morning prayers and breakfast, before making the lengthy journey from the Bronx to the Empire State Building in mid-town Manhattan. This meant, among other things, numerous lunches at the expense of his boss, Edward Swanstrom, since Flynn often received from his Order only train fare for the week. He returned by seven p.m. in the evening, often in a state of "complete exhaustion."[5]

What funds Flynn did have he saved for visits to his relatives in Massachusetts. For twenty years, "Uncle Phil" had been an occasional presence in the life of his relatives. They saw him only during his annual returns to the United States, which usually occurred at Christmastime or the summer. Flynn would also bring as presents toy soldiers, dolls, cuckoo clocks, and other goods from master craftsmen from either Salzburg or Munich. The other times Flynn returned to America for fundraising CRS tours and/or to meet with religious and government figures he was too busy to see them. During the 1950s and early 1960s,

4. Ibid. The decision to name the retreat center after Francis Spellman was also Flynn's idea.

5. Ibid.

when they had the opportunity to travel to Europe, Flynn served as their guide in either West Germany, Austria, or Italy. Now Flynn used his expendable income from CRS, which included extra financial assistance from Swanstorm, to travel to his original home, was a semiregular visitor to Boston, attended Red Sox games, enjoyed meals of club sandwiches with coffee ice cream for dessert, and made visits to the Atlantic coast. Nearly all of his younger relatives asked him to officiate at their weddings, which Flynn also agreed to.[6]

Besides composing press releases concerning various CRS activities throughout the world, Flynn also helped create advertisements and information bulletins concerning the role CRS played both in the United States and abroad. One example comes from March 1964, when Flynn wrote "Where Does Your Catholic Relief Donation Go?" for the NCWC news service. Remarkably his writing style and theme resembles his pamphlets of the 1930s, perhaps even to his articles for the Boston Latin School's *Register* back in the late 1910s and early 1920s. The message of Christian charity as a method to help people achieve economic and physical independence again was still there. As he argued, "In the CRS we do not run a dole system. We do not give handouts; we deplore that expression. We are trying to help people, to bring them back to health, so they can go to school or study, or go to work every day."[7]

Flynn went on to give a specific example of this policy, pointing to CRS efforts to distribute food and medicine in Senegal to those suffering from leprosy. Flynn pointed out there were at least 48,000 unregistered lepers in the country who received aid from CRS, many living in rural areas, or to put it another way, "bush country". The mission in the country had determined: "there was no point in giving a leper medicine if he could not sustain himself with food as well." Thus, the CRS officials adopted a policy of not giving food to any community that did not accept medicine. To enforce this policy, the CRS officials traveled to isolated communities accompanied by local doctors; the drivers of

6. Patricia Chisholm, Interview with the author, Natick, Massachusetts, June 8, 2015. Flynn also had money to spend on cigarettes; he had smoked a pack a day since the late 1930s and never was interested in giving it up.

7. Fabian Flynn, "Where Your Catholic Relief Donation Goes," *NCWC News Service*, March 13, 1964.

the trucks loaded with food and medicine would be Senegalese who had been cured of leprosy and could testify on the effectiveness of the medical treatment. Thus, CRS resolved two problems at the same time.[8]

Flynn traveled throughout the country with Swanstrom during fundraising tours, as well as yearly visits to Chicago for the meetings of the U.S. Catholic bishops. This enabled him to visit a number of his relatives, some of whom had relocated there. On a few occasions, in various parts of the country, both Flynn and Swanstrom dropped in on family members for dinner and games of Scrabble, which had become a pastime for Flynn and one at which he had become proficient.[9]

The Roman Connection: Service as a Peritus at the Second Vatican Council

By all accounts, Flynn quickly got used to life back in America and his role as public relations director for CRS. During this time, he took a leave of absence from CRS to fulfill his appointment as a *peritus*, or official expert, at the Second Vatican Council. Appointed by the National Conference of Catholic Bishops, Flynn served as one of the delegates representing the NCWC; others were Andrew Landi, the director of the CRS mission in Rome from 1944 to 1968, as well as Norris and Swanstrom. Flynn was one of the few appointed *periti* who did not have a doctorate in theology or philosophy.[10]

Pope John XXIII announced the convening of the Second Vatican Council, on January 25, 1959, three months after his election as pope. The Council met periodically from 1962 to 1965. In Rome, on September 9, 1959, Flynn—along with Swanstrom, Landi, and Edward McKinney—had an audience with John XXIII. The pope thanked all four men for the work CRS performed, especially their effective use of material resources.[11] Described by many Italians who worked with him

---

8. Ibid.

9. Patricia Chisholm, Interview with the author, June 8, 2015.

10. François Weisler, "The *Periti* of the United States and the Second Vatican Council: Prosopography of a Group of Theologians," *U.S. Catholic Historian* 30, no. 3 (Summer 2012): 65–91, at 71.

11. "Pope Is Grateful for American Aid," *The Anchor*, September 10, 1959. By this point, CRS was operating in more than 61 countries.

as *furbo*—astute, canny, and sharp-witted—John XXIII was a large man with a gregarious personality and an adventurous background, having served as a medic with the Italian Army during the Alpine campaign of the First World War. What he desired, more than anything else, was a restoration of the Church's image and renewed flexibility in dealing with the modern world. In this sense, his closest predecessor was the pope of *Rerum Novarum*, Leo XIII.[12]

That Flynn was appointed a *peritus* shortly before the Council commenced in October 1962 can be deduced from the fact that none of his correspondence prior to the end of his work in Austria even mentions it. John XXIII's announcement of the Council came as a surprise, for the Catholic Church still played a prominent, if reduced, role in political and social life in Europe, and there did not appear any burgeoning crisis that demanded a global assembly of Catholic bishops. Following the announcement of the Council, a number of issues came to the fore. Many bishops from Germany, France, Belgium, and the Netherlands wanted to discuss broader moves toward ecumenism with Protestants and, with the legacy of the Holocaust in mind, with Jews as well. Some clergy from North and South America desired a move away from the use of Latin in religious services, and changes to certain aspects of the liturgy. Both clergy and laity involved in missionary work desired this as well. Thus, the stage was set for what would become the most important assembly of Catholic leaders since the Council of Trent in the mid-sixteenth century, which began the Catholic Counter-Reformation.[13]

Whether Flynn shared these same beliefs about the need for the Catholic Church to "change with the times," or, in the words of John XXIII, to "open the windows of the Church and let some air in" is unclear. None of his writings illustrate any kind of problems with the Latin liturgy; he was also, unsurprisingly, strongly opposed to any form of rapprochement between the Vatican and any of the communist regimes in Eastern Europe. His writings for *The Sign* and his criticism of the anti-Semitic policies of the Nazis do, however, show support for

12. Henri Fesquet, *The Drama of Vatican II: The Ecumenical Council June 1962-December 1965*, trans. Bernard Murchland (New York: Random House, 1967), 3–5.

13. John O'Malley, *What Happened at Vatican II* (Cambridge, Mass.: The Belknap Press of Harvard University Press, 2008), 13–15.

ecumenism. Like many other northeastern Catholics of the early twentieth century, Flynn grew up in a largely Catholic environment, but his experience in the Boston Latin School, and especially, his time in military uniform during the Second World War, meant interacting daily with people from different religious backgrounds. This, in turn, convinced him the Catholic Church not only should but must pursue closer relations with other religious institutions in order to play a leading role in social, economic, and political life in the modern world.

Four sessions composed the Second Vatican Council. The first was from October to December 1962; the second, from September to December 1963; the third, from September to November 1964; and the fourth, from September to December 1965. Pope John XXIII died on June 3, 1963, a few months before the second session; his successor, Paul VI, continued John XXIII's work by presided over the remaining three sessions.[14] The Second Vatican Council left the Church forever changed, the consequences of which are still being dealt with today. The Church permitted the use of the vernacular and allowed the priest to face the congregation; endorsed religious liberty; called for changes to Church artwork and music; made several decisive steps toward ecumenism, especially toward Jews and the Eastern Orthodox and certain Protestant churches; and urged Catholic clergy and laity to take a more active role in fighting poverty and injustice, at all levels.[15]

Unlike standout figures like Joseph Ratzinger (the future Benedict XVI) or Alfredo Ottaviani, Flynn is not mentioned in the numerous historical accounts of Vatican II, although the same holds true for most of the more than 2,500 participants and observers. The American *periti*—nearly all of whom had knowledge of Rome in general and the Vatican in particular—worked as translators, secretaries, and advisers for the American bishops. Also, following morning religious services and the time from 10 am to 1 pm, which was set aside for speeches, the *periti* would meet with various bishops at the "bars" (where refresh-

14. Fesquet, *The Drama of Vatican II*, 110.

15. O'Malley, *What Happened at Vatican II*, 387. Not only were the Council proceedings covered by the press from all over the world, but non-Catholic observers were invited to attend, and many did, especially from Europe's Anglican, Lutheran, and Orthodox churches.

ment stands had been set up) or in conversations around Saint Peter's Basilica and other Vatican landmarks, where many actual decisions on proposals were made. For his part, Flynn and the other representatives from the NCWC held an important meeting during the second session on October 28, 1963. At that meeting, they decided they would dedicate their efforts to keeping the American bishops informed and advised about all the proceedings. The headquarters of the CRS mission in Rome, on the Via Conciliazione, served as the regular place for the American *periti* to compare their notes on the day's speeches and compose a daily publication on the day's proceedings to be distributed to the American bishops in the evening.[16]

For his part, Flynn enjoyed his time in Rome for the first three sessions; whether he attended the fourth session is not clear from the historical record or from the recollections of those who knew him. By all accounts, Flynn found the experience most satisfying, Rome did not have the same appeal for him as Salzburg or Munich, but meeting with old colleagues from CRS, as well as with so many prominent Catholic clergymen, including those from the Vatican, had an almost intoxicating effect for a man who had spent better than twenty years at the center of historical events in Europe and had been thrilled by every second of it, despite all the hardships he had endured.[17]

The Agony of Vietnam: CRS, Flynn, and Controversy over Aid to South Vietnam, 1966–1968

Flynn was involved in another of the pivotal events of the 1960s, the Vietnam War. Unlike the Second Vatican Council, this experience brought him no enjoyment at all. Instead, although Flynn was not in physical danger (as he had been as an Army chaplain during World War II or during his time in Hungary while working for CRS), it would be difficult to point to another event that caused him as much emotional damage.

The tragic story of America's, and by extension CRS's, involvement

16. Weisler, "The *Periti* of the United States and the Second Vatican Council," 71–77.

17. Columkille Regan, Interview with the author, February 5, 2014.

in Vietnam goes back to the Second World War, specifically the Pacific theater of the conflict. Vietnam, along with Laos and Cambodia, was part of French Indochina, the center of France's imperial presence in Asia, which the French army had gradually conquered between 1873 and 1900. Much as it had in Dutch Indonesia, British Singapore, and the American Philippines, the Japanese Army overran Indochina in the spring of 1942. The French government, following Japan's defeat in 1945, was determined to reassert its former power, and the French fought an eight-year war, from 1946 to 1954, against the Vietnamese independence movement, whose most prominent leader was the head of the Vietnamese Communist Party, Hồ Chí Minh. Despite American support, French military forces were unable to defeat the Vietnamese. They vacated control of the country following their defeat at the Battle of Điện Biên Phủ.[18]

Vietnam was subsequently divided along the 17th parallel between North and South. Much like Korea after 1945, two provisional governments were set up: North Vietnam became a communist dictatorship under Hồ Chí Minh, while South Vietnam came under the semi-authoritarian rule of Ngô Đinh Diệm, a Catholic nationalist. The original United Nations plan was to hold elections for the entire country in 1956 under UN supervision, but, because of pressure from the South Vietnamese government and the Eisenhower Administration, these elections never occurred. Instead, Minh and Diệm became rivals for two alternative futures for Vietnam. Diệm built a staunchly anti-communist regime in Saigon with considerable American support, while Minh, who received support from the Soviet Union and China, sponsored a sizeable communist insurgency—the National Liberation Front (NFL), better known as the Viet Cong—to destabilize Diệm's regime. Difficulties between Diệm and his military officers, as well as his American advisers, convinced the American ambassador to South Vietnam, Henry Cabot Lodge Jr., to persuade President Kennedy in November 1963 to sponsor a coup against him. Kennedy authorized the coup, which led to Diệm's overthrow and assassination. This action

---

18. Richard Gribble, *Navy Priest: The Life of Captain Jake Laboon, SJ* (Washington, D.C.: The Catholic University of America Press, 2015), 208–9.

condemned South Vietnam to continual political instability; a consequently larger role for American military forces became necessary to fight the communist insurgency in the south. In November 1965, the situation turned into open warfare with the Battle of Ia Drang Valley.[19]

Catholic Relief Services had been involved in Vietnam since 1946, providing food, shelter, clothing, and medical supplies to the tens of thousands of people displaced by the French-Vietnamese War. Following the French withdrawal and the establishment of communist rule in the north in 1954, Hồ Chi Minh's regime expelled all the representatives of CRS. The organization continued its work in South Vietnam, which, given the staunchly Catholic nature of Diệm and his regime, was unsurprising. It also provided aid for more than a million refugees from North Vietnam who fled as Hồ Chi Minh created a communist political, economic, and social order. An NCWC press release from March 28, 1956 depicted Swanstrom, Flynn, and the director of the CRS mission for Vietnam, Pakistan, and India, Alfred Schneider, at the New York Headquarters of CRS viewing an "escape raft" constructed by North Vietnamese refugees to escape across the 17th parallel into South Vietnam.[20] Certainly South Vietnam was not the most prominent country in CRS promotions throughout the 1950s, although it rose to prominence from the early 1960s onwards, much as it did for the Kennedy and Johnson administrations. By 1965, South Vietnam became one of the largest recipients of CRS aid, receiving between $1,500,000 and $2,000,000 annually; in the peak years of the North Vietnamese refugee exodus, in 1957 and 1958, CRS distributed $20,000,000 worth of aid during that fiscal year.[21]

Flynn had little experience with the country of Vietnam or with the region of southeast Asia. With the exception of trips to Mexico in 1940 and South America in 1955, he had divided nearly all of his sixty years between North America and Europe. Like many other Americans of his generation, Flynn accepted the need for America to protect and defend South Vietnam from communist aggression—the situation was

19. Gribble, *Navy Priest*, 210–12.

20. "Vietnamese 'Escape Raft' Displayed," *NCWC News Service*, March 28, 1956.

21. National Catholic Welfare Conference, Report to the Board of Trustees—Catholic Relief Services, NCWC, October 1, 1964 to September 30, 1965. CMS 023—6.

much like that of South Korea a decade earlier. The alternative was to give North Vietnam's allies, the Soviet Union and China, a major geostrategic victory and thereby imperil the rest of region. In addition to his strong support of Cold War containment policies, Flynn's view of Vietnam had a more personal foundation: he had observed the communist seizure of power in Hungary, and he did not wish to see any other people suffer the fate of those in Eastern Europe after the Second World War.

South Vietnam was one of the most difficult countries in which CRS operated. Even Diêm's regime in Saigon did not have complete control over the mountainous and jungle terrain that made up much of South Vietnam. Following his overthrow and assassination, subsequent governments—often dominated by the military—were plagued with corruption and inefficiencies. Furthermore, because certain rural areas in the country were controlled either by bandits or by the Viet Cong, CRS was utterly dependent on either the American or the South Vietnamese military to assist them in distributing aid. The assistance was intended both to safeguard the CRS personnel operating in the country and to ensure that the aid reached the people for whom it was intended. Unfortunately, this approach led to a number of public relations problems with CRS, tied to rising discontent in the United States concerning American involvement in the Vietnamese conflict.

In April 1964, a series of stories from the *Los Angeles Times* alleged that the U.S. ambassador to South Vietnam, Henry Cabot Lodge Jr., received reports detailing widespread corruption connected with the distribution of food for the needy in South Vietnam, especially for those who had fled the communist regime in the north. These reports further alleged South Vietnamese military and government officials simply took the food from CRS officials and sold it on the black market. The report concluded there was no evidence anyone from CRS had profited from these arrangements, but Lodge suppressed the report anyway, because it would have caused a political scandal.[22]

Flynn, in a subsequent press release by the NCWC, acknowledged that CRS officials had met the previous May to determine how to police

22. *Los Angeles Times*, April 24–26, 1964.

the distribution of aid more closely and to make sure it went to everyone in South Vietnam who needed it, not just the country's Roman Catholic population. He denied any CRS officials in South Vietnam had deliberately placed food aid on the black market or knowingly given it to government officials who planned to do so. He did concede: "Given the great amount of food distributed all over the world by Catholic Relief Services, it is impossible to have 100% effective control right up to the end."[23]

That some of the CRS aid was stolen and/or sold on the black market was nothing new to CRS officials—it was a recurring problem on every continent where they operated. Jean Chenard in Geneva dealt with these issues multiple times each month back in Europe. One crucial aspect of the training of every CRS employee, especially those who engaged in field work, was how to spot and avoid someone trying to sell stolen goods, or goods donated by another aid agency. While loathe to waste money and aid supplies, Swanstrom, Chenard, and Flynn recognized this problem was not always avoidable. Added to the growing controversy of the Vietnam War, and increasing CRS involvement in this conflict, this was just one more criticism to add on to those already disapproving of CRS actions in Southeast Asia.[24]

The *Los Angeles Times* story was not the only one reporting that CRS aid was ending up somewhere other than where it was intended. A bizarre story entitled "Drugs Donated by U.S. Catholics Shipped to Vietcong by Algeria" appeared in April 30 issue of the *New York Times*. It told of the Algerian government donating four tons of medical supplies to the North Vietnamese regime, which had promptly donated it to the Viet Cong. The bulk of the medicine was Aspirin, part of an enormous, 24-ton shipment from Catholic Relief Services to Algeria in the brutal winter of 1963, a year after that country had gained independence from France. The NLF Central Committee sent a thankful telegram to Algiers claiming the gift was "another magnificent token of the fighting solidarity between the heroic peoples of Vietnam and Algeria and an effective contribution of the Algerian people to the

23. "Corruption in Food Aid Is Cited," *AP Press Release*, April 28, 1964.
24. Christian Chenard, Interview with the author, August 16 2016.

struggle of our people against the American imperialists for the salvation of our fatherland." Called on again to explain matters to the press,
Flynn said: "There was a great deal of confusion in Algeria at the time
and supplies were given out where they were needed. The Government
apparently stored the rest in a warehouse and only now disposed of
it." He acknowledged the urgent appeals for medicine meant it was
"doubtless in shorter supply in North Vietnam," but he added his concern that the Viet Cong would use this for propaganda to demonstrate
to the South Vietnamese that American Catholics were "secretly aiding
their enemy."[25]

A few years later, an even larger controversy emerged over the CRS
aid program to South Vietnam. It dragged on from late 1967 to early
1968 and contributed to Flynn's decision to ask Swanstrom if he could
transfer back to Europe. Most American Catholics supported the war
effort in 1965, but a substantial group of the American Catholic left
had been strongly opposed to the war from its outset. As hostilities
dragged on with victory nowhere in sight, and as the South Vietnamese
government struggled to maintain its political legitimacy, their protests became increasingly loud and more numerous. Among the most
prominent of the protestors were two Jesuit priests, Philip and Daniel
Berrigan, as well as the journalists Michael Novak and Adolph Schalk.
These men rejected the Johnson administration's position—that the
war was just and necessary in the context of the Cold War containment
of communism and to prevent a "domino effect" in Southeast Asia
as the Philippines, Indonesia, and Thailand, which were also fighting
communist insurgencies. The protest movement argued that, at best,
the United States had foolishly inserted itself into an Asian civil war
that never should have been an American concern; at worst, American
forces were blatantly imperialist, propping up a corrupt, authoritarian regime in Saigon and denying the Vietnamese people the right to
unite their country under the leadership of Hồ Chí Minh.[26]

25. "Drugs Donated by U.S. Catholics Shipped to Vietcong by Algeria," *New York
Times*, April 30, 1966, 3. Algeria had won its independence from France in 1962.

26. "We Shed Our Blood Willingly," *Catholic Peace Fellowship Bulletin*, December
1967, 1–2. This analysis tended to ignore the reality that Hồ's regime in Hanoi was
much more repressive than the government in Saigon, and that there was little popular support for communism in South Vietnam.

Their criticisms of CRS were threefold. First, the agency was far too dependent on the United States government for funding, making it basically a branch of the State Department and/or the Pentagon. Consequently, CRS was complicit in the United States' "unjust imperialist policies." This led to the second criticism—the refusal of CRS to provide humanitarian aid to the people of North Vietnam. Thus, the aid group was "taking sides" in the Vietnam War and ignoring the suffering of the people north of the 17th parallel. The third and most prominent critique, that CRS gave food and medicine to the "Popular Forces" in South Vietnam. In the eyes of Flynn and Swanstrom, these were village self-protection societies formed to defend their homes and loved ones from attacks by the Viet Cong; in the eyes of the Berrigans and their supporters, these were paramilitary auxiliaries of the South Vietnamese Army (SVA), and they were guilty of numerous human rights violations.

On September 22, 1967, Flynn wrote a letter to John Deedy, the editor of *Commonweal,* an American Catholic magazine. His letter was written in response to Adolph Schalk's article "Samaritans in Hanoi," which had appeared in the September 8, 1967 issue. Flynn wrote directly to the editor, not to the correspondence section of the magazine, as "it would be useless to do something that might merely spark another one of the undignified and divisive free-for-alls that disgrace so many Letters-to-the-Editor columns of the Catholic Press these days." He attacked Schalk's criticism of the CRS's decision not to provide direct aid to North Vietnam—also, for quoting Edward Swanstrom out of context and for to naivete regarding the regime in Hanoi.[27]

Flynn conceded Caritas Internationale, an international group of Catholic charities, sent a small amount of aid to North Vietnam—mostly microscopes and other medical equipment—but announced that they had already decided not to send any more to the country, since further donations would go, not to civilians, but to the North Vietnamese Army (NVA). A report from the International Red Cross headquarters in Geneva, dated September 18, implied it was far from clear that North Viet-

27. Letter from Flynn to Deedy, September 22, 1967. UND, Catholic Peace Fellowship Records, Box 1 Folder 19.

nam would use foreign aid only for civilians, and based on this information provided by the Red Cross, Caritas Internationale would send no
more aid to Hanoi. Recent experience suggested this policy was correct,
said Flynn: aid that had been given by the United Nations and Catholic
Relief Services in 1940s and 1950s to communist countries such as Yugoslavia, Hungary, and Poland had ended up strengthening dictatorial
regimes. Flynn had seen this happen "with my own eyes." Furthermore,
Flynn added that CRS *was* assisting people from North Vietnam, not
only the million refugees who had fled south since 1954, but also those
who continued to the flee the country and the effects of the war, as
well as NVA and Viet Cong POWs, all of whom were receiving aid from
CRS facilities. The CRS representatives had been expelled from North
Vietnam as "American spies" in 1954, Flynn wrote; would CRS's critics
require these refugees to arm themselves and return to the communist
dictatorship to "force the Vietnamese Communists" to receive aid?[28]

Flynn defended the CRS aid program for the families of the "Popular Forces" (as Flynn noted, an Anglicization of their original French
name "Force Populaire"), who were not military; he declared that
"most are village elders and others not fit or not yet called up for military service, who when an alarm sounds drop whatever work they are
doing, pick up a gun and defend their homes, their path of ground,
their loved ones and their own lives against marauding Viet Cong."
Quoting Swanstrom at the end of the letter: "No one in his right mind
would suggest that we give assistance to the armed forces of a government that is directly locked in battle with American troops," adding,
"Would the editors of *Commonweal?*"[29]

This was not the end of the matter. Swanstrom, who was in Rome
at a meeting with other CRS representatives, explicitly denied on November 27 that CRS provided direct aid to Hanoi, nor would it for the
time being. While Swanstrom conceded that Caritas Internationale
had given a limited amount of medical supplies to North Vietnam,
this aid had been provided by Catholic charitable agencies in West
Germany and France, not by CRS. The most that could be claimed, he

28. Ibid.
29. Ibid.

said, was that donations from the American bishops to the Holy Father over the previous two years might have been used to provide aid to North Vietnam, but only in a limited capacity.[30] Six days later, Caritas Internationale issued its own clarification, with the 17-member board of trustees expressing regret over "misunderstandings in the Catholic press" about its aid to North Vietnam. Although it had provided some medical supplies to Hanoi, it had not and would not send any funds to the International Red Cross in North Vietnam, as "no control over the use of money would be possible."[31]

American critics of CRS remained unconvinced. Three subsequent issues of *The Catholic Peace Fellowship Bulletin* reveal the growing animosity of the Catholic antiwar movement to CRS and to its leadership. The December 1967 article "CRS in Saigon" began: "Nobody questions the goals of the Catholic Relief Service. They are honorable. Their justification is accentuated by the human misery that everywhere mocks American abundance and taunts its best-laid schemes. Nor is there any doubt about the dedication of the people who work for CRS, their competence, their genuine accomplishments in relief work. They are not forgotten or ignored. CRS has earned its considerable stock of public confidence." The article, though, went on to argue that CRS had profoundly lost its way. Its decision not to give aid to North Vietnam but to distribute U.S. government surplus material to "South Vietnamese militias" reduced the CRS slogan "needy equals help" to "only *our* needy equals help."[32] Catholic journalist Michael Novak further alleged that Swanstrom and Flynn lied when they claimed that South Vietnamese "Popular Forces" were village elders or those "not fit" for military service, for they were actually healthy young men for the most part. While

30. "Direct Aid to Hanoi Is Denied by Head of Catholic Relief Unit," *New York Times*, November 27, 1967, 18. Monsignor Angelo Valainc, a Vatican press officer, informed the newspaper that South Vietnam had received $80 million in Catholic aid; North Vietnam had received considerably less, and that aid was restricted to medical supplies.

31. "Caritas Denies Direct Hanoi Aid," *New York Times*, December 3, 1967, 3.

32. Michael Novak, "CRS in Saigon," *Catholic Peace Fellowship Bulletin*, December 1967, 3–5. 4. The fact that much of the CRS aid given out in South Vietnam was U.S. government surplus was, in itself, nothing new, since much of the food aid Flynn had helped distribute in Germany, Hungary, and Austria was also from the American government.

they were intended to defend villages from the Viet Cong, he said, they were a supplemental force of the SVA, and Catholic Relief Services was their food supplier.[33]

The April 1968 issue of *The Catholic Peace Bulletin* dropped even the pretense of complimenting CRS, stating in its opening editorial: "The CRS has managed to feed about half of the South Vietnamese Army and has avoided facing the issue of helping the civilians the U.S. government is bombing in North Vietnam." It accused CRS of acting as a branch of the American government and "Race, color, and religion play no part in its programs, according to CRS, but it says nothing about politics."[34] The June 1968 issue hit even harder, stating that the CRS mission in South Vietnam was "perpetuating human misery" with its partner, the American government, callously helping to "eliminate or wreck lives."[35]

Flynn was, alternately, furious and heartbroken by these charges, mostly due to his intense anticommunism, clearly present since at least the early 1930s and intensified by his experiences in Hungary and in dealing with Hungarian and Yugoslavian refugees. He was convinced the CRS mission in South Vietnam was a continuation of its work in the 1950s, both in containing communism and in helping its victims—in this case, North Vietnamese refugees and South Vietnamese villagers under attack by the Viet Cong. These beliefs led him to support the American war effort in Vietnam, if for no other reason than to protect the Catholic population of the country from the communists. It was unfathomable to him that some American Catholics, especially clergy, defended the atheistic North Vietnamese regime against the Catholic population of South Vietnam, and, by their words and actions, morally support the Viet Cong, who were killing American soldiers. Difficulties with UN bureaucrats or European government officials he considered to be "part of the job"; to be attacked by fellow American priests for providing aid to a country under attack by communists he found infuriating and something he felt he should not have to deal with.[36]

33. Ibid., 5. By the 1980s, Novak had become a conservative Catholic political and social commentator.

34. "Tangents," *The Catholic Peace Fellowship Bulletin*, April 1968, 2.

35. "Tangents," *The Catholic Peace Fellowship Bulletin*, June 1968, 13.

36. Columkille Regan, Interview with the author, June 5, 2014.

In March 1968, Flynn put out another NCWC press release, this one announcing that all CRS staff in South Vietnam were still alive following the Tet Offensive. Shortly afterward, after receiving approval from his Passionist superiors, he sent Swanstrom a transfer request, asking to be sent back to Europe. Swanstrom agreed to make Flynn the deputy director to Joseph Harnett, who was the head of the CRS mission in Rome. Flynn had served in the thankless job of public relations director of CRS for six years, and he had done a commendable job. As a World War II veteran, though, and a staunch anticommunist, he had little interest in engaging the new political trends in both America and the Catholic Church; to at least some of the staff he appeared to be a fossil, or at least a man who would be better returning to the familiar comforts of Europe.[37]

Slowing Down: Deputy Director of the CRS Mission in Rome and Retirement, 1968–1972

Flynn enjoyed his time back in Rome. Frequent visits from 1946 to 1962, not to mention his time as a *peritus* during Vatican II, made him familiar with the Eternal City. His work as Harnett's executive secretary followed a regular routine; office work lasted from 9:30 in the morning to 4:30 in the afternoon. These reduced hours represented a recognition by CRS of his increasing age and continuing health problems. The jurisdiction of the CRS mission in Rome stretched far beyond Italy, as it supervised CRS activities in North Africa, the Middle East, and the Balkans. Flynn lived at the living quarters in the Passionist Monastery of Saints John and Paul, located between the Via Claudia and the Via Celimontana, not far from Vatican City. The work was intended to be Flynn's final assignment, and he found it more enjoyable than his previous six years, although he missed the field work that had charac-

37. "All CRS staff are safe after the Tet Offensive," NCWC Press Release, March 18, 1968. The Tet Offensive was a full-scale rising by the Viet Cong throughout South Vietnam, supported by the NVA crossing the 17th parallel. On the one hand, it was a military disaster for the North Vietnamese, as they failed to achieve any of their military objectives. Yet it also had a demoralizing effect on support for the war among the American people, who had been assured by the Johnson administration that victory had been achieved.

terized his time in Austria, Hungary, and Germany. The trips back to relatives in Boston now occurred three to four times per year, and he still was willing to serve as a tour guide to any friend or relative who arrived in Rome.[38]

By early 1971, Flynn's health problems had become more severe; they now involved back pain and weight loss, as well as stomach cramps. These symptoms marked the earliest stages of the illness that eventually took his life—pancreatic cancer—but the diagnosis was not made until later the next year. His work was gradually reduced to a few days a week, and by the early fall of 1972 it had ceased altogether. Flynn departed Europe and returned to America for the final time in late September 1972.[39] He spent six weeks in October and early November making a final series of trips to New England and the mid-Atlantic states to see his relatives. He carried out an old tradition one last time, distributing hand-crafted goods from Italy and Austria to his family members for Christmas. He received a gift from them as well—an electric blanket to help him deal with the coming winter in New Jersey, as one of his constant complaints about Saint Michael's was its draftiness, especially during the harsh northeastern winters.[40]

The World in 1973

As Flynn's health deteriorated under the strain of pancreatic cancer, the world remained turbulent. Richard Nixon had been easily re-elected in 1972 over his Democratic challenger George McGovern, and—in a move that perhaps only he could have made—opened up ties with the People's Republic of China, while also reaching a series of agreements on arms control with Brezhnev's Soviet Union. Nixon and his Secretary of State Henry Kissinger even succeeded in addressing the most vexing issue in American politics: reaching a settlement with the North Vietnamese negotiating team in Paris that essentially restored the 1965 status quo, with the two different Vietnamese states

---

38. Columkille Regan, Interview with the author, June 5, 2014.

39. Mary and Victor Hoagland, Interview with the author, Jamaica, New York, May 14, 2016. CRS records for Flynn's time in Rome are sparse, unfortunately.

40. Patricia Chisholm, Interview with the author, June 8, 2015.

divided along the 17th parallel. The arrangement lasted only two years, after which North Vietnam overran the south and united the country under a communist dictatorship.

In Moscow, Leonid Brezhnev was in his ninth year in power after having overthrown his mentor, Nikita Khrushchev, in October 1964. He weathered the Czech and Chinese crises of 1968 and 1969, although not without cost, having developed an addiction to sleep medication that would plague him for the rest of his life, as his physical and mental health gradually deteriorated throughout the decade. Hungary under János Kádár, now in his seventeenth year in power, had largely been exempt from the political and social turmoil that had shaken his communist neighbors in Poland and Czechoslovakia. Like the other Warsaw Pact countries, with the exception of Romania, the Hungarian military had participated in the invasion of Czechoslovakia in 1968—a bitter irony, given the country's experience in 1956. Kádár's substantial economic reforms created "goulash communism," which placed slightly more emphasis on consumer goods than on heavy industry and resulted in a standard of living that was higher than that in most other parts of communist world. His doctrine—which, to use the words of Jesus, ironically enough (and almost certain inadvertently) was "those who are not against us are for us"—meant also that his regime was less repressive than the governments of most of its neighbors. A similar situation—a semi-totalitarian political order with moderate economic prosperity—prevailed in Yugoslavia under Tito, whose seemingly endless rule since the end of the Second World War pointed to the permanence of the post–World War II order both in his country and in Europe.

Willy Brandt, the Social Democratic chancellor of West Germany, had, like Nixon, worked to reduce Cold War tensions, in this case with *Ostpolitik* (eastern politics)—a large-scale strategy on the part of the Bonn Republic to improve relations with its eastern neighbors, especially Poland, Czechoslovakia, and the German Democratic Republic. This strategy was carried out through a number of different tactics, from establishing diplomatic relations (or sending a "permanent representative" rather than an ambassador, in the case of the GDR), to relinquishing claims on territories that had produced the millions of

Volksdeutsche, such as Silesia and East Prussia, to the expansion of financial and trade links between East and West. There were also symbolic acts of reconciliation, such as Brandt's famous prayer in front of the Warsaw Ghetto Memorial on December 7, 1970.

In Austria, the Social Democratic Party (SPO) had, through holding onto their electoral majority, controlled the government since their initial victory in 1970, and for the next thirteen years its leader, Bruno Kreisky, served as chancellor. As had happened in West Germany, the political, cultural, and social trends of the late 1960s and early 1970s had brought the Social Democrats in Austria to power. Under Kreisky's leadership, the SPO expanded the benefits and reach of the Austrian welfare state; it extended language rights to the country's small Slovenian and Croatian minorities; in foreign policy, it worked to make Austria a bridge between the two sides of the Cold War. In another parallel development with West Germany, Austria saw a decline in church attendance and a slightly less visible role for the Catholic Church in public life. Despite this, Innitzer's successor as the bishop of Vienna, Franz König, was good friends with Kreisky and remained a powerful figure in Vienna. While Europe seemed less at risk for another war than it had ten years before, the Cold War divisions seemed as permanent as ever.

Flynn's Final Days, November 1972 to January 1973

On November 13, 1972, Flynn arrived at Saint Michael's Monastery in Union City, headed by Father Dominic Papa. It served as his retirement destination and his final home. This had been agreed to by Papa and the provincial of Saint Paul of the Cross, Flavian Dougherty, who had taken over from Gerard Rooney in 1968. Flynn expressed his approval of the arrangement, in a statement released by the NCWC: "I started in a monastery and I think I should end there."[41] Thirty years (almost to the day) after Flynn had left Saint Gabriel's in Brighton for service to the U.S. military, and almost fifty years since he began his seminary work at Saint Mary's in Dunkirk, Flynn was finally returning to full monastic life as a Passionist. Although it was not made public,

41. Saint Michael's Monastery Chronicles 1972–1973, Subsection-Flynn. PHA Record Group 379—28/C.

Flynn had received a highly pessimistic diagnosis of pancreatic cancer and it was clear, especially if the planned surgery to remove a cancerous tumor from his pancreas failed, he did not have much time left. He still contributed to religious life at Saint Michael's Monastery and even dropped in on staff members of *The Sign* whenever he could. Reverend Papa wrote that Saint Michael's was greatly enriched by his presence, especially since Flynn was among the Passionists' "most distinguished members." He marveled Flynn had lived as long as he had, given his numerous brushes with death, in particular the stomach surgery in 1938, the shrapnel injury and malaria during the Second World War, and the kidney and eye problems during the mid-1950s.[42]

After enjoying Christmas and New Year's celebrations with the members of his order, Flynn received approval from Saint Mary's Hospital in Hoboken, New Jersey, for surgery on his pancreas. The surgery was scheduled for January 17, 1973. Although the surgery went through without too many difficulties, it was clear to the medical staff that the cancer had spread throughout many other organs in his body, and his condition was dire. His doctors concluded a few days later his condition was "grave and terminal," and it would be best for him to stay at Saint Mary's Hospital until the end came.[43] By January 25, it was clear Flynn had, at most, a few days left, and his doctors informed him as much. By this time, numerous people with whom Flynn had interacted during the course of his long life of service came to pay their respects. These included numerous Passionists, such as Dougherty and Flynn's former provincials, Carrol Ring and Ernest Welch; veterans from the 26th Infantry Regiment; officials from the West German and Austrian embassies; representatives from German, Hungarian, Slovenian, and Croatian refugee and exile organizations; a delegation from the Catholic Church in Austria; and numerous CRS officials from both sides of the Atlantic, including James Norris and Jean Chenard, both of whom wanted to pay respects to the man with whom they had worked during some of the pivotal events of the twentieth century.[44]

42. Ibid.

43. Ibid.

44. Susan Birdsall, Interview with the author, February 12, 2015. According to one of Flynn's relatives who also came to see "Uncle Phil" one last time, walking through

Perhaps the most important visitor came toward the end. Bishop Edward Swanstrom arrived in the evening of January 26. By this point, Flynn did not want to see many more visitors, as he was in terrible pain, despite the medication he was taking, and, as is typical of those in the last stages of pancreatic cancer, his skin had turned yellow from jaundice. According to his nurse, Mary Hoagland, he made an exception for Swanstrom. His former boss asked Flynn if there was anything he could do, and Flynn asked if he could obtain some beers, turkey club sandwiches, and coffee ice cream, as the hospital food was "simply awful." Swanstrom left to search for these items in Hoboken, and returned to have a final meal with his friend. The two talked about old memories of CRS in the 1940s and 1950s, and what they had accomplished during the last thirty years. Swanstrom remained at the hospital for the next two days, and he, along with Dominic Papa, were the first to be informed, on the morning of January 28, 1973, that Fabian Flynn had passed away peacefully at approximately 5 o'clock that morning.[45] A life of adventures across the world and charitable service to the victims of the horrors of the twentieth century—which took Flynn from the Boston Latin School to the offices of *The Sign* at the height of the Great Depression, to the shores of Omaha Beach, the courtrooms of Nuremberg, the streets of Budapest during the Hungarian Revolution, to Saint Peter's Basilica during the Second Vatican Council—had come to an end after 68 years.

Flynn lay in state in the central parlor of Saint Michael's Monastery on January 29th and 30th. Hundreds of people came to pay their respects, including Flynn's former commanding officer in the 26th Infantry Regiment, the retired Lieutenant General John Corley; his former Passionist seminary classmate Jerome O'Grady; Arno Halusa, the Austrian ambassador; relatives from Illinois, Maryland, New York, and Massachusetts, including Susan Birdsall and Patricia Chisholm; and more than 90 staff members from Catholic Relief Services, including James Norris and Jean Chenard. The funeral Mass—in excess of one thousand people attended—was held on January 31, 1973. Flavian

---

the diverse international crowds at the hospital who wanted to thank Fabian Flynn reminded her of the ending of the 1946 classic film *It's a Wonderful Life.*

45. Mary and Victor Hoagland, Interview with the author, May 14, 2016.

Dougherty and Edward Swanstrom led 40 other concelebrants, most of whom were from the Passionist order. The principal homilist at the funeral Mass was O'Grady, who described Flynn as "an essentially shy and reserved priest, who loved the poor of the world." Graveside at Flynn's burial in the cemetery of Saint Michael's Monastery, an honor guard from the Big Red One fired a volley and presented an American flag to his relatives. Swanstrom gave the main remarks; blinking away tears, he referred to Flynn as a "loyal and dear friend," whose "service to the Church and his fellow man is difficult to calculate." It is not known who selected the farewell song at his funeral Mass, "For All the Saints," but it served as a fitting epitaph.[46]

> For All the Saints, who from their Labors Rest,
> Who Thee by Faith, before the World Confessed.
> Thy Name O Jesus, Be Forever Blest!
> Alleluia! Alleluia!

> Thou wast their rock, their fortress and their might,
> Thou Lord, their Captain in the well-fought fight;
> Thou in the darkness drear, their one true Light.
> Alleluia! Alleluia!

> O may thy soldiers, faithful, true, and bold.
> Fight as the saints, who nobly fought of old.
> And win, with them, the Victor's Crown of Gold!
> Alleluia! Alleluia!

46. Saint Michael's Monastery Chronicles 1972–1973, Subsection Flynn. PHA Record Group 379—28/C. Later, following the closing of Saint Michael's Monastery, Flynn's remains were moved to the Holy Cross Cemetery in North Arlington, New Jersey.

CONCLUSION

Philip Fabian Flynn, a middle-class youth from the Boston neighborhood of Dorchester, had an impact that stretched over two oceans. While it is impossible to give a precise impact of the influence of *A Catechism of Communism for American High School Students* and *Catholicism, Americanism, and Communism*, released during the Great Depression, they were read by tens of thousands of Roman Catholics all over the United States, as was *The Sign* magazine. The First Infantry Division from 1943 to 1945 spearheaded the invasion and conquest of Sicily from the Axis powers, which in turn precipitated the fall of Mussolini in Italy; the landing on Omaha Beach on D-Day followed, helping to ensure the success of the Allied Expeditionary Force's invasion of Nazi-ruled Europe. Aachen, the first German city in the West to fall to the Allies, was captured by the Big Red One, which also fought in the key battle of the fall of 1944, that of the Huertgen Forest.

The International Military Tribunal in Nuremberg, for all its imperfections, established a model for war crimes trials which is still followed today, and provided some sense of justice for the millions of victims of National Socialism. Catholic Relief Services found food, medical care, and shelter for the millions of ethnic Germans expelled from Poland and Czechoslovakia after the end of the Second World War, as well as for the thousands of Eastern Europeans who fled the imposition of communism in the late 1940s and onward. After the tragedy of the Hungarian Revolution, when the Red Army crushed the dream of an independent and democratic Hungary, CRS, in cooperation with the UNHCR and other charitable agencies, helped almost 200,000 refugees find a new home in the West. The assistance provided at that time became one of the greatest success stories in the history of international charitable aid. The Second Vatican Council was the most important assembly of Catholic clergy since the Council of Trent four hundred years earlier, whose effects are still felt and debated today.

Philip Fabian Flynn played a substantial role in these events. His life symbolized the "coming of age" of the United States as global superpower and the corresponding growth of the American Catholic Church as an international institution. For all their flaws, both helped liberate half of Europe from fascist rule, and then both helped rebuild Europe's political, economic, and social foundations, leading to an unprecedented period of peace and prosperity. Although Flynn did not live to see the fall of communist governments in the years 1989 to 1991, his efforts on behalf of both his country and his Church to contain communist influence, and to assist the refugees from its tyranny, helped to bring about that collapse. In a twentieth century filled with villains and despots, Flynn played a heroic and vital role in extraordinary times. It was a legacy John and Julia Flynn would scarcely had envisioned for their son in 1905, but it was one of which they would have been proud.

BIBLIOGRAPHY

Archives

AUSTRIA

AES—Archiv der Erzdiözese Salzburg (Archive of the Salzburg Archdiocese)

Bestand 2.17 Erzbischofliches Ordinariat 18/56 Fluchtlingsseelsorge

Bestand 2.17 Erzbischofliches Ordinariat 18/57 Fluchtlingsseelsorges

Bestand 2.1 Rohracher 19/2 Korrespondenz

Bestand 2.1 Rohracher 20/94 NCWC

Bestand 2.1 Rohracher 19/6: Fluchtlings u Evakuierten Seelsorge

Bestand 2.1 Rohracher 19/16: Fluchtlingsseelsorge 1950–1954

OSA—Österreiches Staats Archiv (Austrian State Archive, Vienna)

Archiv der Republik Bestand BMI (Bundesministerium für Inneres) 1945–2002: Präsidentschaftskanzlei

Archiv der Republik Bestand BMI (Bundesministerium für Inneres) 1945–2002: U.S. Hilfe

Archiv der Republik Bestand BMI (Bundesministerium für Inneres) 1945–2002: Flüchtlingswesen 1946–1990 Referat 10 UH, 1956–1959

Archiv der Republik Bestand BMJ (Bundesministerium für Justiz) 1920–2013: ZR Konv Jugoslawien 1954–1960

Archiv der Republik Bestand AA (Auswärtigen Angelegenheiten) 2. Rep Politische Angelgen 5

SLA—Salzburg Landesarchiv (Salzburg Provincial Archive)

Präsidalakten 1949, Karton 49, PRÄ (Personalangelegenheiten für Landeshauptmanns Salzburgs)

Präsidalakten 1956 Karton 187 PRÄ (Personalangelegenheiten) 1956

Präsidalakten 1957 Karton 195 PRÄ (Personalangelegenheiten) 1957

Präsidalakten 1959 Karton 250 PRÄ (Personalangelgenheiten) 1959

Präsidalakten 1960 Karton 273 PRÄ (Personalangelgenheiten) 1960

SWITZERLAND

UNHCR—Archives of the United Nations High Commissioner for Refugees, Geneva

UNHCR 47—Records of the Office in Austria

UNHCR 4/39—Voluntary Agencies, National Catholic Welfare Conference

UNITED STATES

ANY—Archdiocese of New York Archives, St. Joseph's Seminary, Dunwoodie, New York

Francis Cardinal Spellman Collection, Collection 007

BLS—Boston Latin School

BLS 1918–1923—Catalogues and Register

BPL—Boston Public Library

MS 617—Boston Latin School's Attendance and Discipline Records

CLA—Center for Legislative Archives, National Archives, Washington, D.C.

Material from the 82nd, 83rd, 84th, and 86th Congress

CMS—Center for Migration Studies, New York City

CMS 023—National Catholic Welfare Conference, Department of Immigration Records

CMS 026—War Relief Services, National Catholic Welfare Conference

CUA—The Catholic University of America Archives, Washington, D.C.

National Catholic Welfare Conference International Affairs Collection

HUA—Harvard University Archives

HUE 4.1542—Records of the Harvard Military Chaplain School

NARA—National Archives at College Park, Maryland

Record Group 407—Records of the Adjutant General's Office

Entry 427—WWII Operating Reports, 1940–1948 1st Infantry Division

Record Group 238—World War II War Crimes Records

NPRC—National Personnel Records Center, St. Louis, Missouri

Record Group 247—Records of the Office of the Chief of Chaplains

0-501-418—Personnel File of Philip Fabian Flynn

PHA—Passionist Historical Archive, University of Scranton, Weinberg Library
 Record Group 379—Personnel Files
 Record Group 322—Passionist Military Chaplains
 Records of Saint Gabriel's Monastery, Brighton, Massachusetts
 Records of Saint Paul of the Cross Monastery Church, Pittsburgh, Pennsylvania

UND—University of Notre Dame Archives
 James Norris Papers
 Joseph Harnett Papers
 Catholic Peace Fellowship Papers

USAHEC—United States Army Heritage and Education Center, Carlisle Barracks, Pennsylvania
 Colonel Burton Andrus Papers

Interviews by Sean Brennan

Birdsall, Suzanne. Arnold, Maryland, February 12, 2015.

Chernard, Christian. Hopkinton, Massachusetts, August 16, 2016.

Chisholm, Patricia. Natick, Massachusetts, June 8, 2015.

Hoagland, Mary and Victor. Jamaica, New York, May 14, 2016.

McMahon, Terence. Clarks Summit, Pennsylvania, December 20, 2013.

Regan, Columkille. Yonkers, New York, February 5, 2014.

Wilson, Laura. Scranton, Pennsylvania, December 13, 2015.

Published Primary Sources

Andrus, Burton. *I Was the Nuremberg Jailer.* New York: Coward-McCann, Inc., 1969.

Bekes, Csaba, Malcolm Byrne, and Janos Rainer, eds. *The 1956 Hungarian Revolution: A History in Documents.* Budapest: Central European University Press, 2002.

Flynn, Fabian. *A Catechism of Communism for Catholic High School Students,* New York: Paulist Press, 1936.

———. *Catholicism, Americanism, and Communism.* New York: Paulist Press, 1937.

Goldensohn, Leon. *The Nuremberg Interviews.* Edited and with an Introduction by Robert Gellately. New York: Vintage Books, 2004.

Mindszenty, József. *Memoirs.* Translated by Richard and Clara Winston. New York: Macmillan Publishing, 1974.

The Trial of Jozsef Mindszenty. Budapest: The Hungarian State Publishing House, 1949.

von Papen, Franz. *Memoirs*. New York: E. P. Dutton and Company, 1953.

von Schirach, Baldur. *Ich glaubte an Hitler*. Hamburg: Mosaik Verlag, 1967.

Secondary Sources

Anderson, Christopher. *The Big Red One*. Mechanicsburg, Penn.: Stackpole Books, 2003.

Applebaum, Anne. *Iron Curtain: The Crushing of Eastern Europe 1945–1956*. New York: Doubleday, 2013.

Balkoski, Joseph. *Omaha Beach: D-Day June 6, 1944*. Mechanicsburg, Penn.: Stackpole Books, 2004.

Baumer, Robert. *Aachen: The U.S. Army's Battle for Charlemagne's City in World War II*. Mechanicsburg, Penn.: Stackpole Books, 2015.

Beevor, Anthony. *Ardennes 1944: The Battle of the Bulge*. New York: Viking Press, 2015.

Beisner, Robert. *Dean Acheson: A Life in the Cold War*. New York: Oxford University Press, 2006.

Borhi, Laszlo. *Hungary in the Cold War 1945–1956*. Budapest: Central European University Press, 2004.

Buruma, Ian. *Year Zero: A History of 1945*. New York: Penguin Press, 2013.

Carbonneau, Robert. *Life, Death, and Memory: Three Passionist Missions in Hunan China, and the Shaping of an American Mission Perspective in the 1920s*. PhD Diss., Georgetown University, 1992.

Collingham, Lizzie. *The Taste of War: World War II and the Battle for Food*. New York: Penguin Books, 2012.

Cooney, John. *The American Pope: The Life and Times of Francis Cardinal Spellman*. New York: Times Books, 1984.

Crosby, Donald. *Battlefield Chaplains: Catholic Priests in World War II*. Lawrence: University of Kansas Press, 1994.

Cross, Christopher. *Soldiers of God: The True Story of the U.S. Army Chaplains*. New York: E. P. Dutton and Company, Inc., 1954.

Curti, Merle. *American Philanthropy Abroad*. New Brunswick, N.J.: Rutgers University Press, 1963.

Dodd, Christopher. *Letters from Nuremberg: My Father's Narrative of a Quest for Justice*. New York: Crown Publishing 2007.

Dorsett, Lyle. *Serving God and Country: U.S. Military Chaplains during World War II*. New York: Penguin Books, 2012.

Egan, Eileen. *Catholic Relief Services: The Beginning Years*. New York: Catholic Relief Services Press, 1988.

———. *For Whom There Is No Room: Scenes from the Refugee World*. New York: Paulist Press, 1995.

Fesquet, Henri. *The Drama of Vatican II: The Ecumenical Council, June 1962–December 1965*. Translated by Bernard Murchland. New York: Random House, 1967.

Goda, Norman. *Tales from Spandau: Nazi Criminals and the Cold War*. New York: Cambridge University Press, 2007.

Granville, Johanna. "1956 Reconsidered: Why Hungary and Not Poland?" *Slavonic and East European Review* 80, no. 4 (October 2002): 656–87

Gribble, Richard. *Navy Priest: The Life of Captain Jake Laboon, SJ*. Washington, D.C.: The Catholic University of America Press, 2015.

Holmes, Pauline. *A Tercentenary History of the Boston Public Latin School 1635–1935*. Westport, Conn.: Greenwood Press Publishers, 1970.

Jelavich, Barbara. *Modern Austria: Empire and Republic 1815–1986*. New York: Cambridge University Press, 1987.

Katcher, Philip. *U.S. 1st Infantry Division 1939–1945*. London: Osprey Publishing, 1978.

Kohl, Christiane. *The Witness House: Nazis and Holocaust Survivors Sharing a Villa During the Nuremberg Trials*. Translated by Anthea Bell. New York: Other Press, 2010.

Lampe, John. *Yugoslavia As History*. Cambridge: Cambridge University Press, 1996.

Lewis, Jill. "Austria 1950: Strikes, 'Putsch' and Their Political Context." *European History Quarterly* 30, no. 4 (October 2000): 533–52.

MacDonald, Charles. *The Battle of the Huertgen Forest*. Philadelphia: J. B. Lippincott & Co., 1963.

MacDonogh, Giles. *After the Reich: The Brutal History of the Allied Occupation*. New York: Basic Books 2007.

McManus, John. *The Dead and Those about to Die, D-Day: The Big Red One at Omaha Beach*. New York: Penguin Press, 2014

Mercurio, Roger. *The Passionists*. Collegeville, Minn.: The Liturgical Press, 1992.

Merwick, Donna. *Boston Priests 1848–1910*. Cambridge, Mass.: Harvard University Press, 1973.

Murray, Damien. *Irish Nationalists in Boston: Catholicism and Conflict, 1900–1928*. Washington, D.C.: The Catholic University of America Press, 2018.

O'Connor, Thomas. *Boston Catholics: A History of the Church and Its People*. Boston: Northeastern University Press, 1998.

O'Malley, John. *What Happened at Vatican II*. Cambridge, Mass.: The Belknap Press of Harvard University Press, 2008.

O'Toole, James. *Militant and Triumphant: William Henry O'Donnell and the Catholic Church in Boston, 1859–1944*. Notre Dame, Ind.: University of Notre Dame Press, 1992.

———. "Prelates and Politicos: Catholics and Politics in Massachusetts 1900–1970." In *Catholic Boston: Studies in Religion and Community, 1870–1970*, edited by Robert Sullivan and James O'Toole, 15–66. Boston: Archdiocese of Boston Press, 1985.

Portier,William. *Every Catholic an Apostle: The Life of Thomas A. Judge.* Washington, D.C.: The Catholic University of America Press, 2017.

Ryan, Cornelius. *The Longest Day.* New York: Simon and Shuster, 1959.

Sebestyen, Victor. *Twelve Days: The Story of the 1956 Hungarian Revolution.* New York: Vintage Books, 2006.

Spellman, Francis. *The Road to Victory.* New York: Charles Scribner's Sons, 1942.

———. *No Greater Love: The Story of Our Soldiers.* New York: Charles Scribner's Sons, 1945.

Steininger, Rolf. *Austria, Germany, and the Cold War: From the* Anschluss *to the State Treaty, 1938–1955.* New York: Berghahn Books, 2013.

Swanstrom, Edward. *Pilgrims of the Night: A Study of Expelled Peoples.* New York: Sheed and Ward Publishers, 1950.

Townsend, Tim. *Mission at Nuremberg: An American Army Chaplain and the Trial of the Nazis.* New York: Harper Collins Publishers, 2014.

Veits-Falk, Sabine. "Fürsorge und Seelsorge der katholischen Kirche für volksdeutsche Flüchtlinge in Salzburg." In *Erzbischof Andreas Rohracher: Krief, Wiederaufbau, Konzil,* edited by Ernst Hintermaier, Alfred Rinnerthaler, and Hans Saptzenegger, 165–82. Salzburg: Anton Pustet Verlag, 2010.

Votaw, John. *Blue Spaders: The 26th Infantry Regiment 1917–1967.* Wheaton, Ill.: Cantigny First Division Foundation, 1996.

Wangler, Thomas. "Catholic Religious Life in Boston in the Era of Cardinal O'Connell." In *Catholic Boston: Studies in Religion and Community 1870–1970,* edited by Robert Sullivan and James O'Toole, 239–72. Boston: Archdiocese of Boston Press, 1985.

Weisler, François. "The *Periti* of the United States and the Second Vatican Council: Prosopography of a Group of Theologians." *U.S. Catholic Historian* 30, no. 3 (Summer 2012): 65–91.

West, Richard. *Tito and the Rise and Fall of Yugoslavia.* New York: Carroll and Graf Publishers, 1994.

Wheeler, James Scott. *The Big Red One.* Lawrence: University of Kansas Press, 2007.

Whitlock, Flint. *The Fighting First: The Untold Story of the Big Red One on D-Day.* Cambridge, Mass.: Westview Press, 2004.

Willis, Frank. *The French in Germany 1945–1949.* Stanford, Calif.: Stanford University Press, 1962.

Yuhaus, Cassian. *Compelled to Speak.* New York: Newman Press, 1967.

INDEX

Aachen, Battle of, 75, 78–80
A Catechism of Communism for Catholic High School Students, 38–41
Actio Catholica, 112, 129, 131, 135, 137–38, 222
Adenauer, Konrad, 150, 174, 251
Allen, Terry, 62, 64–66, 71
Andrus, Burton, xix, 65, 85, 89, 93, 95, 98–99
Andrus, Clift, 81–82
Austrian Communist Party (KPO), 151–53, 158–59
Austrian People's Party (OVP), 151–52, 189, 252
Austrian Socialist Party (SPO), 151, 158–59, 274

Barkeley, Camp, 55–56, 58–80
Beermann, Albert, 177–78
Boston Latin School Register, The, 13, 15–16
Brandt, Willy, 251, 274
Brooklyn Tablet, The, 129, 139, 155, 185, 189n, 201–2, 207, 230, 232–34
Brown, Dick, 214–17
Bulge, Battle of the, 81

Carey, John, Reverend, 19–20, 29n
Caritas, 124, 146–47, 153–54, 160, 166, 169, 176, 187, 198, 200–201, 209, 214, 221, 224–26, 229, 238, 245, 248
Caritas Internationale, 267–69
Catholicism, Americanism, and Communism, 38, 41–44

Catholic Peace Fellowship Bulletin, The, 254, 266, 269–70
Catholic Relief Services/War Relief Services (CRS/WRS): activities in Africa, 210, 257–58; activities in Allied-occupied Germany, 129, 139–41, 143, 154; activities in Europe, 103n, 109–12, 125n, 163; activities in French-occupied Germany, 117–128; activities in Haiti, 253; activities in Hungary, 129–31, 135–38, 185, 193–94; activities in Rome, 271–72; activities in Vietnam, 261–71; administrative structure: 113–17; amount of aid distributed, 128, 141, 146, 157, 176, 186, 201, 205–7, 210, 213, 221, 224, 238, 248, 263; attempts to resettle European refugees in South America, 178–79; collaboration with the CIA, 169–70; conflict with UNHCR, 217–20, 239–41; conflict with USEP, 214–216; criticism of, 267–70; dependence on U.S. government aid, 111, 128n, 166n, 169, 173, 205, 213, 225, 238n, 267–70; fund-raising appeals, 144–45, 202, 207–8, 234, 257; historical origins, 42n, 112–14; number of refugees resettled, 160, 162, 165, 175, 187, 204, 207, 209, 212, 217, 242–43, 278; scholarship on, xviii–xix; view of Flynn, xvi–xvii, 58n, 162, 166, 214. *See also* Flynn, Philip Fabian
Chenard, Jean, 116–17, 217–20, 226, 240–45, 248, 265, 276
Corley, John, 68, 70, 82, 90–91, 98, 117, 276

287

℘ *The Priest Who Put Europe Back Together: The Life of Father Fabian Flynn, CP* was designed in New Baskerville and composed by Kachergis Book Design of Pittsboro, North Carolina. It was printed on 60-pound Maple Eggshell Cream and bound by Maple Press of York, Pennsylvania.